D1134755

THE UNCONSCIOUS
MOTIVES OF WAR

THE UNCONSCIOUS MOTIVES OF WAR

A Psycho-Analytical Contribution

BY

ALIX STRACHEY

London

GEORGE ALLEN & UNWIN LTD

RUSKIN HOUSE   MUSEUM STREET

FIRST PUBLISHED IN 1957

PRINTED IN GREAT BRITAIN

in 12-point Spectrum type leaded

BY UNWIN BROTHERS LIMITED
WOKING AND LONDON

CONTENTS

Chapter I

THE PERSISTENCE OF WAR

THE dawn of the atomic age which we are at present witnessing will undoubtedly bring many blessings in its train, since it will enormously increase man's mastery over his environment. With the help of the new techniques which it will increasingly put at his disposal, he will be able, in due course, to produce all the power and heat and light he needs with little labour and at small cost, to construct an abundance of materials precious for health, pleasure and instruction, to conquer space and prolong his years—in short, to live a much happier and better life than today.

At the same time—as our first introduction to it has all too clearly shown—this new-won power can be put to destructive uses as well as to constructive ones, and its possibilities in this field are even greater and much more immediate than in the other. True, the atom bomb hastened the end of the last war, thus saving many lives in the long run; but it did so at the cost of killing tens of thousands of persons and creating miles of desolation at one blow. And this was obviously only the beginning of the story. Such a destructive weapon and others like it have since then developed by leaps and bounds and are no longer in the hands of one nation. Already by now the use of only a few hydrogen bombs in a war between the major Powers would put an end, if not to mankind altogether, at any rate to human civilization; and a couple of thousand of them will destroy not only mankind but every form of life on earth. And behind them there looms the still more awful cobalt bomb, a single one of which, launched anywhere, is said to be enough to annihilate the world. Who knows, too, how soon the smaller Powers may not also all of them acquire these formidable weapons, so that even a small war anywhere can end everything?

This being so, it is clearly a matter of the most urgent practical importance that the occurrence of war should from now on be prevented. And this is the firm belief of every reasonable and informed person today and the subject of his earnest wish.

Indeed, the desirability of preserving peace, or at any rate of reducing the frequency and extent of war as well as its ferocity, had begun to be apparent to the civilized countries long before this. As fighting between them gradually became more destructive and there was more to lose by it in the way of material wealth and intellectual culture, and as people became increasingly sensitive to the physical and mental suffering it inflicted on them, they began to look for means of mitigating the evil. As early as in the seventeenth century the Dutch lawyer, Grotius, drew up a code of behaviour between nations, both in peace and war, with the aim of promoting the first and mitigating the second. This code was accepted and developed by most of the European States, with considerable benefit to them. Later, at the end of the last century, the Hague Tribunal was set up to interpret this body of international law and to give judgment upon points of dispute brought before it by contestant nations; and this, too, has proved of no little value on many occasions.

In addition to this, and once more owing to the growing conscience of the civilized world, much work of mercy went on along with the barbarity of war. The sick and the wounded, be they friend or foe, were better cared for, and, under the auspices of the International Red Cross, the fate of prisoners of war was greatly alleviated.

During the latter half of the last century, indeed, there arose a tendency among the progressive countries—based no doubt on their growing material well-being, scientific achievements and refinement of manners—to assume that mankind everywhere was steadily moving forward in every way and that this movement was bound to go on, whether as a part of the grand design of Providence or as a result of some inner necessity; so that wars would fade away of themselves, as being seen by all to be inexpedient or contrary to their sense of justice and humanity.

This complacent attitude was rudely shaken by the advent of the First World War. All the supposedly civilizing influences of education, religion, arts and wealth went for nothing; and we were presented with the spectacle of the most advanced peoples on earth reverting, on a gigantic scale, to man's oldest occupation of killing and being killed.

The amount of material damage which the 1914–18 war inflicted upon the belligerents, victors and vanquished alike, as well as upon the world at large, and the millions of dead or mutilated soldiers and sorrowing survivors which it left behind, made it clear, even then, that the repetition of such an event—a repetition which was almost certain to be on a still larger scale, having regard to the ever-increasing destructiveness of modern armaments—would be nothing short of a disaster. This the victorious Powers were determined to prevent. Their first care, therefore, was to make sure that those whom they regarded as the aggressor nations (and who were fortunately also the losers) should not soon be in a position to repeat their attack. Accordingly, the Treaty of Versailles imposed crippling reparations and total disarmament upon the defeated Germans.

But this was plainly not enough. If history has shown anything, it has shown that armed aggression has not been confined to one, or even a few, nations. Practically every country has, at some time or other in its history, indulged in military adventure. China, in her hey-day, subdued many outlying tribes and added them to her provinces; ancient Egypt, under the Eighteenth Dynasty, spread far outside her natural boundaries by force of arms; the Persians, in the reign of Darius, attacked Greece; Greece, led by Alexander, overran the East; Rome, during her periods of expansion, engulfed vast areas of land and subdued many proud nations. Nor is such aggression confined to the distant past. England, under her good King

*

Harry, carried fire and sword through France and sought to wrest the French crown from her natural sovereign; sixteenth-century Spain, in the fullness of her power, proclaimed the whole of the New World her possession, cruelly oppressed the Lowlands and sent an Armada to conquer England; under her *Roi Soleil*, France wantonly pillaged the German States and took Alsace; and under Napoleon's military genius she laid all Europe at her feet. Even Sweden has had her moments of martial greatness when she seized Russian soil. Neither have we and other Powers been guiltless of dubious acts of colonial expansion in modern days. Thus there was good reason to fear that at any time some country other than Germany—some country, perhaps, which was at this moment a model of peacefulness and neutrality—might start out on the road of conquest. It was not enough, therefore, to ensure the elimination of Germany alone as a military Power. *No* country ought in future to be able to start an offensive war.

Moreover, it was also plain that in many cases neither side in a war had been the sole aggressor or the sole instigator of it. Before Spain sent her Armada against us, she had been subjected to many insults and minor attacks upon herself by us; and doubtless the illiberal treatment by the Boers towards our own people in South Africa at the time provided strong extenuating circumstances for our war upon them. Indeed, it not seldom happens that the aggressor is in the right of it and that he has only resorted to arms because he could not get justice in any other way. When, in the last century, the Italians threw off the yoke of Austria it was they who started the war of liberation; yet no one can doubt that theirs was the righteous cause.

For these reasons the victors of the Kaiser war were not content with the Treaty of Versailles but created alongside of it an organization for effecting a gradual disarmament of all nations and for ensuring justice between them. This organization was the League of Nations.

As we know, the League of Nations failed. It neither effected all-round disarmament nor ensured justice between the weak and the strong, nor restrained expansionist States from going their way. Unscrupulous governments made use of it for their own ends, and dissatisfied ones openly flouted it or walked out on it. After the outrage of the Abyssinian war its doom was sealed. In due course it was officially wound up, and its end went unhallowed and unsung amid the general welter of the Second World War.

The failure of the League of Nations was of course very largely due to its physical weakness—to its lack of any military force with which to back its decisions. This physical weakness, too, often led it to make unjust decisions in favour of stronger countries at the expense of weaker ones, rather than make just decisions which it could not enforce. This greatly lowered its moral prestige in public opinion and may have contributed as much as anything to its final extinction (though possibly if it had been more uncompromising, its obvious inability to enforce its just decisions might have equally lowered its prestige based on power and have led to the same result). But one of the most important factors of all was the indifference with which most ordinary people received the idea of a League of Nations. The newness of the circumstances that necessitated it and the suddenness with which they had arisen made it a distant and unreal thing to them, to be viewed with suspicion if not hostility, or as something slightly comic and only fit for idealists, cranks and highbrows—who indeed were among its strongest adherents. Thus it lacked a broad and a firm foundation in the belief and imagination of the people.

Nevertheless, the experience of the Second World War and the causes which led up to it made it more certain than ever that some such authoritative international body as the League of Nations was indispensable to the preservation of peace—a peace which was now absolutely vital. This time there was no lack of whole-hearted support on all sides. Accordingly, as we know, the United Nations Organization has been set up to take the place of the extinct League of Nations and to carry on its work. This organization embraces most of the countries of the world, all of which are pledged to the cause of peace; and it provides ample machinery for airing and settling differences between them which might endanger international relationships. In addition, there are attached to it a variety of international bodies for the promotion and pooling of cultural, economic and scientific interests in the member States. Stress, too, is being laid on the material and political well-being of the population of the poorer or more backward States, seeing that a starving and discontented people is more likely to resort to arms than a well-fed and contented one.

There seemed, therefore, every reason to be more confident this time of establishing peace on a permanent footing. Yet things did not work out as well as was hoped. Almost at once the great Communist State of Russia began to show her hand. Her vast military might, her doctrine of world-revolution, and her openly expansionist policy soon constituted a serious threat; and in so far as that threat has for the moment been checked, we have up till now only had the sheltering arm of America to thank for it.

But it is not only Communism—or Communism *versus* Capitalism—which is a potential source of war today, although it is the strongest and most imminent. If we look round on the contemporary international scene there is much else to cause uneasiness. The upsurge of violent nationalism in many of the new States, and in many instances its irresponsible exploitation by their leaders, are bringing about an explosive state of affairs all over the world. Israel against the Arabs in Palestine, Pakistan *versus* India over Kashmir, a quarrel between Peru and Panama about fishing rights—any one of these and like situations might sooner or later light the fatal spark. Again, the growing restlessness of peoples still under the dominion of a foreign power presents another danger spot. The discontents of the North Africans under French rule, or even such a small thing as our unwanted occupation of Cyprus, might well be the beginning of the end. Finally, there seems to be nothing to prevent one Communist State from going to war with another, in spite of Marx's dictum to the contrary. Yugoslavia has been at daggers drawn with Russia and may be again, and a still greater cloud is beginning to gather in the shape of rivalry between Russia and the vast rising power of Red China. If all the world were Communist, we should still not be safe.

Indeed, if we survey the history of mankind from its earliest known times to the present day, we see that it is a more or less unbroken chronicle of strife and killing. Tribes, clans and nations have fought with one another ever since recorded time and pretty certainly all along before. They have fought for all sorts of motives, good, bad or indifferent, reasonable or unreasonable, expedient or inexpedient, important or trifling. They have fought for scalps, for heads, for food, for land, for survival, for freedom, for gold and material wealth, as well as for dominion, honour and glory, an idea, a religion, revenge, philanthropy—for anything or nothing. Often, too, they have fought in the face of certain defeat, and even total extinction, willing for that if they could inflict some wounds upon the hated foe.

In view of all this, it begins to look as if the necessity to fight was something indigenous to man—something ineradicably implanted in the human mind; and the attempt to end war threatens to be a hopeless task.

It is here, I think, that the comparatively recent science of psychology—and in especial that branch of it which is concerned with the deeper levels of the mind—has a contribution to make. For the discoveries of psycho-analysis, as this depth-psychology is called, give us the clue to many hitherto unknown and unsuspected motives which cause peoples, even the most civilized ones, to be violent towards other peoples or to excite violence in them; and it is to be expected that a knowledge of those motives will put us in a better position to tackle the problem.

What I propose to do in this book, therefore, is to devote the first part of it to a rather long and detailed description of the unconscious factors of the mind that come into the picture; and I shall point out in what ways they influence the conscious ideas and attitudes of the individual in his private and domestic life. In the second part I shall try to show how their influence is altered or increased by certain aspects of his social and public life in such a manner as to work to the detriment of his international relationships and to encourage the phenomenon of war. In the third and final part I shall go on to discuss how far our new knowledge can help us to obviate that phenomenon.

PART ONE

UNDERCURRENTS OF INDIVIDUAL PSYCHOLOGY

Chapter II

THE PRESSURE OF THE INSTINCTS

AS the reader doubtless knows, the psycho-analytic theory of the unconscious is almost entirely the work of one man, Sigmund Freud. It is so called partly because it is largely concerned with separating out the various elements of the mind, and partly because of the method of discovery upon which it is based (a method about which we shall learn something in the later part of this book).

Freud regarded his theory as in no sense final and absolute but as a working hypothesis designed to give the most likely explanation of the facts so far known. He was fully aware of its shortcomings and he was always ready to amplify it, cut certain parts of it out and alter others, in order to make it agree better with the material to hand and with new material which came his way. He was not interested, either, in rounding it off and clarifying it at the expense of fidelity to the known facts. Thus it is in many places obscure and incomplete and not without internal discrepancies. Freud, too, regarded the relations which he postulated between his psychological findings and the biological and physiological facts with which they were connected as purely tentative and schematic; nor did he think that the truth of those findings was in any way dependent upon the truth of such facts and relationships but stood on its own merits. Finally, although he liked to reflect upon the ultimate nature of certain mental phenomena, he did not view his reflections as anything but a speculative flight of thought. And their correctness or incorrectness did not, in his opinion, in any way affect the validity of his theory, which took its stand upon empirical fact alone.

The following account of the Psycho-Analytic Theory is necessarily very simplified and incomplete, owing to lack of space and to the difficulty of making some parts of it intelligible to the uninstructed reader. Nor, of course, is a knowledge of the whole of it necessary for the purposes of this book. Its more abstruse parts, fascinating as they are, have been omitted altogether, as being too difficult and as having no direct bearing upon the subject in hand. No attempt can be made, either, to describe the gradual evolution of the theory; nor can full justice be done to contributions made to it by later workers in the field. I shall try to make good these deficiencies by referring the reader to Freud's own writings or to the more important writings of other psycho-analysts, most of which have been translated into English, whenever amplification of what is said in these pages seems necessary, or in case the reader should be interested to go deeper into the matter; and I shall indicate very briefly some of the major points upon which other analysts have added to, and sometimes differed from, Freud's views, and also some of the more important respects in which Freud himself changed his views in the course of this work.[1]

*   *   *

According to the psycho-analytic theory the most powerful elements of the mind spring from instinctual sources. The theory starts from the assumption that the mental activities of a living organism proceed in the first instance from certain physical events which occur in it. It is the recipient of large quantities of physical stimuli which impinge upon it from the external world—such things as light, or sound, or heat-waves or chemical emanations from foreign bodies or contact with their surfaces. These stimuli set up nervous excitations in

---

[1] Freud's own essay, *An Outline of Psycho-Analysis*, which is almost the last thing he wrote, gives a clear and simple account of the theory as it stood at the end of his life. For a fuller, though not so recent exposition of the subject, his *Introductory Lectures on Psycho-Analysis* should be read. Ernest Jones's exhaustive and important biography of Freud (*Sigmund Freud, Life and Work*), which is now appearing, also gives a very full account of his theories and the history of their development.

specific sensory organs—in the retina of the eyes, the taste-buds of the mouth, the receptor organs of the skin, and so on—and these excitations travel along the afferent nerves to the brain where they give rise to elements of a mental order in the shape of appropriate sensory percepts—to sights, sounds, tastes, smells, tactile sensations, etc. These sensations and percepts enable the individual to know something about the sources of the stimuli, so as to be able to deal with them in an expedient way—to remove himself from them or alter them or destroy them if they are damaging or unpleasurable, or to increase or continue them if they are beneficial or pleasure-able.

But some physical stimuli arise within the organism itself. These cannot so easily be dealt with. To begin with, the sense-perceptual system is not nearly so well designed to register internal stimuli accurately as it is to register external ones. Thus the individual is much less able to know the nature of their sources and to deal adequately with them. A man who has a pain in his stomach cannot tell whether it comes from a growth and calls for the surgeon's knife or from wind and only needs a couple of soda mints. In the second place, the ability of the individual to act effectively towards his internal stimuli, even if he knows their nature, is very small. He cannot run away from their source, since it is a part of himself, nor can he always change or destroy it with impunity. A man with cancer of the stomach cannot leave his stomach behind, and he cannot have it operated on without grave danger to himself. In the third place, the organism is more exposed to the force of internal stimuli than it is to that of external ones; for it is to some extent shielded from the latter by the outer layers of the skin which are insensitive to them and form a kind of protective barrier against them. No such shield exists against internal stimuli.

Many internal stimuli are slight and passing and arouse no strong excitations. But others are powerful and constant and do arouse them. Of these, a large and important class arises from the physiological needs of the organism. These set up large quantities of excitations which also have their psychic off-shoots. The body, for instance, requires food in order to live and if it goes without food for a certain length of time particular stimuli (probably of a chemical nature) arise in the stomach, which, when they reach a certain pitch, cause feelings of hunger, and a desire for food.[1] These large sums of excitation press for discharge. This the organism achieves by putting an end through appropriate means to the stimuli that arouse them. The hungry man, e.g., puts food into his stomach and so ends the stimuli there that have caused him to feel hungry.

But the subsidence of these stimuli is short-lived. For the bodily needs which give rise to them are perpetual or perpetually renewed. The body, for instance, is using up the food inside it all the time, so that the appeasement of its need for food does not last long. It is soon a prey to fresh excitations due to renewed stimulations from its empty stomach, and it must once more look about for nourishment. Thus cessation of such stimuli can never be more than a temporary affair. They constantly recur and as constantly need to be allayed by appropriate action. This class of internal stimuli thus sets up a psycho-physical process of a recurrent kind. This process constitutes what Freud calls an *instinct*.

According to Freud, there are a great number of instincts, many of which are as yet unknown and unspecified. For he includes among them short-ranged processes with limited objectives as well as long-term ones, having more comprehensive aims. These limited instincts are such things as the instinct of possession, of aggressivity, of dominance, of acquisitiveness, etc., as compared to the wider instincts of hunger or sex.[2] These minor instincts are independent processes which act irrespectively of one another. They are, however, able to

[1] For this and what follows cf. Freud's paper, 'Instincts and their Vicissitudes'.
[2] Many of these are, as is seen, hardly recognizable as instincts in the ordinary sense of the word. This is due to a fault in English psycho-analytic nomenclature. The German word for them is '*Triebe*' ('drives'), which can mean 'impulses' or 'urges' as well as 'instincts'. They are in fact often called by us 'instinctual impulses' or simply 'impulses'. American psychologists often give them the truer name of 'drives'.

enter into combination with other minor instincts to form a major one, or to become a more or less integral part of it. Thus, for instance, the greater instinct of hunger involves a lesser so-called 'oral' instinct which impels the individual to put food into his mouth; and it may also involve an instinct of aggression which impels him, if necessary, to fight for his food, and a minor instinct of curiosity which impels him to look about for the right kind of food, and so on. Accordingly, the minor instincts are often called *component*, or *part*-instincts, and the major ones *whole* instincts. In any given whole instinct there is often one component instinct which is the predominating one. Thus, in the instinct of hunger the oral instinct is the most important. The same whole instinct does not always contain the same component instincts, or the same proportion of them. In a land of peace and plenty, for instance, the instinct of hunger need contain no instinct of aggression: the food is to hand. But in hard times it contains a lot of that instinct, for the food can only be got by struggling for it. Again, the same component instinct may appear in different whole instincts. The instinct of aggression, for instance, enters into the major instinct of sex as well as of hunger. It may help a man to beat his rival in love, or overcome a lady's reluctance to his suit as much as it helps him to gain his daily bread.

The parts of the body from which the stimuli activate an instinct are called its *somatic source*. Each instinct has one or more somatic sources, according to its importance and complexity, of which one is usually the most powerful. Thus, e.g., the instinct of hunger is based mainly upon stimuli arising in the stomach; but stimuli from the mouth also add their quota—these being, incidentally, specific for the oral component instinct.

The physical excitations created by those stimuli provide the instinct with the necessary *impetus*, or driving force, to overcome the obstacles in the way of its gratification. The strength of the impetus varies in direct proportion with the strength of the stimuli. A man who is rather hungry will walk two miles for a meal; but a man who is very hungry will walk ten.

Every instinct also has an object. This is the being or thing in respect of which it seeks to obtain gratification. The objects of the oral instinct, for instance, are food and drink, and the objects of the sexual instinct are persons of the opposite sex. Almost anything or anyone can be an object of some instinct. A man may want to ruin a rival or acquire a dog or hoard soap, in which case the object of his instinct to destroy or acquire or hoard are, respectively, a rival, a dog, and soap. Instinctual objects, furthermore, may be the whole of a being or thing or only part of it. A man may be attracted by a woman as a living and beautiful creature; but he may be attracted only by her feet or by certain tones of her voice. The objects of many component instincts are of the latter sort. These are known as *part-objects*. The part-objects of some of the most powerful instincts are, as we shall see later, certain regions of the body.

Instinctual objects can be either someone or something which is not the subject (or a part of him), or the subject himself (or a part of him). A man may have instincts of curiosity about a neighbour or a neighbour's nose; but he may have them about himself or his own nose. Instincts are liable to change their objects from self to non-self ones and *vice versa*. This often happens if the one kind of object is not available and the other is. In consequence, the reversal tends to take place from non-self objects to self objects rather than the other way round, since the self is always present to the subject. Nevertheless, as we shall see later on, other factors, especially developmental ones, work in the opposite direction.

Instinctual objects do not, of course, have the sole function of allaying an instinct by providing it with a means of discharge. They also have the opposite effect of increasing the strength of an instinct through the addition of the external stimuli coming from them to the internal stimuli which create it. A hungry man usually feels more hungry than ever when he smells food, and a sexually-starved one becomes still more lustful at the approach of a woman. Conversely, the external stimuli supplied by the object may detract from the strength of the instinct by being of a kind which acts against it. Provided he is not absolutely ravenous, a hungry man may feel a little less hungry than he was if nasty food is put before him, and a moderately lustful one may have his ardour somewhat damped if the partner of his joys turns out to have a false leg. But this aspect of objects as providers of stimuli rather than as a means of discharging them does not concern us at the moment.

Every instinct also has an *aim*. As can be seen from what has been said, the ultimate purpose of all the instincts is to get rid of the excitations present in them, and this is most successfully done by abolishing the stimuli that give rise to those excitations. But since each kind of instinct is set going by a different kind of stimulus, each calls for a different method of abolition. The excitations that cause hunger, for instance, and that arise from gastric stimuli are allayed by eating food; and sexual excitations are removed by copulation. These specific means of getting rid of the excitation are called the *immediate aim* of the instinct, as distinct from its *end-aim*, and they are usually what is meant when we speak of the aim of an instinct.

This aim may be either *active* or *passive*. If it is active, the subject desires to do something to his object. If it is passive he desires to have things done to himself. When a woman wants to eat, that is an active aim; but when she wants to be made love to, her sexual instinct, forceful though it may be, has a passive aim. The first is called an *active* instinct, the second, a *passive* one.

Instinctual aims tend to be interchangeable in regard to their activity and passivity. A desire to do a particular thing to someone or something else can be replaced by a desire to have that thing done to oneself. A man with aggressive impulses, for instance, may, on occasion, seek to be attacked by others; and a domineering person sometimes gets pleasure from being domineered over. Such a reversal of aim is apt to occur if, for one reason or another, the original aim cannot be carried out.

But it is also facilitated by the fact that every instinct tends to be dual in this respect and to have both an active and a passive aim, though the one is usually much stronger than the other and keeps it out of sight and action. This duality or reversibility of aim may in some instances be based upon the fact that the instinctual object is part of the self, so that the individual, in gratifying his instinct, perforce plays both an active and passive role. A man, for instance, who enjoys contemplating his sexual organs is also having his sexual organs contemplated. This may arouse the opposite aim in him, or at any rate, it may give him easy recourse to it if his original aim cannot be satisfied.

*   *   *

The mental representatives of an instinct—those psychical elements to which the excitations give rise—are known as *instinctual presentations*. Each such presentation possesses an *ideational content*. This consists of the perceptions, images, thoughts and memories which are concerned in the satisfaction of the instinct. The man who wants to kill his enemy is filled with ideas of encompassing his death; and the man who desires to possess his mistress imagines her in his arms. Owing to the conative character of instincts, much of their ideational content thus depicts things not as they are but as the subject wants them to be. We have here, as we see, all the ingredients of wishful thinking.

Each instinctual presentation also possesses *mental*, or *psychic*, energy. Freud distinguishes two main kinds of psychic energy. One is a uniting, creative and preserving force. It predominates in the sexual instincts, whose aim is to join the subject with his object and which engenders new life and keeps the species going. This was the psychic energy with which Freud became acquainted first, since those instincts play by far the largest part in hysterical affections, from which he obtained his earliest data; and this energy is still the one about which most is known. It is, however, not restricted to sexuality in the narrow sense of the word. It also informs wider erotic instincts which do not principally concern the genital organs, and whose aim is not that of copulation—instincts which cover very extensive ground, and are the substratum of countless human activities, and about which we shall have a great deal to say as we go on. It is also very strongly present in the parental instinct, and more specially in the maternal one. For mothers, and to a lesser extent fathers, cherish and care for their children, whose life and well-being depend on them. The same psychic energy also underlies all feelings of love, affection and kindness that animate the human breast.

Freud calls this psychic force *libidinal energy*, or *libido*,[1] and the instincts which it governs, the *libidinal instincts*. When libidinal instincts of an erotic sort are directed to external objects—to objects that are not the person's own self or some part of it —they are often called 'allo-erotic instincts'. When they are directed to parts of the subject's own body, they are described as 'auto-erotic instincts'. But when libidinal instincts are directed to his self as a whole, and include love of the self, they are called 'narcissistic instincts' (after the Greek myth of Narcissus who fell in love with his own reflection in the water), and the libido residing in them, 'narcissistic libido'.[2] Such self-ward directed libido causes the subject not only to love himself and prefer his own company to any other but to take care of himself and look after his own interests. It is thus a powerful adjunct to his self-preservative trends (except, of course, if excess of narcissism should render him so oblivious to all else save himself that he fails to observe dangers about him and falls victim to them—as happened in the case of the luckless Narcissus).

The other kind of mental energy is almost the direct opposite of libido. It is a disuniting and destructive force which

[1] In accordance with the term widely used by German psychologists for all manifestations of sexual life. Jung, the eminent Swiss psychologist, who was at one time a follower of Freud, still regards libido as the sole form of mental energy, but he gives it a much wider meaning than does Freud. (Cf. his book, *The Psychology of the Unconscious*.)

[2] The word 'narcissism' was used by Havelock Ellis to designate abnormal manifestations of self-love. Freud has enlarged its meaning to cover its normal manifestations as well.

impels the individual to separate himself from his object (or it from him) or to abolish it; and it is at the bottom of his attitudes of hatred and repulsion. This kind of psychic energy is accordingly called *destructive energy* (or sometimes *destrudo*), and the instincts in which it predominates, *destructive instincts*. If the object of a destructive instinct is another person or being or thing, the subject, as has been said, seeks to harm it or do away with it. The instinct leads him to repel his friends or turn away from them, to neglect his neighbours, to spoil whatever he comes in contact with and to commit homicide and murder; and it leads him to hate and despise others. Once more, however, its effects can be self-preservative; for it is often necessary to protect oneself from dangers—a mad dog, a resolute rival, a ruffian or a poisonous mushroom —not by combining with them or cherishing them, but by destroying them, or putting a distance between oneself and them. If, on the other hand, the object of a destructive instinct is the subject's own self or a part of it, it makes him hate and despise himself or that part of himself and impels him to injure or destroy or remove it. This on the whole militates against his self-preservative trends, since it often makes him do himself an injury or even kill himself. Nevertheless, it, too, can have its uses, if it is directed to a part of himself which is harmful to him, and which he can do without safely. Destructive impulses towards a bad tooth in one's head which encourage one to get rid of it are decidedly beneficent—much more so than libidinal ones which make one cling to it.

Both libidinal and destructive energy are present in almost every instinct, but the amount of each varies very greatly from one instinct to another. Thus the parental instinct probably possesses the highest proportion of libido, and the instinct to kill the highest proportion of destrudo. The sexual instincts, again, have a great preponderance of the former, and the instincts of aggression and domination a comparatively large quantity of the latter, whereas in the instincts of possession or acquisition they are much more evenly balanced. The proportion in each instinct may vary, too, from person to person. One man may want to know a great deal or to dominate his fellows or to possess many goods mainly in order to benefit and please all concerned; another may want to do these things mainly in order to spread ruin and dismay. Furthermore, the proportion of libido and destrudo in any given instinct may vary in the same person. Thus it can happen, especially if the two sorts of energy are pretty equally matched, that a decrease in the stronger one or an increase in the weaker suffices to tip the balance of force between them, so that what was a libidinal instinct becomes a destructive one and *vice versa*.

In addition, it seems as though mental energy itself was reversible or *polarized*, as Freud terms it, and was apt to change its nature from the one sort to the other. This characteristic is called *Ambivalence*; and instincts in which there is a nearly equal proportion of these two qualities of energy, so that a change of ascendancy is liable to occur, are known as *ambivalent instincts*.[1]

If the ambivalence is not very great the predominating sort of mental energy may keep the lesser one out of sight and away from overt action, so that its presence is not felt. Nevertheless it may be operative in the sense not only of making the manifest energy more liable to be reversed, should a suitable occasion arise, but of decreasing its strength or efficacy. A mother whose attitude to her child is not entirely free from destructive instincts may, for instance, feed her children fairly adequately, but not so well as she would have if her maternal instincts had been completely libidinal; and a man with an ambivalent attitude to his rival may be content to cause him small annoyances instead of seeking to ruin him outright, as he would if his destructive instincts towards him were unmixed.

Often, too, a person's instinctual ambivalence towards his

---

[1] The name and the concept of ambivalence were taken from the Swiss psychiatrist, E. Bleuler, who first invented them and applied them to the reversibility of feelings and emotions. To begin with, Freud seems to have used the words to denote the reversibility of instincts in respect of their activity and passivity, rather than in respect of their libidinal and destructive content, but he soon dropped this earlier meaning. It was not till later, however, that it got the meaning of the co-existence of the two forms of psychic energy.

object finds expression, not in that each side of it mitigates the other on every occasion—in every manifestation of the instinct, that is—but that each finds unrestricted outlet in one or more of its manifestations by turn (unrestricted, of course, by the opposite kind of mental energy, not by all other considerations). Thus a mother with ambivalent impulses towards her child may at one moment love and pet it to the top of her bent, and at another hate it whole-heartedly and slap it hard; and an ambivalent shop-keeper may be ready utterly to ruin his business rival one day and equally ready to set him completely on his feet the next.

On the other hand, libido and destructive energy may become so intimately fused together as to create what amounts to a new variant of psychic energy. This force causes the individual to obtain erotic gratification from giving pain to, injuring or destroying his object. It is called *sadism* (after the novels of the Marquis de Sade, the eighteenth-century writer, who recounted various sexual perversions to which it gives rise); and the instincts in which it prevails are known as the *sadistic instincts*. As we know, destrudo pure and simple moves the subject to get rid of his object, either by destroying it or by disconnecting himself from it; it does not matter which. Situations in which he is obviously out to destroy or injure it for the pleasure of doing so and would not for the world be deprived of this gratification nor be removed from the object of his hatred and destruction—such situations, which are very frequent, argue the fusion of a good deal of libido with his destrudo—and the presence of sadistic rather than purely destructive instincts. In fact, wherever feelings of hatred and persecution rather than indifference or repulsion accompany a person's attitude to the object he wishes to destroy, it is a sign that such a fusion is present.

Sadism has a passive counterpart which causes the individual to obtain erotic gratification from *receiving* pain or *being* injured or even destroyed. The passive form is called *masochism* (this time from the works of the nineteenth-century Austrian novelist, Sacher-Masoch, in which he describes the sexual perversions arising from it); and the instincts in which it prevails are known as *masochistic instincts*. These, no less than the sadistic instincts, play a considerable role in the mental life of many individuals; and both are responsible for many acts of cruelty and destruction, either done to others or suffered by the self.—Sadism turned back upon the self is also a frequent cause of pain or injury to the subject.

The psychic energy existing in an instinctual presentation is attached in amounts of varying quantity to the elements of its ideational contents. These amounts are called 'charges', or, more technically, *cathexes*;[1] and we speak of the ideational contents or their elements being 'charged' or 'cathected' with such sums of energy.

We have already seen that the ideational content of an instinctual presentation tends to be unrealistic, owing to its conative character. The psychical energy which informs it also operates in an anti-realistic sense. In the first place, the quantity of cathexis of the ideational elements determines the forcefulness with which they appear in the subject's mind and act upon it. If an idea or image or sense-percept or memory are highly cathected—have a large amount of psychic energy attached to them—they will be exceedingly vivid and strong and will dominate his mental horizon to the detriment of other ideas; if they have only a low cathexis—a small sum of energy attached—they will be weak and colourless and edged aside by stronger interests. A man who is hungry thinks of nothing but food and eating it, and a man who is aggressive, of nothing but his intended victims and how to attack them. On this level of the mind, moreover, no critical assessment of ideas in the light of reality is possible. Thus what occupies the subject's mind seems to him *ipso facto* to be important and true. Anything about which he thinks or feels *must* exist; and

---

The word 'cathexis' is a translation of the German word *Besetzung*, meaning 'occupation' or 'investment'. It is taken from the Greek *katekhein*, 'to occupy', 'fill', 'spread over'. This gives the notion of these sums of mental energy being lodged in the ideational content much as a charge of electricity might be in the matter which it charges.

the more strongly he feels and thinks about it the more certainly and vigorously does it exist.

In the second place, the *quality* of the cathexis attached to the ideational elements determines the light in which the subject sees the objects about which his idea is, in respect of their goodness and worth. If his idea of an object is cathected with libido, he will not only love that object but will over-esteem it as good, lovable or beautiful, even if it is none of these. Conversely, if his idea of it is cathected with destrudo he will not only hate it but will regard it as bad, hateworthy and ugly, regardless of what it is really like. And the stronger his libido or destrudo are, the more admirable or odious will it appear to be.

We can see that, left to themselves, a person's instinctual presentations would create a strange world of ideas in him and would lead to disastrous actions on his part. They have to be modified and counteracted by other ideas and modes of thought coming from other parts of his mind before they can be allowed to come to the fore or be put into execution.

Nevertheless, many of them, or large portions of them, do not become adequately adapted. These, accordingly, are repressed and remain unconscious and unimplemented. Moreover, they are joined by many other mental elements which have undergone repression and by yet others which have become attracted to them through association. These additional elements receive the cathexes and obey the laws which govern them. There thus exists in every person an extensive and powerful underground system of the mind, as it were, which differs very greatly from the surface, conscious system with which we are ordinarily acquainted. This Freud calls the *Unconscious system*, or, for short, the *Ucs.*[1]

This system has various distinctive characteristics. To begin with, it is not at all closely integrated, so that its elements have little influence upon one another. A desire to cherish an object may exist there alongside of a desire to harm it, and each may be just as strong as though the other did not exist. Similarly

[1] For this and much of what follows here, cf. Freud's paper, 'The Unconscious'.

a belief in the complete goodness of an object can co-exist with a belief in its complete badness, neither belief shaking the firmness with which the opposite one is held.

Next, as has been said, processes of criticism or judgment or rejection do not occur in this system. Ideas that are present in it are believed in simply from the fact that they are present. No denial or doubt of their truth is possible to it. If it thinks of the moon and of dragons, the moon and dragons are equally real.

Then, again, the cathexes of the ucs. are not firmly secured within the ideational content to which they are attached. They spread with great ease on to other ideas which are connected with it by associative paths. A man who hates another may get to hate his belongings as well; and a girl who is afraid of a bull may feel a spasm of fear when she nears the field in which it commonly browses, empty though she sees the field to be. Indeed, the cathexis often moves away in its entirety from its original ideas so that they are completely emptied of it in favour of the new ideas. The cathexis, too, frequently moves along a whole series of associated ideas, so that the ideational content in which it finally lands is very far removed from the content from which it started. (But if it has left any part of itself behind at any of the intermediate ideas, these, too, acquire value.) Where mental presentations with a conative content are concerned, this *displacement*, as it is called, can take place in regard to their aim or their objects. A man who wants to kick his aunt downstairs may become possessed with a desire to kick her dog instead. That is a displacement as to object. Or he may feel a desire to give her a hearty slap on the back. That is a displacement as to aim. And if he wants to pat her dog rather hard that is a displacement as to aim *and* object. When displacement of object alone takes place, it does not change the person's attitude to the object which has replaced the original one. He has the same emotions and ideas about the former as he has (or had) about the latter. Thus he tends to regard it in the same light. If, say, a man has an aversion to his wife because she has a harsh voice and if he

displaces his aversion on to her dog, he may feel that her dog
has an exceptionally harsh bark, when in fact its bark is comparatively inoffensive. Thus we see that the substitutive object
is apt to become a *representative* one. It can take on many of the
characteristics of the original object and may even stand for
it altogether.

This aptitude for displacement in the ucs. offers the subject
a very useful way of satisfying desires and indulging feelings,
in part at least, which would otherwise have to be altogether
put away. For whenever an instinct is debarred from finding
discharge along its original route—whether from a physical
impossibility or because such a route involves ideas and actions
that are obnoxious to his conscious self or to society—it can
usually find a partial gratification along some alternative
route. To kick one's aunt downstairs is not permissible; but
to pat her dog is. And, in point of fact, instincts make great
use of displacement for this very purpose.

As a result of displacement, ideas which originally had
importance for the subject lose their importance, or much
of it, and ideas which had no importance acquire it. Moreover,
displacement frequently involves the shifting of a cathexis
from one ideational content on to another which already has
a cathexis of its own, or the convergence of cathexes from
more than one content on to a single one. This greatly
enhances the strength and importance of the idea in question.
Such a process is known as *condensation*.

Displacement and condensation lead to modes of thinking
and feeling which are highly characteristic of, and unique to,
the unconscious system. Freud classes them together under
the name of the *Primary Process (of thought)*.

*   *   *

In contradistinction to the ucs., there is another system of
the mind, whose contents and functioning are very different
to it. The mental presentations belonging to this system are
largely derived from psychic excitations arising from physical
stimuli which reach the body from outside, as opposed to

psychic excitations arising from physical stimuli which reach it from within. Consequently those presentations are much more numerous, since there are many more external stimuli than internal ones; and their ideational content is far more precise and accurate, since the sense-perceptions which they receive can give a much more detailed and faithful account of what they are about than can the sense-perceptions arising from the inner world. Moreover, a more realistic attitude to them is encouraged, for the individual is able to take effective steps to deal with them. He is able to escape from, or destroy, unpleasurable ones, and approach and enhance pleasurable ones, and so it is worth his while to study them and make true judgments about them.

This system, unlike the ucs., is a closely organized whole in which the various elements influence and modify one another very extensively. It is here, too, that ideas can be subjected to criticism in the light of other ideas and that doubt and denial are able to enter the mind.

But, in addition to its external presentations, the system contains many internal ones as well. These include instinctual presentations, or at any rate off-shoots and derivatives of them, which, by commingling with the external presentations that abound here and characterize the system, become to a great extent subdued to them and it. Again, externally caused excitations presumably also evoke psychic energy, and this energy, like instinctual energy, is attached in sums of varying amounts to the relevant external presentation in the form of cathexes. Now the cathexes of this system have a different relation to the ideational content of its presentations and behave in a different way in respect of them from what the ucs. cathexes do, and in so far as the latter enter the system and conform to it they, too, follow this model. These cathexes, namely, are much more firmly bound to the ideas which they invest. They are not so freely displaced from one content to another but adhere to the one to which they properly belong. In so far as they do move from one to another, this is due to a voluntary effort of attention on the part of the subject. Then,

B

too, the paths which the cathexes follow in this system are less primitive. The basic associative principles of mere contiguity or similarity of perceptual or affective experience give way to, or are improved upon by, considerations of causal connection or significant likeness or some other kind of relevant connection. These modes of thought Freud calls the *Secondary Process (of thought)*.

This system contains nearly all the ideas that are capable of being conscious, provided they are attended to—i.e., receive a certain amount of cathexis. It is accordingly called the *Preconscious System*, or more shortly, the *Preconscious*, this part of the mind being viewed as a kind of antechamber to consciousness.

With the preconscious we feel ourselves once more on firm and familiar ground; for this system seems to coincide with what we are accustomed to regard as the human mind. Nevertheless, there is a region of it, or just outside it, which consists of mental elements that are not capable of being conscious even if they are substantially cathected. This is because, without belonging to the unconscious in their nature and mode of behaviour, they are yet obnoxious to the subject's conscious mind and have been repressed from it. Many of them, moreover, tend to be drawn down into the unconscious system itself through associative links with elements in it, and owing to their dissociation from consciousness.[1]

The unconscious, however, is not so easily kept in its place. Those of its elements which are highly cathected are continually pressing forward for discharge in action or expression in consciousness, and they often succeed in influencing the conscious thought and behaviour of the subject to a noticeable degree. One man, for instance, may firmly and consciously believe that the Loch Ness monster exists, not because he has good evidence for his belief, but because he unconsciously

---

[1] Ideas which are not cathected or not sufficiently cathected, are, of course, unconscious even if they belong to the preconscious, and to that part of it which is admissible to consciousness—though, once more, the fact of their being unconscious does not preclude them from being operative. Here, there is no question of repression. Absence of attention is one of the most obvious mental factors in their lack of cathexis.

very much wants it—or what it stands for—to exist, or simply because he has strong unconscious ideas about it; another man may, on equally slight evidence, firmly and consciously believe that the monster does *not* exist, because he unconsciously very much wants it not to, or because he is fending off highly cathected ideas of it which make him believe in its existence unconsciously but which, for one reason or another, are intolerable to his conscious mind; while yet another may be unable to decide whether it exists or not, not because the evidence is inconclusive either way, but because one set of powerful unconscious motives draws him in one direction and another set of equally powerful ones in the other. Again, a man may feel suspicious of all red-haired people as being treacherous, not because he has good reason to suppose that there is any inherent connection between red hair and treachery, but because a person who once acted treacherously towards him happened to have red hair; and so, by an irrelevant association through external similarity, he casts the same suspicions upon all people with hair of that colour.

It may happen, too, that an idea is consciously believed, or disbelieved, quite correctly and for quite correct reasons, but that it is believed or disbelieved with much more violence than its nature warrants. One can understand a person's believing passionately in some humanitarian cause or his forcibly denying the supposition that he is cruel to his cat. But that he should support the abstract notion of determinism with great heat or deny the existence of spontaneous generation with personal abhorrence seems uncalled for. It is only to be explained by the fact, once more, that such conscious ideas are substitutive ones and have become injected with disproportionate amounts of unsuitable cathexes displaced from powerful impulses and ideas which cannot emerge in their original form.

Chapter III

MODIFYING FUNCTIONS OF THE EGO

IN view of the distinctive qualities and high importance of instinctual presentations Freud decided to class them into a separate province or major agency of the mind. This he called the 'id' (Latin for 'it')[1] because not only are its elements not directly conscious to the person to whom they belong; in so far as he recognizes their existence in himself he feels them to be alien to his mind. And, indeed, many of them, as we shall see, seem scarcely human at all.

Over against this, Freud postulated a second major agency. This he called the 'ego'. The ego, as its name implies, coincides to a great extent with what is usually regarded as the mental self or personality of the individual and is felt to be so by himself; for it contains much of the psychic material and modes of thought which are conscious and familiar to him. Yet it by no means coincides entirely with that self. For on the one hand, although many of its presentations and thought-processes belong to the preconscious, many do not; and, on the other, as we have seen, much that is preconscious is in good part a derivative of the id. Moreover, as we shall learn in Chapter VI, no small portion of the conscious self belongs to yet a third psychic agency. Thus the ego is at once much more and much less than the conscious (or conscionable) self.

[1] In German, *das Es*. Freud took this word from Groddeck, a contemporary German author who, carried away by the discoveries of psycho-analysis, wrote a somewhat fanciful work entitled *The Book of the Id (Das Buch vom Es)*, in which he maintained that all the things which a person did or which happened to him—even railway accidents —were caused by wishes in his unconscious.—In regard to the classification of the mind into separate agencies, an account of which follows in this chapter and Chapter VI, the reader is recommended to consult Freud's book, *The Ego and The Id*, and the chapter on 'The Anatomy of the Mental Personality' in his *New Introductory Lectures*.

Unlike the id, the ego does not appear to possess much mental energy of its own. Notwithstanding, it is of vital importance to the organism as an adaptive agency. Its main task is to fit the individual to his environment or his environment to him.

One of the things it must do for this purpose is to deal with external stimuli in such a way that they shall not injure the body. In order to achieve this it must be able to know the nature of those stimuli and the sources from which they come. This it does through the organs of sense—of sight, hearing, taste, smell and touch. Thus it is in control of the sense-perceptual system. The ego must, in addition, be able to direct the outward behaviour of the individual in relation to those stimuli and their sources, so that he can act in accordance with the knowledge it has obtained about them. Thus it is in charge of the motor system and initiates or inhibits external action as occasion requires.

The ego also copes with internal and instinctual stimuli and with the excitations which they arouse. It is its business to see to it that these shall not be discharged till they have found an outlet which is expedient for, or at least not detrimental to, the subject. Suppose a man looks out of a third-floor window and sees a ten-shilling note lying on the pavement. His instinct of acquisition is activated and urges him to get hold of the note. If his ego exerted no inhibitory functions he would jump out of the window straight away—this being the quickest way of getting at the note—and break his neck. But if it is carrying out those functions adequately it intervenes to save him from his fate. It causes him to postpone the fulfilment of his desire long enough for him to run down the three flights of stairs and out into the street to fetch the note. Again, if he notices that another man is approaching the note and will see it and pick it up before he can run down the stairs, his ego may counsel him to lean out of the window and call out 'Hi, that note belongs to me!' or, 'Take care, that note is infected', or anything else which will make the man hesitate to pick it up, so that he has time to run down the stairs and get it himself.

(Thus, incidentally, also altering the external world to suit his wish.)

The ego, furthermore, adapts the various component instincts to one another, so that they shall not clash too severely or get too much in one another's way. Suppose a little girl wants to gratify her instinct of curiosity by taking her doll to pieces in order to find out what it is made of, but also wants to gratify her instinct of possession by keeping it whole and intact. Left to itself, her id would make her do whichever of these two things appealed to it at the moment, as the spirit moved it, oblivious of the fact that if she gives way to her instinct of curiosity and destroys her doll, she will never again be able to gratify her instinct of possession with respect to it. Or her instinct of possession may be so strong that her instinct of curiosity is totally and forever frustrated. Her ego, however, may be able not only to decide which of the two instincts it is best for her to indulge at the expense of the other, but to effect a compromise between them by restricting the aims of one or both. In that case she may on the one hand content herself with taking off her doll's clothes, so as to inspect, if not the inside of its body, at least its outside; and, on the other, she may allow its clothes to be rumpled by this process, provided she can protect it from more serious harm.

Thus the ego is an integrating force as well as an adaptive agency. It brings together the various elements of the mind into a harmonious and intercommunicating whole.

*   *   *

As we should expect, it is the ego, too, which carries on the intellectual activities of the mind. Here, and here only, does the secondary process of thought—that is to say, rational thinking which characterizes the preconscious—take place. Nevertheless, the ego does not pursue pure reason alone. It often yields to pressure from the id and other constituents of the unconscious system, and descends to the primary process —i.e., to irrational thinking in which displacement and condensation play a major rôle.

Moreover, the ego is not only the seat of thought. It is also the seat of feeling. It is here that the sentiments and feelings, such as hope, despair, envy, pity, tenderness, respect, awe, gratitude, disappointment and so on take shape. It is here, too, that the more primary emotions and feelings of love, hatred, anger, joy, grief, and fear are experienced. To these states of mind Freud, in common with many of his contemporaries, gives the name of *affects*.

Although affects belong to the ego, they can possess a great deal of force. Anger, fear, grief, love, hatred, remorse, pity, envy, vengefulness and all the rest of it may visit the subject in only a very mild degree, so that he is only faintly annoyed or apprehensive, or mildly happy or sad, or has the dimmest of likes and dislikes, or suffers hardly perceptible twinges of conscience or entertains but a passing feeling of compassion or a momentary grudge; on the other hand, they may reach almost any degree of strength and can fill him with violent rage, or panic-stricken terror, or a sea of misery, or ecstasies of love or hate, delirious joy, agonies of remorse, and so on, to the exclusion of all other feelings and thoughts. This force must clearly be supplied from some source of energy. As clearly, too, much of it has the same quality as the two kinds of psychic energy which inform the instincts (or rather, their mental representatives). Feelings of love, affection, tenderness, compassion and remorse, for instance, are obviously mainly derived from the libido, whereas feelings of hatred, rage, envy, revenge, contempt, etc., get most of their colouring from the destructive principle. It is thus legitimate to assume that the affects draw the bulk of their energy from the id. Nevertheless, the ego has greatly modified this id-energy from its original instinctual form. Moreover, although, as we know, the ego is not supposed to possess much energy of its own, it undoubtedly has *some*—evoked, most probably, by psychic excitations arising from external stimuli (or even internal stimuli of a non-instinctual kind) rather than by instinctual ones; and this it may contribute to the emotions. In his later writings Freud regards fear, for instance, as a response by the ego to an excess of excitations rather than an echo of the excitations themselves; and fear can be an exceedingly powerful emotion.

Affects seldom exist as pure states of feeling divorced from all ideas. They nearly always go along with perceptions and ideas connected with the situation in which the emotion is involved. A man may be so furious or frightened that he does not think about what he is furious or frightened at, or why; but most often, he does. His mind is filled with images and ideas about the person he is furious with or the thing he is frightened of, what it is that makes him furious or frightened, why he should be so affected, and so on.[1]

Most affects carry with them conative attitudes. A person can hardly be in a towering rage with another without wanting to attack him or wishing him harm; grief for a lost object usually entails a desire to have it back; envy makes a man wish to be at least as well off as the person he envies; and fear makes him want to be in a safe place. Many of these conative attitudes and ideas are concerned with the fulfilment of id-aims, as, for instance, is obvious in the case of love and hatred. This is only to be expected in view of their predominantly instinctual origin. Though others, like fear once more, do not seem to proceed from the id but the ego.

The presence of conative attitudes in affects means that their ideational content, like that of instinctual presentations, is apt to be of the wishful kind; it tends to represent things to the subject as he wants them to be rather than as they are, and failing any subsequent correction of those ideas in the light of reality he accepts them as being true. The stronger his affect, of course, the more likely this is to happen, since his wishful ideas are correspondingly forcible. Such wishful thoughts do not necessarily involve the primary process; but they do involve unrealistic thinking.

Some affects, on the other hand, are not of a conative nature

---

[1] Yet the word 'affect'—and 'emotion', too, for the matter of that—is commonly used sometimes to mean the feeling alone, sometimes the feeling plus its accompanying ideas. It is thus advisable, when necessary for the sake of clarity, to call the feeling plus the ideas an *affective presentation*, the feeling alone its *affective cathexis*, and the ideas alone its *ideational content*, just as is done with instinctual presentations.

and do not carry any wishes with them. Sadness or joy, for instance, seem often to be pure states of feeling, or if they have an ideational content it is more concerned with what the subject's joy or sadness are about than what he wants to do about them. These states of mind do not entail wishful thinking by the subject. Nevertheless, they influence not only his feeling about things but his view of them. They do so in the direction of making him see them in a way which accords with his mood. Thus, if a person is feeling gloomy he is apt to think that everything is worse than it is, and if he is joyful he is inclined to view the world through rose-coloured spectacles. Such emotions therefore also lead to unrealistic thinking, though of a different kind.

Many of the affective cathexes, like the instinctual ones, find discharge in motor innervations leading to appropriate actions. The angry man hits out at what he is angry at, or if he cannot do that, at the next best thing or the empty air. The fond mother caresses her child or smiles at its picture. Such movements, of course, are to a large extent caused by instinctual elements in the affect; but sometimes, as when a person sighs from sadness, it seems a matter of feeling only. Expressive movements can also take place in the automatic or vegetative systems of the body. Joy makes the heart bound; anger brings on a rush of blood to the head; the bowels of compassion are moved, we are told; and grief lends itself to tears. It is for this reason, doubtless, that so many of the affects are commonly called 'emotions'.

These physical concomitants moreover, arouse various sensations in the subject which play no small part in the picture. The frightened man who has palpitations feels his heart pounding in a most uncomfortable and disconcerting manner; the man whose voice is choked with grief has a painful sensation of a lump in his throat; the angry man whose blood rushes to his head and who grinds his teeth, feels his face getting hot, the muscles of his jaws contracting, his teeth gritting together, and so on.

*

These sensations are so intimately connected with the affect from whose bodily concomitants they proceed that they are often regarded as part and parcel of the affect, not the least so by the subject himself. And this, too, no doubt, is why affects are no less commonly called 'feelings'.[1]

Many of these bodily concomitants serve, as we can see, to diminish the strength of the affect. A person finds relief from his grief in tears and he unburdens himself of some of his anger by grinding his teeth and clenching his fist. This may be because he is having the satisfaction of partially enacting his affective aims or simply because a portion of the cathexis involved is being discharged in the innervations concerned, or for both reasons. Some somatic signs, however, like having a lump in the throat when one is grieving, do not seem to have this cathartic effect. The griever is not relieved by it.

*　　*　　*

In addition, the ego experiences two special qualities of feeling in regard to a large number of mental presentations. These are of an opposite nature to each other. They are *pleasure* and *unpleasure*. The first accompanies all sensory (or 'physical') enjoyments such as eating good food, or sitting in a comfortable arm-chair, as well as non-sensory (or 'mental') ones—such as being happy or hopeful or self-satisfied about something; the second accompanies all sensory and non-sensory pain or discomfort, such as sitting on a pin or shivering with cold or despising oneself.

These two qualities of feeling can vary greatly in degree. They range from what is barely noticeable to an intolerable intensity.

Freud calls the influence exerted by pleasure and unpleasure on the behaviour of the subject the *Pleasure Principle*; and in so far as the ego is under the sway of this principle he names it the *Pleasure-Ego*.

The pleasure principle has extensive dominion over the ego, and, through it, powerfully controls the subject's actions.

---

[1] According to the James–Lange theory, indeed, an affect is nothing else than the sum of its somatic concomitants plus the sensations of them.

For his pleasure-ego forms a very large part of his whole ego, and it urges him to shun everything that gives or is likely to give him unpleasure, and to go for everything that gives him pleasure or holds out a promise of it. Moreover, pleasure and unpleasure come from many sources, so that they regulate his actions almost all the time. To begin with, the ego gets unpleasure from the tension set up by large quantities of undischarged cathexes, and it gets corresponding pleasure from the relaxation of tension which ensues from the discharge of those cathexes. Other things being equal, the greater is the tension, the greater is the unpleasure, and the more complete the relaxation the greater the pleasure. This being so, the pleasure and unpleasure which the ego gets from instinctual gratifications and frustration, respectively, can be very great, since the cathectic quantities involved in the instincts may be exceedingly high. Eating food when one is hungry, having sexual intercourse when one is lustful, hoarding one's goods when one's possessive instincts are in operation, getting hold of other people's goods when one's acquisitive instincts are aroused, attacking others when aggressive impulses come uppermost—all these activities can afford the ego much pleasure and their frustration much unpleasure, and the ego accordingly does what it can to promote them and to remove obstacles in their way. Then again, the ego obtains pleasure and unpleasure, great or small, from countless non-instinctual sources. Thus, for instance, the scent of a rose gives it pleasure and a kick from a boot or bending a stiff knee, unpleasure; consequently, it impels the subject to smell a rose, to get out of the way of a kick, and to avoid bending his stiff knee. Or, to speak of higher things, it may get pleasure from apperceiving the happiness of a friend and the distress of an enemy and unpleasure from the reverse, so that it moves the subject to help his friend and harm his enemy on both counts.

But it often happens that what gives the ego pleasure for one reason, gives it unpleasure for another. For one thing, as we know, the aims of one instinct are frequently incompatible with those of another and both may be activated at the same time. In such cases the subject cannot have it both ways completely. To the extent to which he gratifies the one instinct and gets pleasure from this, he frustrates the other instinct and gets unpleasure from that. Again, pleasure or unpleasure from instinctual sources may be accompanied by unpleasure or pleasure respectively from non-instinctual ones. Say a hungry man is offered a plate of rotten food; if he eats it the pleasure he gets from indulging his appetite is offset by the unpleasure he gets from its nasty taste, and if he does not eat it, the unpleasure he experiences from not indulging his appetite is diminished by his perception—supposing he smells the food—of what he is being spared in the way of a nasty taste. Then again, a non-instinctual pleasure may go along with non-instinctual unpleasure, as when a person who feels very cold steps into a bath that is too hot for him and so gets pleasure from the sensation of heat and unpleasure from the sensation of too much heat; or, to rise once more to superior heights, as when a person who feels cold pushes his way into the bathroom past another person who, he knows, feels equally cold, and so gets physical pleasure from a warm bath, but moral unpleasure from remorse at having acted selfishly. In all such cases the ego chooses that course of action which it expects to provide on balance most pleasure or least unpleasure.

The ego also experiences unpleasure from the existence of conflicting mental elements, and it strives for that reason to bring them into harmony with one another by making suitable modifications of them or compromises between them or by dismissing one or the other.

Again, the ego gets unpleasure from the presence in consciousness of mental elements which are obnoxious to the rest of the conscious mind, and for this reason, it often represses them.[1]

---

[1] Indeed, it may well be that unpleasure is the sole reason for repression and the pleasure-ego the only cause of it. Admittedly, there can be other reasons besides why obnoxious ideas should not be accepted or expressed or carried out; but rejection or condemnation and inhibition would suffice for this.

There is yet another way in which the ego operates under the influence of the pleasure principle. If things are not to its liking it may, instead of striving to make them so, or to adjust the subject's demands to them, permit his wishful mental presentations about them to come to the fore in consciousness and gain a footing there, so that they provide some of the pleasure which they would provide if they were true. If, for instance, the man on the third floor who sees a ten-shilling note on the pavement below, fails to get it, and so experiences unpleasure from the frustration of his aroused acquisitive instincts, he may decline to escape from that unpleasure by switching his desire for the note to more obtainable things or by rejecting or repressing it, but may instead go one better, as it were, and still obtain pleasure from it, by *imagining* that he has got hold of the note; and he may expand this idea and indulge in all sorts of visions of what he will buy with the note. This method of obtaining pleasure by fictitious means through the powers of the imagination, is of great importance in the economy of the mind, for it provides a most useful method of discharging instinctual excitations that cannot find an outlet in real life.

But the ego is by no means wholly under the sway of the pleasure principle. As we know, the ego's main business is to ensure the subject's welfare and to make him behave in an expedient way. Now it is true that what is pleasurable to him is frequently also good for him and what is unpleasurable, bad, so that the pleasure principle largely assists the ego in this matter. An abscess in a tooth, for instance, may injure a person's health if it is neglected; but even when he knows this, it is often only because the abscess is very painful that he goes to his dentist, as the lesser unpleasure of the two. (This correspondence between what is good or bad for the self and what is pleasurable or unpleasurable respectively is, of course, not accidental. For, but for it, the organism would have had so much less motive for acting in its own interests, and often such a powerful motive for acting against them that it would probably not have survived at all.) Nevertheless, not all that is unpleasurable is injurious nor all that is pleasurable beneficial. Morphia is a pain-removing drug, yet constant indulgence in it is harmful to the health; and cold baths, horrible as they are to many, do sometimes improve their health.

One of the first prerequisites for the ego, therefore, if it is to obey the dictates of self-preservation, is that some part of it should be unaffected by the pleasure principle so that it can withstand the demands of the pleasure ego. Moreover, in order to recognize what is good for the subject, the ego must be able to know reality, and also to test the subject's ideas in the light of that reality and recognize what is false in them. This system of evaluations Freud calls the *Reality Principle*, and that part of the ego which subscribes to it, the *Reality Ego*, in contradistinction to the pleasure principle and the pleasure ego.[1]

Nevertheless, the ego's ability to withstand pleasure or unpleasure and to apply the reality principle is often put at the service of the pleasure principle. For it is frequently a question of forgoing a present experience which is pleasurable or incurring one which is unpleasurable, for the sake of having a future experience which is so much more pleasurable or less unpleasurable, as the case may be, that it is worth doing so. If one is hungry, it is pleasurable to eat one's food even before it is quite cooked; but it is much more pleasurable to have waited till it was quite cooked. Similarly, if one feels cold in bed it may be more disagreeable to get up and make oneself a hot water bottle than to stay in bed, but not so disagreeable as to develop a cold in the head from not having got up. Left to itself, the pleasure-ego might not be able to forgo present pleasures or incur present unpleasures for the sake of as yet non-existent pleasures and unpleasures, superior as these may be. It is only in so far as his reality-ego, with its longer vision and its emancipation from the pleasure principle, lends a hand

---

[1] Cf. for this his paper 'Formulations on the Two Principles of Mental Functioning'.

that the subject can embark upon this course. Thus, just as the operation of the pleasure principle often helps him to attain his self-preservative ends, so, in turn, does the operation of the reality principle often help him to attain his hedonic ones.

Chapter IV

THE EGO-DEFENCES AND THEIR EFFECTS

THE inhibitions and repressions which the ego carries out from motives of pleasure or expediency are in the nature of protective measures, since they save the individual from suffering or injury. They are therefore called *mechanisms of defence*.

Inhibition and repression are, however, not the only methods by which the ego wards off obnoxious mental elements. It has many other ways of doing so, of which only the most important can be described here.[1]

One of these is known as *Reactive Formation*, or, more shortly, *Reaction*. In this, impulses and affects which are not in keeping with the conscious self are changed into their opposites. A boy who—whether from natural kindness, ethical considerations, fear of the consequences, or for whatever reason—repudiates his impulses of cruelty to cats and his desire to torment them, reverses those impulses and that desire into kindness to cats and a desire to be nice to them; a man who, out of shame or from motives of hygiene, condemns his liking for dirty habits such as going unwashed or never changing his underclothes, transforms that liking into a loathing and delights in baths and clean underclothes; a young woman, who, from a sense of decency, or love or fear, or a mixture of all three, cannot tolerate her feelings of hatred towards her step-father and her wishes for his death, turns that hatred into love and those death-wishes into wishes for his prolonged life and fears lest he should die; one girl who will

---

[1] In her book *The Ego and the Mechanisms of Defence*, Anna Freud, a daughter of Freud and herself a psycho-analyst, has given a very full and clear account of these methods, together with many illustrations from case material.

not give in to her greedy appetites, for fear, perhaps, of getting fat, takes a dislike to food, and another, who rejects her vanity about her personal appearance, because, say, she thinks it immoral, hates being well-dressed and prefers shabby clothes. Ambition turns into diffidence or the other way round, meanness into generosity or *vice versa*; cowardice gives place to courage, recklessness to caution; domination becomes subservience and subservience domination; and so on and so forth.

The original, obnoxious, affect or wish gives rise, needless to say, to a whole number of corresponding ideas, images and perceptions. The boy who feels cruel to cats has all sorts of thoughts about tying tin cans to their tails, letting them starve, or seeing dogs set on them, and so on; and if at any time he gives way to his impulses, and enacts them, he will have sense-perceptions as well of those events. Similarly, the dirt-loving man entertains many ideas, and perhaps some perceptions, too, concerning the smell and feel of dirty clothes next his body or concerning his own greasy, unwashed skin. The hating step-daughter has visions of many ills befalling her step-father—some helped on by herself—and the vain or greedy girl sees in her mind's eye charming pictures of her person or mountains of delectable food. And as the feeling undergoes various modulations and spreads to other contexts, so does the stock of ideas arising from it increase. When the attitude is reversed, it in its turn evokes many consonant ideas (including a great many perceptions, since, being now acceptable, it is freely enactable). These ideas are naturally the opposite of the ideas belonging to the original feelings.[1] The boy who turns his cruel feelings towards cats into kind ones is full of thoughts for their welfare and happiness and how he can ensure their good treatment and make friends with them; the step-daughter who reverses her hatred of her step-father

---

[1] For the sake of brevity, I often use the single word 'idea' to mean any ideational element—sense-perceptions as well as images and thoughts. For the same reason I also often use the word 'feeling' for all conative or affective states—impulses, wishes, feelings, etc.; and in this particular passage, this latter set of words excludes all ideational elements.

into love of him entertains a quantity of ideas about all the nice things that might happen to him and how she can promote them; the man who reacts to his bent for personal dirtiness with a bent for personal cleanliness is taken up with a multitude of images and sensations of wearing clean clothes and having baths; and the reactively abstemious girl or the reactively modest one has a lot of notions concerning plain living or plain looks, as the case may be. Many of these new ideas correspond specifically to ideas which the original feeling gave rise to. If, for instance, the boy's feelings of cruelty to cats made him have thoughts of starving them, his reverse feeling of kindness to them will make him have thoughts of feeding them up; and if the step-daughter's hatred of her step-father led her to have ideas of some public disgrace befalling him, her reactive love of him will lead her to have ideas of his receiving some public honour; and so on. Such ideas might well be called 'reactive' not only in the sense of being products of a reactive feeling but of being themselves reversals of the original ideas.

With the supersession of the old feeling by the new, moreover, many of the ideas generated by the former disappear. The boy no longer thinks about ways of ill-treating cats but about ways of doing them good, and the clean man drops his thoughts of dirtiness in favour of thoughts of cleanness. And if the old set of ideas are put before the subject from outside —as when the boy is told stories about starving animals, or the man is forced to be dirty through lack of facilities for washing—he will be most disagreeably affected and he will do his best to remove himself from the situation or alter it.

The reactive feeling is, of course, attached to many elements of the old ideational content, in the shape of reactive ideas, and these are combined in new ways and introduced into fresh contexts which give them an opposite sense to the old. Cats still hold the cat-cherishing boy's attention, though now they are well-treated cats, and the cleanly man continues to think a lot about his underclothes, albeit his thoughts are about clean ones. Indeed, parts of the old ideational content are often preserved in more significant units, which point to the original feeling and depict its aims as fulfilled; but these, too, are woven into the new aims and ideas so as to give them a contrary direction. The kind boy may still think of starved cats but now he pities them and thinks of feeding them up. The cleanly man continues to have ideas about dirty clothes, but they fill him with disgust, and he has ideas of getting out of them into clean ones.

Nevertheless, the old significant ideas often continue to exist apart from any such remedial ideas. And in any case they tend to possess a high degree of intensity, as if the subject were quite as much interested in them as in their opposites. Our kind boy may plague himself with pitiful notions of starving cats and yet not have many notions of anything being done about it, and our cleanly man may think with disgust about wearing dirty underclothes without thinking much about wearing clean underclothes or even getting out of his dirty ones. Considering the unpleasurable nature of the ideas, this is surprising. It looks suspiciously as if the original feeling which generated them had not been altogether given up after all, but was continuing to nourish them in secret. And this, in fact, is what analysis often discovers to be the case. We find that a greater or lesser portion of the original feeling nearly always still persists in attachment to the old ideas and that all the ego has been able to do with that portion is not to *exchange* it for opposite feelings but only to overlay and *combat* it with them. Beneath the surface, the old feeling struggles against the new, and although its force is reduced by the conflict, and it itself is relegated to unconsciousness, it manages to push many of its ideas into consciousness, though they are coloured there only by the contrary feeling which is now also attached to them. Some of its ideas, however, are usually not capable of becoming conscious in any case, owing to the fact that their very content betrays its nature. This is so wherever they depict the subject's favourable attitude to his obnoxious ideas. Thus, for instance, it is all very well for a step-daughter to have conscious thoughts about the ills that might befall her step-father or even about how she herself might accidentally cause his death; but it will not do for her to have conscious thoughts about how she might purposely contrive his death, or images of herself laughing and dancing at his funeral.

In so far, too, as the original feeling has not been reversed but merely repressed and opposed by contrary feelings, the resultant reactive feeling is apt to be excessively strong and somewhat demonstrative. For the subject is obliged to exaggerate the reactive feeling in order to make head against the still existing old feeling, and he must make a great show of the former in order to disguise from himself and others the continued presence of the latter. Only by loading her step-father with affection and thoroughly spoiling him can the step-daughter, for instance, who still unconsciously hates him, hide her hatred from herself and persuade herself that she truly loves him.

This method of warding off mental presentations is one of out-balancing or *counteraction* rather than true reversal, and whenever it is important to make the distinction, I should like to use the term 'overcompensation' for it, in preference to 'reaction'.

In overcompensation, the repressed portion of the original feeling, moreover, is incessantly seeking outlet in consciousness and motility, and it does not cease its displacements till it has come upon ideas in attachment to which it finds such an outlet.

The overcompensating step-daughter, for instance, may not be able to manifest her hatred and death-wishes which were originally directed to her step-father when they are directed to his friends (in regard to whom, therefore, they are once more reversed or repressed); but she may be able to manifest them when they are directed to people who do not like him. And these she will consciously hate and wish harm to with strange intensity.

Just as we give the name of 'cathexis' to the sum of psychic energy which forms part of an original mental presentation or its derivatives and which is attached to their ideational content, so do we give the name of 'anticathexis' to the sum of psychic energy which forms part of these reactive or counteractive presentations and which is attached to *their* ideational content. The anticathexes supply these new presentations with the necessary force to withstand the force, whether actual or potential, of the old ones. (The concept of anticathexis, however, is employed in a wider sense than this, as we shall see more fully later on. It is used to mean not only the investment of psychic energy in mental presentations which are the opposite to the original presentation, but its investment in ego-syntonic mental presentations[1] which shall take up some of the original cathexis as well, and, by mingling it with the new, make a kind of absorbent zone for it rather than a repelling barrage against it. Thus, for instance, a man who cannot bear the idea of dying may deal with it not by asserting to himself that he will not die, nor by denying the existence of death or becoming reckless of it, but, say, by the philosophic reflection that all mortals must die, or by telling himself that it is better to die than to grow old and infirm and see one's friends die; or he may invent grand scenes—and even enact one in reality—in which he dies for such a good cause or in so noble a way that half the sting of death is removed.)[2]

Reactive formation can be applied to intellectual judgments and attitudes of every sort. A person may, for example, counteract his disbelief about certain things by cultivating an extra strong belief in them instead. The small boy whose faith in Father Christmas is beginning to be shaken but who very much wants Father Christmas to exist, may keep his scepticism at bay by redoubling his faith in that personage and by thinking and talking about him all the time as if he were just round the corner; and this reactive belief may extend to associated persons or things—to Loch Ness monsters or little green men.

[1] i.e. mental presentations which are in keeping with the conscious ego. The term is sometimes shortened to 'syntonic'.

[2] This wider concept of anticathexis is, incidentally, more in line with Freud's earliest view, according to which anticathexes were sums of libidinal energy which had been displaced from an unconscionable idea to the nearest conscionable one and caused it to be extra forcible.

Conversely, the subject may counteract his belief about certain things if it offends his sense of probability or if he does not want them to be true, by fostering in himself a complete disbelief in them, and one which may be impervious to reason whatever the topic he extends it to. Thus, a man who has reacted against his childhood belief in fairies may not be able to believe in a giraffe when he sees one. In the same way, a person thinks what he thought good or beautiful or useful, bad or ugly or useless as the case may be, and *vice versa*. The subject's own intellectual capacities or interests or experience can also come in for reaction. He may strive to make up for his natural stupidity or ignorance about certain things or in general by forcing himself through hard work to become extra clever or well-informed in those fields of knowledge; conversely, he may counter his native sharpness of mind or his too much knowledge of certain matters or his too great curiosity about them by becoming dull-witted or ignorant or uninterested in them.

This defensive mechanism is furthermore applied to bodily properties of the subject. If his ego cannot bear to observe certain physical defects in him it moves him not merely to make them good, but to more than make them good, so that he excels in what before he fell short in. The puny man, for instance, will work at his dumb-bells until he becomes a minor Sandow; the man with a crooked back will exercise until he is ideally straight; and the man with a poor circulation will harden himself to withstand the bitterest cold. History tells us how Demosthenes, from being a wretched stammerer, trained himself to become the greatest orator in the world.[1]

Often, however, the ego fails to effect the required counteraction of the attribute, whether mental or physical, which it repudiates. The coward cannot always become a hero, or as much of one as he wants to be, although he may make himself

---

[1] Adolf Adler, a one-time analyst and disciple of Freud, lays great stress upon this application of the mechanism to the somatic sphere, and has shown how wide are its ramifications and how important its effects. Indeed, he regards it, very exaggeratedly, as one of the mainsprings of human behaviour. (Cf. his book *Studie über Minderwertigkeit von Organen*.)

less cowardly than he was, or even reasonably brave; the dunce, study as he may to become brilliant, rarely attains more than an ordinary amount of intelligence, if that; and the puny man may not achieve all he wants in the way of Sandowism. A hunchback cannot straighten his back, nor a dwarf reach gianthood, let alone average height. In such cases, the subject frequently helps himself out by having recourse to his imagination and *pretends* to himself that his properties are the opposite of what they are. Thus the coward who cannot turn hero thinks of himself as performing deeds of daring; the dunce who cannot shine dreams of astounding the world with his brilliance; and the dwarf who cannot be taller than others, has phantasies of towering head and shoulders above them. And if he should delude himself into *believing* his imaginings, this can have strange results.

The feelings and ideas which are reacted against or over-compensated for are, of course, mostly of an ego-dystonic kind.[1] To want to be cruel to cats is not up to the standards of nice young persons, nor is it well looked on by one's companions if one is dirty in one's habits; whilst for a step-daughter to hate her step-father and desire his death is not the thing at all, unless he is a fiend in human shape. Greediness is bad for health and figure alike, and vanity is discouraged on all sides. Nevertheless, the mental attitudes which undergo reactive formation often seem harmless enough, not to say commendable. A person may reverse his curiosity about quite innocent and interesting things into a dislike of knowing anything about them, or he may transform a liking to be decently turned out into a cult for dowdiness. Or again, he may not be able to tolerate in himself the slightest severity towards a friend or any adverse criticism of him, but must be affable and compliant to him all the time, with the result that he can never make use of those often so necessary means for helping or advising him.

---

[1] I.e. out of keeping with the conscious ego. The shorter word 'dystonic' is often used.

Such an application of reactive formation to psychic material which does not appear to call for it is due to its meaning in the unconscious. There the innocent attitude is connected with attitudes that are not so innocent and is being banned on their account. Wanting to be neatly dressed may stand for wanting to cut everyone else out in the matter of dress; being interested, say, in plant-life, or the habits of insects may represent a devouring curiosity about horrific matters or about things to do with one's own sex-life; and being severe with a friend or critical about him may be the reflection of highly hostile feelings towards him.

Grossly inappropriate reactive formations do not occur in normal psychology, for they are brought to bear on properties which are dystonic to the ego on more or less reasonable grounds. Thus they work predominantly in a civilizing direction and do much to make the individual a good and useful member of society. Indeed, they have no small hand in producing its most shining examples. The tireless philanthropist, the devoted hospital nurse, the zealous official of the R.S.P.C.A., the selfless hero, the thorough scavenger, the punctual employee, the incorruptible servant of the public, the conscientious worker, the devotee of hygiene—all these good and useful types usually owe something at least of their admirable qualities to a reaction against opposite ones. Without it, the philanthropist might be a callous egotist, the R.S.P.C.A. man himself a torturer of animals, the hospital nurse a Sarah Gamp, the hero a coward, and the employee always late at his desk; the scavenger might fail to clean the streets, the public servant might take bribes, the worker play truant, and the hygienic man spread germs right and left.

Yet, even so, reactive attitudes can have considerable drawbacks, as they are often overdone or uncalled for. The philanthropist from reaction tends to be too kind to people who do not deserve it and who might be the better for a little severity; the overcompensating nurse gives more care to her patients than they need or than is good for them; the hero who reacts against his cowardice often throws away his life when it would have been more profitable for his country if he had run away to fight another day.

The mechanism also has serious drawbacks for the individual himself. The over-assiduous nurse wears herself out in her work of mercy, the too-kind philanthropist goes short of necessities to supply them to others, the hero's life is likely to be cut short and the tireless worker heads for a breakdown. Nor must we leave out of account the large amount of unpleasure which the subject experiences from the continuance of ideas belonging to his original feelings. The reactive nurse is especially sensitive to the suffering she sees about her, the reactive hero dreads the possibility of cowardice in himself and loathes any sign of it in others, and the reactive scavenger shudders at the filth he loves to clear away.

Another drawback is this: Although the reactive formations are so largely directed against the id, their task is in many cases facilitated by that very agency. For the ego makes lavish use of the energy and modes of behaviour of the ucs. in warding off the dystonic material. It changes a person's cruel feelings into kind ones and *vice versa*, with the help of the mutual reversibility of his libidinal and destructive instincts, and it overcomes his love with hatred and or the other way about, in virtue of their ambivalence.[1] This holds equally good with repression, which takes advantage of the displaceability of unconscious cathexes to keep unwanted ideas out of consciousness, and it is also true of inhibition, which, as we know, often frustrates one instinct by calling in another.—The same, as we shall see,

---

[1] The preponderant role played by ambivalence and the mutual reversibility of libidinal and destructive attitudes in reactive formation is clear enough where the feeling that is reversed is obviously and primarily one of hostility or friendliness towards the object, as we see, for instance, in the example of the daughter who changes her hatred of her step-father into love of him. And such cases are very common. But the same factors are also at work where those attitudes are less openly and less exclusively involved in the feeling. Take, for instance, our other example of the dirty man turned clean. He once liked dirty things and his experience of them was libidinally cathected. In reacting against this, he transfers some of his liking to things of the opposite sort and reverses the rest into its opposite quality. The situation now is not merely that he likes cleanliness and is indifferent to dirt—as, say, one might like jam and be indifferent to bread—but that he actually dislikes dirt. In so far as this is so, it argues an underlying change of his libidinal attitude to dirty things into a destructive one.

applies to most, if not all, defensive mechanisms. Indeed, they could scarcely function without thus exploiting the ucs., seeing how small is the force of the ego compared with that of the id. It is clear that the most advantageous method of dealing with ego-dystonic mental presentations is one in which the largest possible amount of the psychic energy belonging to them is able, in modified form, to enter the preconscious system, and the least possible amount of energy belonging to other presentations is lost to that system in the process. In this respect reactive formation, at least in its over-compensatory aspect, leaves much to seek. It cannot but put considerable amounts of psychic energy out of commission for free adaptive use by the ego. The energic quantities adhering on the one hand to inadmissible presentations and, on the other, to the presentations designed to counteract them— the cathexes and anticathexes—are bound in a perpetual deadlock and unable to leave those ideas for any others. A person, for instance, who is busy combating thoughts of death by dwelling on thoughts of immortality or safety first can hardly give his full attention to a round of golf or to business at the office; nor, other things being equal, can a boy who is occupied with keeping off his desire to be cruel to cats with a desire to be kind to them display as much zest in other fields of activity that come his way, as can the boy who is troubled with no such conflicts. The amount of psychic energy thus 'frozen', as it were, and withdrawn from currency, depends, of course, on the quantities of the cathexes and anticathexes implicated.

Finally, it must not be forgotten that in reaction—and still more in over-compensation—there is the same danger as in repression of the dystonic trend becoming too strong for the opposing mechanism and, in part at least, breaking its way through. An R.S.P.C.A. official, for instance, may feel more eager than most mortals to flog persons who are cruel to animals, not so much on account of his pity for the animals as because of his latent cruelty to them which now finds an excellent substitutive object.

*   *   *

Some of the disadvantages outlined above seem to be largely absent in another ego-mechanism, known as *sublimation*. This mechanism is applied to the instincts and consists in inhibiting their aim, so that they cannot be gratified in their unmodified form, and in supplying them instead with non-instinctual aims which are not only admissible to consciousness but positively useful or valuable; but instead of achieving this through a reversal or counteraction of the instincts in question, it does so by refining them and deflecting their course into channels which are a continuation of them on a higher plane.

In sublimation, for instance, a man deals with his homicidal impulses, not by turning pacifist, but by becoming a criminal lawyer, or a war correspondent, or a crime reporter, or a writer of blood-and-thunder books, or a surgeon or a student of war—in all which activities he can gratify no little of those impulses in a to a very large extent aim-inhibited way (since he kills no one), and this not only legitimately but with considerable profit and enjoyment to himself and others. Similarly, when a woman sublimates her exhibitionistic impulses she does so not by dressing so as to attract as little attention as possible, but by dressing so as to please the artistic rather than the sensual eye; or she develops an intelligent interest in fashions generally and, perhaps, becomes a designer of clothes. Again, a person with strong eating instincts sublimates them by becoming a good cook, or cultivating the aesthetic or scientific aspect of food—such as how to plan a nutritious meal or combine its courses into a harmonious whole—rather than by becoming indifferent to food or ascetic about it.

Sublimation plays a very important part in the erotic sphere. It deprives the libidinal instincts of their sexual aim; but it develops instead the non-sensual side of love in the form of feelings of affection and friendship. Moreover, it encourages its idealistic aspects and enables the subject to entertain Platonic friendships and romantic attachments to persons and devotion to causes, and it fills his heart with a fund of tender imaginings.[1]

In the absence of any head-on collision, as it were, between the impulse and the defensive forces—and with the pursuit by the latter of a policy of attenuation and deflection of the former rather than suppression or counteraction of it—we should expect to find that sublimation does not need nearly so much expenditure of mental energy as either reaction or repression. Nor should it be so liable to involve unpleasure or to remain affixed, along with what it fends off, to unconscious modes of mentation, seeing that the preconscious ego works in alliance with rather than opposition to the id as a whole. Indeed, it would hardly be justifiable to call sublimation a defensive mechanism at all, were it not for the ego's determination to ward off the instinct even though it does this by, as it were, less oppositional means.

This is true enough as far as it goes; and many sublimations are indeed characterized by an ease, a fitness, a pleasure and a stability which are often wanting in the other mechanisms. Nevertheless, sublimation is usually taken to imply a pretty high level of achievement in the adult. It is not enough to displace the instinctual aim on to what is merely *admissible* to the subject's conscious self; it must be on to something that is regarded as valuable and *good*. To modify one's instinct to kill, for instance, into a desire to watch a fox-hunt or a habit of tearing paper to bits is not enough, innocent as those activities are; one must modify it into at least an interest in the history of war or a study of military strategy, or writing crime stories or painting scenes of death and destruction or hunting down criminals. The attainment of such elevated standards necessitates a great deal of realistic modification and adaptive displacement, and this requires no little activity and effort on the part of the ego, so that relapses from sublimation,

[1] Freud originally used the word 'sublimation' exclusively for such a de-sexualization and elimination of the libidinal instincts. But this was before he turned his attention to the destructive instincts. At the start, too, he did not make a very clear distinction between sublimation and reaction, and often called by the latter name what we should now call by the former.

no less than from repression or reaction, may occur if, for any reason, the instinct in question becomes very strong or the ego much reduced.

Sublimation, like reaction, is responsible for many virtues, both private and public. Often, too, it leads to the same product, though by a different route. A nurse's devotion to her patients may equally well be based on a sublimation of her libidinal impulses as on a reaction against her destructive ones; and a man's affection for his wife can be the result of a reversal of his hostility to her no less than of a desexualization of his erotic feelings for her. Such products are indeed more often than not the outcome of a mixture of both mechanisms.

* * *

A much more superficial compromise between the conscious and the unconscious is effected by yet another defensive mechanism. This is called *Rationalization*.[1] As its name implies, rationalization consists of giving an air of truth and plausibility to false and absurd ideas and in making inappropriate actions and feelings seem appropriate by adducing specious motives for them, this being done in perfect good faith by the subject. A cook, for instance, may be afraid to touch the new electric cooker which has just been installed. The reason which she gives, and believes consciously, is that the kitchen is damp and that one of the wires is frayed, so that there might be a short-circuit and she might get a shock. This is true enough. The kitchen *is* damp and the wire *is* frayed. But the kitchen is not so damp nor the wire so frayed that there is any but a very remote chance of a short-circuit and this she is in a position to know. Psycho-analytic investigation (or questioning under hypnosis) may reveal that what the cook unconsciously believes, and what motivates her fear, is that the electric cooker is a magic box with a malevolent demon inside who will strike her dead if she touches it. Such a primitive notion was unacceptable to her conscious intelligence, which clothed

---

[1] This mechanism was first described and named by Dr. Ernest Jones. (Cf. his paper, 'Rationalization in Every-Day Life'.)

it in scientific language, without, however, fundamentally altering it.

The facts and arguments which are adduced to support a piece of rationalization often betray the unconscious origin of that attitude, not only by the falsity of the facts and the fallacy of the logic upon which it is based, but by the violence with which it is held and by its imperviousness to all counter-argument or evidence to the contrary. The cook's fear of getting an electric shock is irremovable; and if her complaint that the kitchen floor is damp and a wire frayed is taken seriously and the floor is dried and the wire mended, she will probably refuse to believe that these things have been properly done, or else she will raise a new complaint, such as that the floor is made of stone and so, dry or not dry, not properly insulated. If a rubber mat is put upon the floor to improve the insulation, she will say that it is too thin to be efficacious, and so on, and so forth.

But often, too, a rationalization is so ingenious and plausible that it appears to be founded on true facts and sound reasoning, and completely veils the ucs. thoughts behind it. Indeed, the facts which the rationalizer brings forward and the arguments he uses sometimes *are* perfectly correct. But they still are rationalizations, because it is not those facts and arguments but his underlying unrealistic ideas which are the operative motives of his conscious attitude. Thus, suppose the frayed wire in the kitchen really was dangerous and the cook refused to use the electric cooker for that reason consciously, her refusal might nevertheless be based upon her unconscious belief in the demon in the cooker, and mending the wire would do no good.

Another reason why the presence of rationalization is not always easy to detect is that it is often used by the subject to mask unconscious ideas from himself which other people are almost as anxious not to be aware of as he—and all the more so seeing that their own unconscious, too, is often manufacturing the same ideas, which are also seeking expression and being denied it as they stand. Thus, if he provides those ideas

with a form of expression which is in not too glaring contradiction with reality they are only too glad to accept it at its
face value and benefit by it. The master of the house may
concur in his cook's assertion that the electric cooker is not
properly wired, though he knows better, because he, also,
believes in the depths of his mind that there is a demon inside
it. Furthermore, to question the validity of the rationalization
would be not only to deny to the criticizers a vicarious mode
of giving disguised utterance to similar unconscious ideas in
themselves; by undermining that mechanism they threaten
to bring to light the undisguised idea behind it in themselves
as well as in the rationalizer. The master of the house concurs
in his cook's assertion about the cooker having dangerously
frayed wires, not only because he shares her belief in the
demon inside it but because he would not for the world
expose *her* and therefore *his* belief in demons to his critical
and realistic ego. Best let sleeping dogs lie, even if they growl
in their sleep.

The work of rationalization is strikingly shown in the
explanations which persons often give of the actions they
perform or the ideas they entertain or the feelings or impulses
they have as a result of post-hypnotic suggestion. If, for
instance, a man is told not to drink his beer at lunch-time
next day because it will have been poisoned, he may, in not
drinking it, adduce as a reason for his abstention that the beer
tastes nasty, or that it is bad for his health, or even that it is
too expensive. Again, if he is told to feel angry when next he
sees his friend, he may account for his anger by saying that
his friend happened to come along just as he was feeling angry
about his income-tax; and if he is told to run away from a
dragon, he runs away, but declares it was a dangerous car in
the offing which made him take to his heels.

Rationalization has a great practical value for real life,
especially on its social side. For by means of it the subject can,
in part at least, indulge his prohibited thoughts and feelings
without giving offence to others, and can, in turn, tolerate
the partial indulgence by others of their inadmissible thoughts

Chapter V

DISTORTIONS IN PROJECTION AND INTROJECTION

OUR list of the main defensive mechanisms is not yet exhausted. There are still other important methods by which the ego deals with dystonic mental presentations.

One of these is known as *Projection*. In this the subject rids himself of an obnoxious presentation by assigning it to another person. If, for instance, a man wants to attack his wife but is unable to tolerate this wish, he may give it up, but become convinced instead that his neighbours want to attack her; or if he knows that his sister is a secret drinker, but cannot face the fact, he may cease to know it, and may imagine that someone else is slanderously accusing her of that vice.

The subject's ego can, of course, proceed in the same way with mental presentations about himself. Thus if he wants to attack himself, he may cease to do so but believe instead that someone else wants to attack him; or if he is a drunkard he may prefer to think that he is no such thing but that other people are falsely accusing him of being one. He can also deal with his dystonic presentations about himself along the same lines, by believing, not that it is someone else, not he, who is entertaining them, but that it is someone else, not he, about whom they are. The man, for instance, who cannot bear to realize that he is a drunkard may, instead of believing that other people are falsely accusing him of it, believe that someone else is a drunkard, and the man who originally wanted

C

to attack himself may now be convinced that he is dangerous to some other person.[1]

Where the person's mental presentation is about himself, both sorts of projection—the one in which he refuses to believe that it is his own and attributes it to someone else, and the one in which he refuses to believe that it is about himself and asserts that it is about another—can occur together. In that case all that remains of his original presentation is that it is somebody else's presentation about someone else. The man who wants to attack himself believes that, say, his friend wants to attack his elder brother; and the drunkard thinks that the man next door suspects his landlady of drinking. When both these sorts of projection relate to the *same* other person, then the subject will believe that that person thinks or feels about himself what he—the subject—originally thought and felt about himself. In that case the man who wants to attack himself may think, say, that his young lady wants to attack *herself*, and be suitably concerned; and the drunkard believes that the man next door both is, and realizes with pain that he is, a drunkard.

A characteristic kind of projection is one in which the subject attributes to his objects ideas and feelings about himself which he himself had precisely about *them*. Thus, for instance, if a man hates his aunt, he may come to believe not simply that she hates someone else, but that she hates *him*; or if he regards his two brothers as a couple of cheats and condemns them accordingly, he may, instead, regard them as (unjustly) condemning *him* as a cheat. Projection in this narrow sense is often found to be at the bottom of what emerges as a projection in one of its wider senses, owing to the occurrence of subsequent further displacement. Thus, for instance, a man who hates his aunt may in fact have projected his hatred of her in such a way that he believes that she hates him; but this belief may itself be intolerable to him, and so he

[1] If the *feeling* of the presentation as well as its ideational content undergoes this change, so that he now not only believes that he may attack other people but actually wants to, then a turning outward of the impulse has occurred. This, though not in itself a projection, obviously often goes along with it and perhaps underlies it.

displaces his idea of someone-who-hates-him from her to another person. He now believes that it is not she but, let us say, her sister-in-law, whom he has never hated, who hates him.

The field of objects upon which a person can project his feelings and ideas is not limited to human beings. The subject's unconscious ego can attribute to dumb creatures and even to inanimate things properties which belong to him. He may think that it is his dog, not he who is suspicious of his friend, or that it was the table, not his own movement, which was clumsy when he stubbed his toe against it. He may, indeed, project his presentations upon thin air. In that case he feels the presence of disembodied influences; or he even creates apparitions to contain them. He makes great use, too, of ready-made imaginary figures and influences for this purpose. The bad airs and sinister elementals of superstition and folklore, the terrifying ogres of myth and fairy-story and the many disagreeable characters of ordinary fiction—all these often help him to displace corresponding properties in himself elsewhere. The sinister figure of the *Doppelgänger* (the Double) exhibits their use very clearly. For it not only reflects the subject's own repudiated properties—his evil side—but dogs his footsteps wherever he goes and is thus obviously a part of him.

The mechanism of projection is very primitive and occurs in early infancy. By the time the individual has grown up he has usually left much of it behind. A good deal of it still goes on in unconscious levels of his mind, but his comparatively well-developed preconscious, as well as his wide experience of reality, tends to modify it or prevent him from giving way to it; and if not, he at least chooses a probable object for it or represses its products or recognizes them as untrue (though even so they make their influence felt indirectly more than is supposed). Children, on the other hand, with their weaker sense of reality and their smaller experience of it, are held back by no such considerations. They freely and openly attribute their dystonic properties to the most unlikely persons and beasts and trees and stocks and stones alike, not to mention imaginary beings, and they seem to have no difficulty in lending credence to them there. The child is as apt to put its wooden horse in the corner as its little sister for its own misdemeanour, and it is as likely to fear its own anger in a lowering cloud or a menacing gnome as in a big dog or a new face. In children, however, there is a more realistic foundation for such a projection of exclusively human attributes onto non-human objects than there is in adults. For they are surrounded by human objects who influence and guide almost the whole of their life, so that it is more plausible for them to expect all objects to be human and capable of possessing human properties. Ignorant or uneducated persons are also more prone to give way to this mechanism, deficient as they are in the necessary knowledge of facts or the mental discipline to modify or criticize its products. Primitive people, too, in whom the preconscious system is so much less developed in comparison with the unconscious system than is the case with civilized people, are greatly addicted to projection. Savages see their own repudiated properties in a hundred and one shapes about them—in fearsome witches flying through the air, in dangerous forces emanating from their neighbours, and in occult influences everywhere. Certain types of mental aberrations, too, as we shall see later on, exhibit this mechanism in great force. The sufferer believes himself surrounded and persecuted by real or imaginary persons and figures whose supposedly bad intentions are often nothing but a distorted reflection of his own.

It goes without saying that projection in itself implies no change whatever in the non-self object in respect of which it is made. When a man regards his friend or his dog as possessing say, his own suspicions or his own crooked toe, those beings are not a whit the more suspicious or the less straight-toed for that. (Projection may *lead* to a change in it—as, for example, when a small boy attributes his naughtiness to his toy horse and throws it into the corner and breaks it. But even so, the object is rarely changed in the *sense* of the projection. The boy's horse is broken, not made naughty, by his belief in its naughtiness.)

Nor does projection necessarily imply any alteration as regards the properties concerned in the subject. It is no good ascribing one's crooked toe to another; one will not thereby get rid of it. (Once again it often alters some properties of the subject, though not in the sense imagined by him. Thus, when the owner of a crooked toe ceases to believe that he has one but believes instead that someone else has, this does not mean that he ceases to have a crooked toe; but it does mean that he becomes happier about his appearance.) On the other hand, projection often *does* alter the property concerned and in the sense he supposes, though not to the extent he supposes. When a man projects, say, his anger or his sadness on to other people, he does, in fact, rid himself of those feelings, though perhaps only on the more conscious levels of his mind.

As we see, projection greatly falsifies the subject's picture of himself and his objects. Yet it does sometimes, and in some respects, give him a more realistic idea of them than he would otherwise have. The property which he projects is often in fact present in the persons upon whom he projects it, though to a far lesser degree than he thinks, or in a repressed and inhibited state. Thus although in ascribing it to them he is mistaken in believing that they possess it strongly and consciously and that they indulge it, he is right in believing that they do possess it. This, incidentally, is what often makes it so annoying to be accused of thinking or doing things which, to the best of one's belief, one has not thought, and which one certainly has not done. The accusation is false as to one's *conscious* thoughts and *real* actions; but it is true as to one's *unconscious* thoughts and *desired* actions. No amount of proof that one has not consciously thought or really done them avails to refute the charge in one's own mind, since one's unconscious knows better.

Then, too, however false the subject's projective view of the external world may be about *it*, it is an excellent clue to properties of *himself*, which often cannot be known in any other way. A man who wrongly feels that another person is unkind to him is very likely fighting against his own unkind impulses (directed, perhaps, to that very person); and a woman who unjustly suspects her neighbours of envying their betters is in all probability choosing this method of fending off feelings of envy in herself.[1]

As so far described, projection comprises two events: a rejection of properties of the self and an ascription of them to the non-self. But it may comprise only one of those events, viz. an ascription of those properties (or exactly similar ones) elsewhere, *without* a rejection of them in the self. Thus, for instance, a man who projects his anger onto another person in the heretofore described sense will believe that that other person is angry and will cease to feel angry himself; but a man who projects it in this new sense will, while believing that the other person is angry, continue to feel angry too.

This limited form of projection does not have the advantage of ridding the subject of his unwelcome properties; but by bestowing them upon others as well, his ego can often ease the unpleasure of possessing them himself. Thus, for example, if a man cannot get rid of his anger against another person or his impulse to attack him by attributing those attitudes to someone else, he can at least feel less badly about them by supposing that someone else shares his feelings towards that person; if he has a crooked toe, it may console him to believe that many other people have crooked toes too, even if he cannot deny the evidence of his eyes and believe that he has

[1] Yet it must not be forgotten that the projector's view, whether of self or non-self properties, are apt, like any other person's, to be untrue. He may, for instance, believe that he is a coward when he is in reality brave, or perceive his straight toe as a crooked one. Certainly, if he projects this false view of himself *qua* view onto some other object—if he allocates to another the ownership of it in his place, so that he now thinks that that person regards him as a coward or as having a crooked toe —then his view of that person does correctly reflect his repudiated view of himself in that respect; but if he projects those views in the sense of believing that someone else is a coward or has a crooked toe—making that object the grammatical object, as it were, instead of the grammatical subject of his mental presentation—then the picture which that object reflects of himself as being a coward or having a crooked toe is as untrue of him as it is of it. In this case, therefore, we must beware of reading into his view of others what he is really like himself.

not got one; and if he knows he is a cheat, it is better to view his companion as a cheat too, than to think he stands alone —though doubtless not so good as to think himself honest.

This kind of projection causes the subject to believe that he and the object upon whom he has projected the property have that property in common. To that extent, therefore, the object seems to him to be exactly like himself. The greater the number, extent or importance of his properties supposed by him to be thus held in common by him and any particular object, the more extensive will this similarity appear. As far as those properties go, the subject thus identifies the object with himself. He sees it in his own image. Such a thing, of course, could not happen if he no longer experienced the properties as his own, as occurs in the type of projection described earlier. This distinguishing feature is perhaps the most marked of them all, and I shall accordingly, when necessary, call this second type of projection *identificatory projection*. Identificatory projection is the more common kind of projection, and it leads to a very extensive anthropomorphic view of things. It is largely responsible for the inclination we all have to regard not only animals but inanimate objects as endowed with human feeling and thought and even shape. To nearly everyone, unwatered flowers are thirsty as he would be if he had nothing to drink; untidy rooms feel dishevelled and want to be tidied up; the windows of a house are its eyes, and when the blinds are drawn it is asleep, or perhaps sightless; the wind is benign when it is soft and unkind when it cuts, just as the sea is cruel when it drowns us and merciful when it floats us safely to the shore; and, as I heard a food expert once say to clinch the argument against keeping loaves in air-tight tins, 'after all, bread must breathe'.

Once again, too, the subject may use existing fictitious entities and figures or create ones of his own to serve as pegs on which to hang his own properties. And *this* time he fills his world with beings who he feels have properties in common with him, and so makes it a more familiar and understandable place to live in.

We can see, I think, that identificatory projection is something more fundamental than a pure defensive mechanism. The pleasure principle no doubt still sets it going on many occasions, for sharing properties is often more pleasurable than having them alone. But something more primary seems in many cases to be the cause—namely the automatic assumption that everything is like oneself until proved otherwise. This attitude may be as much based on a basic principle of saving effort of thought as upon lack of experience of external objects in an undeveloped mind.

* * *

The next and last mechanism we come to is in many ways the exact opposite of projection. In it the ego takes properties which it observes in other objects away from them and assigns them to the self. Thus, for instance, if a poor man sees a rich man eating an expensive meal or sitting in good seats at the theatre or driving about in a grand car—things which he, the poor man, cannot afford—he may, instead of suffering the pangs of useless envy, imagine that it is he and not the rich man who is eating the expensive meal or sitting in the good seats or driving in the car; or if a boy realizes that his companions are brave and he is not, he may make himself believe that it is he instead of them who is brave; or if a plain woman has a handsome brother she may persuade herself that she, not he, is the handsome one. Again, if someone hears another strike out an idea that appeals to him, he may accaparate that idea for himself and produce it in all good faith as his own invention. (This, incidentally, accounts for many plagiarisms which bear all the marks of deliberate fraud, but are nothing of the kind.)

Moreover, the ego may ascribe to the self properties belonging to others which it dislikes; for if the subject is fond of his object, it may be less painful for him to believe that *he* possesses some bad quality than to believe that *it* possesses that quality. If, for instance, a boy observes that his best friend is a coward or a thief, he may find this so harrowing to his feelings that he prefers to regard himself as the coward or the thief, dis-agreeable though this is to him.[1]

Once more, the field of external objects in regard to which the ego carries out this operation is not limited to human beings. It may attribute to the self physical or mental pro-perties which it cognizes, rightly or wrongly, in animals, vegetables or even inanimate things. A man may, uncon-sciously at least, regard himself as literally having the insensi-bility or stiffness of a poker, the pride of a lion or the com-pliance or grace of a waving tree.

This mechanism is known as *Introjection*. A person is said to *introject* a mental or physical property of a foreign object when he allocates this property to himself.

Introjection, like projection, can take place on primitive levels of the mind. It is also in full force at a very early age and it is largely based upon certain component instincts which are in the ascendant at that time and about which we shall hear in a later chapter.

Like projection, too, introjection obviously effects no change whatsoever in the object, but only in the subject's idea of it. Ascribing one's friend's courage to oneself and denying it in him does not detract in the least from that friend's courage in fact, nor does taking over one's brother's good looks make him any less handsome for that.

In many cases, too, introjection effects no more change in the subject than does projection. The only change is that he now *believes* that the property belongs to him instead of its true owner. A cowardly boy who feels that he is the possessor of his companion's courage may nevertheless find his heart fail him at the least danger, and a woman who has the illusion that her brother's good looks are hers has not in fact increased her good looks in the least. Naturally, such convictions often alter the subject's demeanour in reality; but they do not do so in the sense of his conviction. Thus, if a man thinks he possesses another person's meanness he will reproach himself

---

[1] The same, of course, is true of projection, where a person may, for similar motives, endow another with *good* properties of his own at the cost of forfeiting them in himself.

*

and feel badly about it in actual fact—but he will not in actual fact *be* mean.

In other cases, however, introjection does effect a real change in the self and in the sense of the introjection. The subject does in fact take on the foreign property in question. He may, for instance, become truly kind or genuinely greedy by introjecting another's kindness or greed.

In so far as the subject tends to introject properties which he likes and admires and to project properties which he dislikes or despises, he builds up a self—partly real, partly imaginary, which he approves of and loves. This process has a large share in reinforcing his narcissism. But, as we have seen, he does sometimes, though much less often, introject properties which he dislikes and disapproves of and project their opposites; and to the extent which he does this, he builds up a self which he dislikes and of which he has a low opinion.

It very frequently happens, too, that when a person is frustrated in his love for an external object, whether because that object dies or rejects his love or disillusions him in some way, or for whatever other reason, he makes extensive introjections of its properties. Such massive introjections are an excellent way of enabling him to get over the loss of his object, seeing that he now to a great extent supplies its place and largely becomes, or thinks he becomes, the object himself; and they are often carried out for that very purpose. But they are also sometimes carried out with the less friendly purpose of taking another person's place out of envy or rivalry.

In its complete form, introjection, like projection, comprises two events. It consists of an assignment, whether real or imaginary, to the self of properties belonging to another object, and of an imaginary removal of them from their owner. But introjection, too, can consist of only one of those events. It may consist of an assignment to the self of those properties without any such removal from their owner. A man who admires another man's cleverness or boldness may take on those qualities from him, in fact or fancy, without ceasing to regard him as clever or bold; a woman who likes her friend's smile may take to smiling in the same way and yet continue to apperceive her friend's smile; and a boy whilst acquiring his pet dog's greediness may nevertheless still recognize that greediness in it.

Much hedonic gain can be got from this more restricted form of introjection too (which also has the added advantage of not flying in the face of reality, at any rate as far as the object is concerned). To be brave with the brave, clever among the clever and as presentable as one's companions is almost as good as having the advantage over them in these matters; and if one cannot cease to notice bad qualities in a loved object one can at least lessen the pain of observing them there by sharing, or thinking one shares, them. A loyal wife who cannot shut her eyes to her husband's meanness might prefer to descend to it herself, or think she does so, rather than despise him for it from the superior eminence of her own generosity.

The result of this sort of introjection is, of course, that the subject becomes, or thinks himself to be, like his object (as he sees it, whether truly or not) in respect of the properties he has introjected from it—just as in the second sort of projection he believes that the object is like himself (as he sees himself, whether truly or not) in respect of the properties he has projected on to it. Accordingly, I shall call this kind of introjection *identificatory introjection*, whenever it is necessary to distinguish it from the other.

When the property concerned is a mental one, such an identificatory introjection is often referred to in ordinary psychological language as 'empathy'. We are said to 'empathize' another person's states of mind when we partake in them in this fashion. Certainly this process is a necessary precondition for sharing in other people's states of mind and for every attitude of sympathy or fellow-feeling, but these are also only made possible by the fact that the subject already has those states of mind himself in a latent or potential condition. On the other hand, there is no doubt that, apart from this, some people are much more prone to make such intro-jections—are much more psychologically infectible than others.

Since identificatory introjection gives the subject a first-hand experience of the properties which he has made his own, and since, at the same time, he does not lose sight of the fact that they appertain to the object from which he has introjected them, he in this way not only obtains a very intimate know-ledge of them, but can assign them to their true source (wherever his observation has been correct and in so far as the properties concerned are such as he is *capable* of experi-encing). This is more particularly the case with states of mind, and it gives him great insight into human affairs. Indeed, introjective identification is no small factor in that apparently miraculous power which some people seem to have of divining what is going on in another person's thoughts—that sixth sense which we sometimes call intuition. But, of course, intui-tive knowledge is by no means a matter of empathy alone. It is based upon innumerable perceptions and apperceptions each of which is too slight by itself to cross the threshold of consciousness but the sum of which is able to do so. That is why the knowledge it gives us seems often to come from nowhere and to be based on no evidence that we can lay hands on. Nor is identificatory introjection a necessary part of it. One can have an acute and even intimate understanding (though perhaps not an immediate, first-hand one—a 'from within oneself' knowledge, as it were) of the character or feelings of another person without empathizing them. More-over, one can have intuitions about other things besides minds and people. One can have an intuitive grasp of machinery, mathematics, insects, the lay of the land, the weather and what not—of whatever one is interested in, clever about and non-resistant to—where empathy would be useless and even downright misleading.

We must not forget, furthermore, that the understanding of others which the subject gains through identificatory intro-jection is liable to the same distortions from the truth which attaches to all intuitive cognition. For this, being mostly based on his unconscious reception of data, is bound to be more influenced by his own feelings and desires (not to mention his projections) as well as by the primary process, and less by considerations of reality and the secondary process than would be the case if it were based on conscious experiences; nor will it be very susceptible to subsequent criticism or rectification by reality-testing. We all know how convincing our 'hunches' seem to us, and how wrong they can be. And this is especially so wherever introjection has had a finger in the pie, for then the subject experiences the property with all the directness and immediacy of what is a part of himself.[1]

Identificatory introjections are constantly being made by the human mind and they form a very important part of the individual's general attitude and behaviour. Moreover, they are an essential basis of his social life, since they enable him to adapt himself to those he comes in contact with, through approximating his ways and notions to theirs.

Nevertheless, the tendency to make such introjections on a large scale is stronger in some kinds of persons than in others. Such a tendency goes along with a passive receptive and dependent cast of mind—a pliable, not to say a weak one —rather than with a dominating, forcible or rigid personality. Possibly, too, it tends to be linked to a feminine type of character and intelligence more strongly than to a masculine one. An amusing illustration of this is to be found in Chekov's short story, *The Darling*, in which an amiable but not strong-minded woman is married three times and each time becomes completely absorbed in her husband's occupation and interests and changes her character and outlook accordingly.

Where identificatory introjection is most strongly found, however, is in children, especially young children, in whom proneness to imitate their elders in thought, act and word is a marked characteristic and often, though not always, a useful

[1] In this connection it may be pointed out that the views which the subject obtains of his object through projection upon it of properties belonging to himself are also likely to bear this stamp of certitude for him, since they are also derived from what he has perceived in himself. Yet they are liable to be still more wrong.

Chapter VI

ORIGINS OF THE MORAL SENSE

THE influence of identificatory introjection makes itself especially strongly felt in one very important part of the mind which has not yet been discussed. This part is concerned with making judgments of right and wrong and constitutes the moral sense and the conscience of the individual.

In view of the great social importance of this part of the mind, as well as its high survival-value for the race—for it even causes the subject to do and endure things which are unpleasurable and even detrimental to himself for the sake of others—we may presume that it is something inborn and inherited. Nevertheless, it has a history of development and undergoes formative influences in each individual. This takes us back to his infancy and early childhood. Throughout that time he is a very weak and helpless creature, and depends for his well-being, comfort and safety and for the gratification of most of his instincts upon the care of those about him, without whom he would perish. Quite to begin with, however, he takes these things for granted; and although he is in fact utterly beholden to those in charge of him for them, he does not know it. Though *physically* dependent on them, he is not *mentally* so,—at least, he has no *felt* dependence on them. Presently, however, he begins to discover that he owes these benefits to them and he develops an attitude of trust and psychological need and dependence upon them. He is also impressed by their size and strength relative to his and by their ability to cater for his wants and to manage his life, and he consequently attributes to them limitless power over himself and—partly from lack of experience to the contrary—over everyone and everything else as well, and boundless knowledge and wisdom, too, so that he looks up to them with awe and veneration as omnipotent and omniscient beings.

Furthermore, the small child loves his elders for their care and love of him and for the pleasure they give him, as well, perhaps, as from natural instinct; and this makes them seem eminently kind and good. Nevertheless, they cannot help frustrating some of his desires and sometimes causing him unpleasure; for he cannot be allowed to do or have all he wishes—to eat everything he fancies or put his hand into the fire or make messes everywhere. Sometimes, too, he must be deterred from these pleasures by being scolded or even punished. In so far as his elders thwart and correct him they seem unkind to him, since he cannot as yet understand the reason for it. Moreover, their behaviour tends to arouse his anger and hostility towards them, and this makes them seem downright bad. In this connection there is another important point to consider, and one which will be discussed more fully in the following chapters. This is that the small child has strong destructive instincts towards his parental objects, alongside of his libidinal ones. These, though not nearly so great as the latter, are much greater than they appear, owing to their being for the most part repressed and inhibited by his love and fear; and they add much to his view of his upbringers as bad and unkind persons, just as his libidinal instincts add still more to his view of them as good and kind ones.

Thus, whereas the small child regards his parental figures as all-powerful, and all-knowing, he does not regard them as all-good—or at least as absolutely good in every respect—though that may be the view of them which occupies the conscious foreground of his mind. Nevertheless, he regards them as beings greatly to be looked up to.

In addition to this, the small child makes extensive identificatory introjections with his parents and upbringers. He copies their actions and makes their view of things his view and their wishes his wishes, and he takes over their affects and impulses—all, of course, as he sees and interprets them, and all to the extent of his limited ability. If his father blows a trumpet he tootles into his fist; if his elder sister has beautiful long hair and brushes it out at night he has phantasies of having long hair and brushing it out, too; and if, when his mother cuts the pages of a book she is reading he thinks she is punishing the book, he adopts a punishing attitude to it, and if he cannot cut its pages he may tear them. For whatever those grand and remarkable persons are and have and do is grand and remarkable, and he wants to be and have and do it too.

In thus identifying himself with his elders, however, the little child acquires many properties that are very different from those of his natural, native self. It may not be out of keeping for him to blow trumpets like his father or brush his hair like his elder sister or attack books like his mother; but when it comes to becoming like them in preferring quiet behaviour to fidgetiness, silence to chatter, or in liking cleanliness and order rather than mess and untidiness, this changed part of himself stands in sharp contrast to the rest. Moreover, the new part also possesses attitudes towards the rest of himself and arouses in the latter attitudes towards itself which reproduce on the one hand the attitudes which he has experienced from his parental objects, and, on the other, the attitudes which he has had to them, in this way internalizing—or, to be more accurate, rendering endopsychic—those external relationships between him and them. Thus, the old part of himself is subservient and admiring and all the rest of it to the new part, and it in turn is patronizing and approving and disapproving, and so on, to the old.

For this reason the nexus of mental presentations thus acquired forms the nucleus of a separate province of the mind, functioning independently of the ego, and, as it were, placed over it. This Freud called the *Super-Ego*, and he set it up as a third major agency of the mind, side by side with the other two.[1]

[1] Freud first mentions the super-ego by name in his book *The Ego and the Id*, published in 1923; but he had already described it under the name of the 'ego-ideal', notably in his *Group Psychology and the Analysis of the Ego*, published two years earlier.

We have said that the child's super-ego is at variance with his ego. But it is also often at variance with itself. One reason for this is that it is not built up from a single prototype. The child is usually surrounded by several elders and betters—by a mother, a father, a nurse, an aunt, a half-grown brother or sister—all of whom contribute, some more, some less, to his superior self. These persons naturally have different characters and modes of behaviour; nor do they always see eye to eye about what is right and what is wrong, and, most important of all, what is right or wrong for the child. His father may be good-natured and indulgent, while his mother is colder and more severe; *he* may be amused at the child's pranks, whilst *she* frowns upon them. An uncle may think it wrong to give him sweets, but an aunt may stuff his pockets with brandy-balls. His governess may let him make mud-pies to his heart's content in the back garden; but along comes the cook and scolds him for his dirty hands. His artless prattle delights his granny; but a ten-year old sister snubs him and reduces him to silence. Many of these differences between his authoritative objects become reflected as corresponding differences within his super-ego, so that while one part of it commends his playing pranks, eating sweets, making mud-pies and chattering away, another part disparages them.

Another reason for the heterogeneity of the child's super-ego is that it reflects divergent attitudes in the same elder. An important cleavage here is once more between that person as a thwarter and an indulger of his desires. This difference may be in part due to inconsequent behaviour on the part of the grown-up. But it is also inherent in the situation itself. For an impulse which can be safely indulged in one set of circumstances may not be able to be safely indulged in another. A small child may shout to his heart's content in a field, but he must not do so in a room; he may throw a rubber ball to the ground, but not a china cup. Until he is old enough to understand the reason for these differing commands he is bound to attribute them to inherently differing attitudes in the person from whom they come. In either case—whether that person *is* changeable or whether he only *seems* so—the child acquires from him a super-ego with two divergent aspects, a permissive and a prohibitive one, and the two act in opposition to each other.

Furthermore, as we have seen, the child tends to regard his parental object as not only kind and good, but unkind and bad. And these two opposed aspects of it he also introjects, so that there emerges alongside a kind and good super-ego, an unkind and bad one. Sometimes the activities of this bad super-ego lead to the curious situation in which the child is forced to feel guilty about all sorts of thoughts and acts which he knows are not wrong, and in which he is constantly struggling in vain against a cruel, unjust and persecuting conscience. (He has a 'bad' conscience, not in the sense of a conscience which makes his ego feel bad, but in the sense of a conscience which is bad to him.)

As well as all this, it must be remembered that the child's upbringer cannot always behave before it in an educative manner. It is true that he can consistently advocate and enforce a certain code of what is right or wrong for it, and he can support much of that code by example. But some of his behaviour is bound to contravene it. The way in which grown-up people behave by nature is often very different, and rightly so, from the way in which they behave before their children when they wish to be a pattern to them; nor can they keep the whole of this natural behaviour from the child's knowledge. A mother, in teaching her little son to be clean of his own volition does well to be clean herself; but she can scarcely be expected to teach him to go to bed cheerfully at half-past six every evening by doing the same, though doubtless if she did it would greatly help. Nor can she very well dissuade him from touching the scissors by never using them when he is by. Yet a child may introject his elder's non-exemplar behaviour as well as their exemplar behaviour, in which case, if they are mutually contradictory, so will his super-ego be on this point. It will, for instance, seem right to our small boy both that he should go to bed early and leave the scissors alone and that he should go to bed late and ply those sharp blades.

This aspect of his introjective behaviour helps to create in the child not only a heterogeneous super-ego, but one whose standards of right and wrong are ill-suited to its needs. For much that is morally right for adults is not morally right for small children and much that is morally wrong for the one is not so for the other. It is reprehensible for the young to be disobedient or to tell fibs; but they do not have to make difficult decisions or endure much danger or pain without fear or flinching. Grown-ups, on the other hand, may go their way freely and they may say 'boo' to a goose and 'not at home' to tiresome visitors; but they must shoulder hard responsibilities and they must face thunderstorms and visit their dentist with at least outward equanimity.

By and large, however, the small child's upbringers usually put before him a sufficiently homogeneous and appropriate scheme of right thought and behaviour by precept and example, and he himself is able to have a tolerably true view of what they present to him, so that the super-ego he forms is reasonably realistic—that is, reasonably adequate to his age and situation.

*   *   *

As the child grows older, his super-ego increases in extent and power, largely by accretion of introjects, and his mental submission to it progressively takes the place of his mental submission to his outside authorities. After a certain age, however, the rate of introjection diminishes, and the super-ego ceases to expand so fast. Moreover, much that once belonged to it dwindles away as the individual grows up, being handed over to his ego, which on its side is steadily gaining in strength and experience. What had once appeared as a matter of right and wrong often now appears as one of practical expediency. Not tying up one's shoe-laces or being late for breakfast are no longer the sins they were, and eating rich food or getting one's feet wet are matters of good sense rather than moral behaviour.

At the same time, too, the growing child's moral standards must undergo considerable change to fit his changing needs, capacities and circumstances. These changes are to a great extent brought about by the changing demands made upon him by his elders. What they expect of him when he is two years old is not what they expect of him when he is five; what they call good or bad at five they do not always call good or bad at ten, and so on. Moreover, his elders themselves change their behaviour to him and in front of him as he grows older, and this, too, goes to change his super-ego, not to mention the fact that new authoritative figures, in the persons of teachers and a wider world of adults begin to appear upon the scene and to influence his mind and increase and vary his store of introjects; and even when he is quite grown up he still has elder statesmen and grand figures from the past and present, in history and fiction, to admire and imitate.

Yet neither the growing child nor even the adult are able entirely to suit their super-ego to current requirements. Some portion of it remains infantile or lags behind the rest and therefore stays, or becomes, unrealistic. The man who must tell the truth in every smallest detail and at all costs and in every circumstance is probably still being guided in this respect by an antiquated early super-ego, and the respected adage 'cleanliness is next to godliness' smacks strongly of the nursery.

So long as the ego obeys the dictates of the super-ego it is filled with happiness and a sense of innocence and security. But if it disobeys them, it is filled with gloom, remorse and fear, or 'moral anxiety', as Freud calls it. Thus the ego does all in its power to fall into line with the super-ego and uses all its defensive mechanisms against the impulses and affects which displease that internal authority. Some desires it inhibits so extensively that the subject is handicapped in performing a quantity of actions which are only remotely associated with them, or cannot perform them at all; some it represses so severely that he is absolutely unaware of them and of many associated ideas as well; some it projects so that he attributes his sins to someone else. Others it rationalizes, so that he manages to believe in their value and necessity; and yet others it sublimates, so that they do in fact become valuable and necessary.

On the other hand, if it should happen that to obey the super-ego is intolerably unpleasant to the ego, either because to do so conflicts with id-impulses which cannot be denied, or with powerful affects or interests or even with strongly held intellectual convictions, the ego may align itself, not with the super-ego but against it. It may employ one or other of its defensive mechanisms against that portion of the super-ego which condemns the impulse or affect or ideas in question. A person may repress that portion, so that he has no conscious sense of guilt about those impulses,[1] or he may inhibit it, so that he implements them in spite of a conscious sense of guilt; or he may react against or overcompensate for it, so that he makes a point of promoting them or even glorying in them and becomes a regular 'tough guy'. Again, he may project the relevant portion of his super-ego, so that he has no pangs of conscience about the attitudes it condemns, but believes that other people strongly condemn him for them; or he may direct its strictures on to other sins of his, or to other people's sins and be extra hard on minor transgressions of his own instead of the real ones, or busy himself with running down his neighbours.

Although it would clearly be better if the whole of the super-ego could be altogether modified so as to become realistic, even an unrealistic super-ego can be useful. In the first place, it often strengthens the ego in enforcing certain kinds of behaviour which are advisable on grounds of expediency alone, by adding moral motives. Most people, for instance, know that they must keep their bodies clean for hygienic reasons and because other people object to them if they look

---

[1] Though making it unconscious does not necessarily make it inoperative, and he may suffer many seemingly inadvertent misfortunes on its account.

dirty and smell bad. Indeed they themselves dislike feeling and smelling dirty. But some people are too lazy to take a daily bath, or they are afraid of water, or their dirt-loving instincts are too strong. Their preconscious ego cannot alone induce them to wash, because its fear of disease or its dislike of offending other people are not sufficiently strong to overcome their motives for being dirty. But the unrealistic super-ego may supply the necessary strength by being very angry with it for not making them wash and by threatening dire punishment if it fails to do so, because not to wash was a cardinal sin in the nursery and punished by the powers that be.

Again, the unrealistic part of the super-ego may range itself on the side of the realistic part and reinforce the commands of the latter with sanctions of its own, though its behaviour is actuated by totally different reasons from those which actuate the behaviour of the realistic super-ego. A man may, for instance, know perfectly well that he ought to give money to an aunt who is very poor. But he may have a miserly character or be in straitened circumstances himself, so that helping her would be inconvenient; and so he does nothing about it. But if his unrealistic super-ego warns him that if he does not help his aunt it will enforce the law of Talion upon him and make him lose all his money, his ego will then have a sufficiently strong motive to make him give her what she needs.

Often, however, the unrealistic super-ego works in a detrimental sense or weakens the beneficent operation of the realistic super-ego. An adult person, for instance, seeing a small child stretch out its hand too near a fire, will be moved by his realistic super-ego as well as by natural compassion to take its hand away from the fire and save it from hurt. But his unrealistic super-ego may view all mortals, even the youngest of them, as steeped in wickedness and almost bound to suffer hell-fire after death; so that a little burning now can make no material difference and may, indeed, be good for its soul and spare it hell-fire hereafter. (Such a ferocious and out-moded view is, of course, likely to be unconscious—having been repressed by the ego, at the behest, perhaps, of a more advanced portion of the super-ego—and it may be concealed by a piece of rationalization, such as that to have its fingers burnt will teach the infant more effectively than anything else not to go near a fire.) If his unrealistic super-ego overrides his realistic one—and his compassion—he will not take the small child's hand away from the fire, but let it be burnt; conversely, if his realistic super-ego triumphs, he will take the child's hand away and save it. But the unrealistic super-ego, though defeated, may not have been rendered wholly powerless. It may be able to delay his action, so that he takes the child's hand away too late to prevent it from being a little burnt. Neither result is so satisfactory as if he had had no such unrealistic super-ego at all.

As the child increases in years and as his range of objects extends, the field of application of his super-ego becomes less concentrated on himself and takes in other objects as well; and on these he lavishes his moral judgments as freely as his elders lavished theirs on *him*. Thanks to his anthropomorphic attitude, moreover, he tends to regard *every* object as morally responsible for its behaviour. He blames the cat for drinking the baby's milk no less than he would blame himself if he had done so; the rain which spoils his picnic has, to his way of thinking, as much intention of spoiling it as has a person who deliberately pours a bucket of water over his sandwiches; and the sun which shines upon him, shines on purpose to please him. In this way, there is hardly a thing in the world which he does not judge (unconsciously if not consciously) as good or bad as well as useful or harmful and pleasurable or unpleasurable—which he does not judge by ethical standards as well as utilitarian and hedonic ones.

Conversely, he tends to feel that he himself is the constant target of moral judgments on the part of everyone about him. This is in part due to the fact that, as a small child, he was in truth almost exclusively surrounded by people who took a very comprehensive moral attitude towards him (often

calling 'good' or 'bad' things that had no ethical significance)
as well as to the fact that he tends to project his super-ego.[1]
And once again he is inclined to extend this moralizing
attitude to non-human objects. The rain may be wetting his
sandwich to mark its disapproval of his playing truant to go
for a picnic, or the sun may be shining on him to reward him
for his independence of spirit in taking a day off from dull
routine.

*   *   *

The nature of a person's super-ego and the position which
it adopts towards the rest of his mind is of first-rate importance
in deciding how successfully his ego can make adaptive modifications of his instincts. Whether this happens or not depends,
of course, to a large extent upon his environmental conditions. If a man with strong homicidal impulses has no opportunities of becoming a surgeon or a criminal lawyer, or is too
genteel to be a butcher, he will find no appropriate channels
into which to deflect those impulses and he may become a
gangster or a political murderer instead. But sublimation also
depends upon his *capacity* for it. This, in turn, depends largely
upon the attitude of his ego towards his impulses—whether
it acts in a prohibitive and repressive way or whether it guides
them rather than opposes them. It is here that his super-ego
comes in. A super-ego which is at once realistic, friendly and
firm—which is modelled, that is, upon his idea of authoritative
objects whose ethical standards were appropriate, in whose
power he had full confidence, and whom he felt to be loving
and careful of his happiness and welfare—such a super-ego
is more likely to enable his ego successfully to direct his
impulses into a useful and pleasurable channel than is a
super-ego which is unrealistic or weak or hostile. For if it is
unrealistic it causes his ego to deflect those impulses into
inexpedient paths; if it is weak it cannot assist the ego to

---

[1] Yet he is not so wrong in this view as one would wish, for in so far as *their* unrealistic
super-ego persists, they, like him, are inclined to make moral judgments where none
apply.

enforce its commands; and if it is hostile it fills the ego with so much fear or hatred of it that the ego either repudiates the impulses altogether or else defies the super-ego and puts them into effect as they stand. None of these courses are conducive to the happiness and well-being either of the subject or of his environment.

Thus we see that a satisfactory super-ego has an eminently social value. Whereas the ego, left to itself, checks only those impulses which are deleterious or unpleasurable to the subject and those it loves, and deflects them into channels which are pleasurable and beneficial to him and them, the super-ego moves it to check impulses which are deleterious or unpleasurable to all and sundry and to deflect them into channels which are beneficial and pleasurable to them. Thus, although the ego achieves social aims among other things—for it is often inexpedient for oneself and those one loves to annoy or injure others—the super-ego does this for their own sake.[1]

But a favourable super-ego can also bring about sublimations or other attitudes which have a private rather than a social value, as, for instance, in a religious life of a contemplative kind. Moreover, their value need not be moral in a narrow sense of the word. They can be good in the sense of having aesthetic or intellectual worth, as in the execution or appreciation of works of art or in scientific achievements. And some of them can even be socially injurious. A child who has been brought up to be a pick-pocket by his elders, who are pickpockets themselves, has the full approval of his super-ego in his thieving activities (besides having sublimated more crudely aggressive instincts into that fine art of acquisition).

The possession by the grown individual of a super-ego ensures his possession of moral standards which can be independent of the wishes and moral standards put before him by his contemporary authorities, not only because he is

[1] For an exhaustive account of the super-ego in its social aspects more especially, the reader cannot do better than peruse J. C. Flugel's excellent book, *Man, Morals and Society*.

no longer so much in their power mentally as he was as a child and because he can use his intelligence better, but because he now has an internal authority of his own, and his introjective processes have greatly decreased. In this way he is able, if need be, to resist external authority and public opinion. If he is required to do what his super-ego thinks wrong, he can refuse to comply with those demands (or, if he does comply with them, he does so out of fear or love or calculation without changing his mind about their wrongness). The conscientious objector who will not fight because he thinks it wicked to kill human beings even in war, and who endures the contempt of his fellows and suffers imprisonment or death for the law in upholding his convictions; the heretic who will not give up his heresy in spite of the exhortations and threats of his church; the vegetarian who refuses to eat meat because he believes that it is wrong even to kill animals, although everyone around him sees no harm in it— all these persons are obeying the dictates of their super-ego in the face of the ideas, or convenience, of the world about them.

On the other hand, the super-ego of every adult within a given society or social stratum, does in fact tend to be similar to that of his fellows so that he accepts the same standards of right and wrong. Every Westerner knows, for instance, that punctuality is a great virtue and that energy and enterprise are highly meritorious; and every Oriental knows that time has little meaning and that repose is generally better than action. This similarity of the super-ego within a given section of society is primarily due to each individual having had parental models which were similar to those of his fellows.

Since these models belong to the generation before him it is not surprising that a person's views of what is good and what is bad are apt to err on the conservative side and that he is inclined to regard new things with a condemning eye. Moreover, his super-ego is fashioned not only by his parents and educators but by *their* parents and educators. For the standards of right and wrong which his elders have implanted in him reproduce the standards which they themselves have received from their elders (once more, of course, in so far as they have not modified them as they grew up). Moreover, those standards, in their turn, reproduce the standards of the generation before that, and so on, *ad infinitum*. In this way, a considerable part of every person's super-ego reflects the morality of his forbears of long ago. It is not merely a paternal institution but an ancestral one. And where it is no longer adapted to present-day conditions, it stands out as a truly archaic heritage.

But more than this. As we know, the subject's super-ego is based not only upon the super-ego of his elders but upon their id and ego as well—their whole personality as observed by him. Thus it contains elements which made no pretence of being moral in *them*. Similarly, many things which his elders view from an ethical standpoint were viewed by *their* elders only from a utilitarian or hedonic standpoint. As a consequence, he regards as good or bad much that was not so regarded at the time by his forbears. He is, as it were, more royalist than the king. Once upon a time, for instance, ancient man had to till his field in the sweat of his brow by pushing and pulling his wooden ploughshare through the hard earth. It was a matter not of virtue but necessity. But his son after him was doubtless supported in that arduous toil by the belief that he was not only carrying out a necessary task but doing something meritorious in itself—for had not his father done the same before him, and was not all that *he* did good? The introduction of the horse-drawn plough or the iron ploughshare would be looked upon by him with suspicion and distrust long after their material superiority over the old handplough had become obvious to him, simply because his father had not used them. (And this attitude would, of course, become invested with a still stronger moral tone in *his* sons, because of its *moral* quality in *him*.) Luckily the super-ego is not so entirely impervious to the representations of the ego or the claims of reality as to prevent it from ever modifying its position; the man-plough did give way to the horse-plough and the wooden plough-share to the iron one, to the benefit of all. But the whole process was once more gone through many years later, in the matter of ploughing by tractor as compared to ploughing by horse. Indeed, the people of some backward countries, and even some people in progressive countries, have not been able to surmount the objections of their archaic super-ego sufficiently to dismiss the old methods in favour of the new, although the advantage of doing so is as plain for them to see as for anyone else. This unrealistic preference for the antiquated over the modern is frequently disguised by rationalization, as when, for example, the pretence is made that horse-ploughing is better for the land than ploughing by tractor because it manures the ground at the same time; or that it is better for the health of the plougher. But what is really meant at bottom is that it is more virtuous.[1]

Indeed, so strong is the effect of ancestral piety that the individual regards as praiseworthy not only actions and states of mind of his forbears which were regarded by them as *non*moral in their day but many which were regarded as downright *im*moral. In the Middle Ages, for instance, a robber baron may have been ignominiously hanged for his lawless depredations and may have been held in contempt by most of his peers; but his descendants may view his exploits with admiration and pride themselves on the fact that some of his predatory blood still flows in their veins.

Thus we see that the super-ego is essentially a traditionalist part of the mind, and forms a strong link with the past. It ensures that certain attitudes of mind and modes of behaviour shall be handed down from generation to generation by a kind of psychological inheritance.

[1] The belief in the moral value of ploughing by hand over ploughing by horse, or of ploughing by horse over ploughing by tractor has, of course, other determinants besides filial piety. But some of these emanate from a parental super-ego, too. The long and hard work involved in the more primitive method means that the individual has less energy and leisure left to do what he pleases; and doing what he pleases involves doing many things which his super-ego disapproves of—for Satan will find mischief still for idle hands to do. Then, too, hard work is often disagreeable—and pain and punishment are what he deserves. 'In the sweat of thy face shalt thou eat bread.'

Chapter VII

EARLY INFANTILE STAGES OF DEVELOPMENT

IN discussing the modifications which the super-ego undergoes in childhood both as to its own nature and its relations to the rest of the mind, we have said that they were largely due, among other things, to the development which the ego was going through at the same time.

The growth and expansion of the subject's ego from the beginning of his life to his attainment of maturity are great and continuous, and it takes up an ever-widening area of his mind and plays an ever-increasing part in it. From being a weak and almost non-existent thing, unable to orientate his perceptions, co-ordinate his movements or control his elementary functions, and incapable of entertaining anything like a coherent idea, it grows into a thinking, integrating and guiding entity, able to sustain appropriate feelings, construct consistent notions and shape much of his own destiny and that of the world about him.

These changes are partly a matter of spontaneous development, partly of experience. Let us take, for example, the child's capacity for testing its experiences in the light of reality, especially as regards arriving at a correct estimate of its own powers and importance in the scheme of things. At the beginning of its life, a baby's various needs and wishes are attended to by those in charge of it. Thus most of its desires are anticipated; and those which are not are usually satisfied soon after they are felt. The breast or bottle are forthcoming at the proper times not too long after it wants to be fed; its napkins are changed at about the time that they begin to feel disagreeably cold and clammy; sore places on its body are at once soothed with powder; as soon as it begins to feel cold it is carefully wrapped in an extra blanket, and so on. The baby is not yet able to realize that this prompt attention to its wishes comes from outside, independent agencies and—in so far as it has any notions on the matter—it assumes that this is all its own doing and that it can make pleasurable things be and unpleasurable things not be by merely wishing them so. In other words, it believes in the omnipotence of its thoughts.

Sometimes, however, the unpleasure which the infant feels is not put right soon enough. A harassed mother or a neglectful nurse may have delayed its feed or forgotten to change its napkins or left it too lightly or too warmly clad. Now no amount of wishing the napkin to be dry or the breast to appear or to feel warmer or cooler is any use. As its distress increases it starts crying and screaming and waving its arms about and kicking with its legs. Instantly its elders are at its side to ascertain what is wrong and bring relief and comfort. As a result of this experience the infant assumes—this time correctly—that its cries and gestures have brought about the fulfilment of its desires. But it still supposes—incorrectly—that those demonstrations have *directly* caused the fulfilment of its desires, not that they have done so *indirectly* because they have drawn someone's attention to them. Thus although it no longer believes that simply to *have* a wish is enough for the wish to be fulfilled, it now believes that to *utter* that wish is enough. In this way the infant shifts its belief in the omnipotence of its thoughts to a belief in the omnipotence of its *expression* of them. And this belief is further confirmed when, later on, it finds that the words it learns to speak are still more efficacious in bringing about the fulfilment of its desires. It is now convinced of the omnipotence not only of its gestures but of its words. It is only gradually, as the child grows older, and as its contacts with the outer world increase, that it gets to know better.[1]

*   *   *

[1] For a fuller account of what has been said above cf. Ferenczi's paper, 'Stages in the Development of the Sense of Reality'.

The instinctual life of the ungrown individual, too, is very different from that of the grown one, and the id undergoes many changes between infancy and adolescence. Many of the small child's impulses, moreover, are exceedingly strong, and even if they are not as strong as those of mature beings, they are often stronger in comparison with his weak ego and newly emerging super-ego, so that they exert a disproportionate influence in his mind. Furthermore, these early instincts are liable to retain much of their original force and character long after they are due to recede into the background, and their preservation in later years colours the adult's instinctual life and affects his mental attitudes as a whole.

For these reasons, it is worth our while to trace in some detail the course of development through which the mind passes on its way from infancy to maturity, having special regard to its instinctual side.

One of Freud's earliest discoveries was that the young child is capable of having, and indeed, regularly has, impulses of a sexual kind. These impulses are already very strong by the time he has reached the age of four or five. But they are by no means altogether absent at a still earlier age; and even the infant in arms frequently exhibits signs of genital excitement in connection with his sucking activities.[1]

In addition, Freud showed that the infant and small child experiences pleasure which, if not of an actually genito-sexual kind, is undoubtedly erotic in character, in connection with the gratification of quite a number of its component instincts.[2] These erotic instincts are not all equally powerful at the same time but come to the fore in turn. The child's instinctual life passes through several stages, each of which is characterized by the supremacy of a different component instinct, and these stages form a continuous series of libidinal positions, which

---

[1] This fact had already been recorded by non-analytic observers, who, however, were inclined to regard it as a pathological phenomenon.

[2] Cf. Freud's *Three Essays on the Theory of Sexuality*, which is his major work on this subject. Much of what will be said here and in the following chapter is based on this important book, in especial the second essay.

finally terminates in the attainment of a sexual position in the accepted sense of the word. That final position constitutes what is called the *genital stage*. The stages which precede it are known as *pregenital stages* and the component instincts which dominate them, *pregenital instincts*.

The first pregenital stage sets in immediately after birth. During its intra-uterine existence the baby was continually receiving nourishment through its mother's blood-stream, so that it never lacked food. But, in its extra-uterine existence, it is only fed at intervals, and towards the end of its intervals of fasting its unsatisfied need for nourishment arouses in it sensations of hunger and a desire for food. This vital need arouses the major instinct of hunger (or the nutritional instinct, as it is also called). The somatic source of this instinct is the digestive tract; its aim is to take things into the stomach, and its object is food.

In activities of eating and drinking the mouth plays an important part as an additional source of stimulus. Freud accordingly postulates a component instinct which forms part of the nutritional one and which he calls the *oral instinct*. Furthermore, the sensual pleasure derived from the mouth in sucking, chewing or drinking is very strong and is to a large extent of an erotic character. This Freud therefore designates as an *erotogenic zone*.

During the first part of its life, the infant's nutritional needs are paramount and its oral instinct outweighs all the others. Its oral erotogenicity is particularly clearly seen in its addiction to sucking at all manner of things besides the breast, and when there is no question of obtaining food. In especial, it likes sucking its own fingers (perhaps because in doing so it obtains sensations in them as well as in its mouth). This contributes no little to its auto-erotism. This stage, in which the oral instinct is dominant, is called the *oral stage*.

As we see, the objects of the oral instinct are part-objects, viz. the breast (or bottle), the nipples and the milk from them.

D

The perceptual activities and affective attitudes of the infantile ego are in consequence naturally centred upon those part-objects; and owing to the weakness of its ego's integrative powers it is not as yet able to relate them to the larger bodily unit to which they belong and to realize that they are part of a whole object—its mother or its nurse, as the case may be. Indeed, although the infantile ego regularly experiences certain other perceptual presentations in connection with the primary object of its desires, it cannot at first relate them with one another at all. It knows the feel of the soft breast, the taste of the delicious milk, the careful, or not so careful, touch of hands, the sound of a voice and perhaps a loving smile or chiding frown; but only gradually, as a result of repeated experience of their simultaneous or successive appearance (and as a result of its own growth) does it come to realize that they belong together.

Just as the infant's part-objects were the target of its instincts and emotions, so now are its whole objects. It begins to desire and love not only its mother's breast or the touch of her hands or the sound of her voice or the smell and warmth of her body or her smile, etc., but herself as the owner of them. The age at which infants begin to recognize and love whole objects as such is put at round about six months; but it varies a good deal from one to another, according to their mental capacities and the treatment they receive.

Nevertheless, the very small child is a self-centred and narcissistic being. This is partly because, as has just been said, its leading instincts obtain a great deal of auto-erotic gratification and partly because, although it is in fact dependent upon non-self objects for the main gratification of that instinct, it tends to believe that those pleasure-giving objects are a part of itself, since they are always there when it wants them, which is mostly when it thinks of them. Thus it prizes in itself what appertains elsewhere, and it thinks of itself as far more self-sufficient than it really is. These factors, together with its exaggerated sense of power over whatever it does recognize as external objects, give it a high degree of self-regard as well as self-love, as soon as it is able to think of itself as a whole person.

Alongside of this attitude of self-sufficiency, however, the small child soon begins to have an opposite attitude of felt dependence on its mother, or whoever is in charge of it, arising from its growing knowledge of its real dependence on them. The two attitudes exist side by side, the dependent one gradually gaining ground from the self-sufficient one as the child grows older and more cognizant of the true state of affairs—though, in *fact*, of course, the child is becoming steadily more independent and self-sufficient.

At first Freud regarded the oral stage as a single one. But it presently turned out to have two distinct successive phases. In the earlier phase the infant's aim is, as has been said, to suck and swallow its objects. But in the later one it is to bite and chew them up before swallowing them. As to those objects, one class of them—the breast and nipples—remains the same; but the other—the milk—is given up in favour of solid food. This partial change of aim and object probably occurs as a result of the appearance of the teeth. Nevertheless the infant already nips at the breast and squeezes the nipple between its bare gums long before. The earlier period of the oral stage, being characterized by sucking instincts, is called the *oral-sucking* stage, and the later one, in which biting predominates, the *oral-biting* stage. This differentiation, with which Freud fully agreed, was first made by Karl Abraham.[1]

In the oral-sucking instinct, libidinal energy preponderates greatly over destructive energy, so that the baby has in the main a loving attitude to its objects. In the oral-biting instinct, on the other hand, the amount of destructive energy has increased very much. This gives rise to impulses to attack the nipple and breast by force and to seize hold of them in a violent way and even to injure them; and the infant's attitude

[1] See his essay, 'A Short Study of the Development of the Libido', p. 450. Abraham carried on the Freudian traditions of psycho-analysis in the best manner, both as a science and a theory, in the importance which he attached to empiric data and in his belief in the instinctual basis of mental processes. A great deal of what is said in this chapter is got from his work as well as from Freud.

of hostility becomes very marked. Moreover, its biting impulses must be more firmly checked than its sucking ones, because they are harmful in effect, even if they are not so in intent. The mother cannot put up with having her breasts torn and hurt. Thus the impulses are bound to undergo a great deal of frustration and this greatly increases the infant's anger and hostility. No doubt, too, the pain and discomfort which accompany teething contribute no little to its annoyance. Seeing, however, that its biting impulses emerge in full force soon after it has been weaned, there is little doubt that much of the anger and hostility which go along with them is due to that grand frustration of its earlier oral stage.

Yet the objects which the child now hates and wants to destroy are the very ones which he loves and wants to cherish. He thus now develops a strongly ambivalent attitude to them; and in so far as a fusion of libido and destrudo occurs he becomes sadistic towards them. On this account, the oral-biting stage is often called the 'oral-sadistic' stage. (It has also been called the 'cannibalistic' stage because in it the infant wants to eat human flesh, viz. the breast.)

Thanks to the immaturity of his ego, the quite small child is not as much put out by his ambivalent attitude to his object as an older child and, still more, an adult would be. The fact that he hates and wants to hurt and destroy the very thing that he loves and wants to please and do good to does not set up a conflict in his mind, since his ego is not as yet far enough advanced in its integrative functions to bring the two attitudes fully into a single mental picture; nor in any case does he as yet realize that if he destroys his object he cannot cherish it any more.

In addition, he does not properly understand that the thing he loves and the thing he hates are one and the same. A person's idea of an object is based upon the many various perceptions and apperceptions he has had of it. These he combines into a single picture, which in psycho-analytical parlance is called an *imago* of it.[1]

---

[1] The word 'imago' is borrowed from Jung, who in his turn took it from the title of a well-known novel by Spitteler. To begin with, this word was used in psycho-analysis to denote an object which stood for another original object. Thus, for

Now, as we know, the subject's unconscious view of his object is coloured by his feelings of love and hatred for it. In so far as he hates it and wants to destroy it, it seems worthless, bad and dangerous to him; and in so far as he loves it and wants to cherish it, it seems valuable, good and helpful. In this way, if he has a very ambivalent attitude to it, and the feelings involved are strong, his unconscious sets up two separate imagos of it, one bad and unkind, the other good and kind; and it is only in his preconscious that these imagos are rectified and merged together. Thus, to the unconscious there are two different persons—a good and a bad—instead of one. In the case of the ambivalent child, with its undeveloped preconscious, such a merging is not yet possible and these two imagos still remain apart. Indeed, the child may once more separate out the single imago of his object that he has formed during his earlier, pre-ambivalent sucking stage. Thus he now thinks that he has two mothers—one who loves him and looks after him in every way, and another who hates him and wants to do him harm.[1] Moreover, he can wholly trust and love the former and wish her well, and he can mistrust and hate the latter and wish her ill, if not without fear, at least without remorse. And all conflict is avoided. These are incentives for making or maintaining the separation.

Gradually, however, the growing ego of the small child begins to make a better synthesis of its imagos. It learns that an object which has diverse aspects is not necessarily more than one. But now it realizes that the object which it loves and wants to be with is also the object which it hates and wants to injure or get rid of, and that the 'good' person is the same as the 'bad' one; and it must endeavour to deal with the conflictual ambivalence which arises from this state of affairs

instance, to a schoolboy a prefect or a school-master might be imagos of his father. Latterly, however, this meaning has been taken over by the words 'substitute' or 'surrogate'. Thus, in the case of the schoolboy the prefect or the school-master would be 'father-surrogates' or 'father-substitutes' for him. An 'imago' now simply means the subject's idea of the object—the object as it appears or seems to him.

[1] He does the same with his part-objects. He believes that there is a 'good' nipple which gives him lots of nice milk and another 'bad' nipple which withholds milk from him or gives him nasty milk.

and which is highly unpleasurable to it. One way of doing this is to transfer the hostile side of the ambivalence to a new object. In this the small child is assisted by the psychological contacts which it is beginning to make with other persons besides its mother. (Indeed, it may well be that the need to sort out its ambivalence in this way is itself an inducement to it to make such new contacts.) Of these its father is as a rule the first to be recognized as a whole object, owing to his constant attendance on its mother and it. Thus he comes in for a considerable share of its hostility—all the more so because he does in fact often interfere between it and its most desired object, its mother. But the small child gets to know other people, too, besides its mother and father. Its family circle may include brothers and sisters, a nurse, an aunt and so on. Any one of these may receive the full brunt of its original hatred of its mother. The grave-looking aunt from whose well-meant advances it shrinks with repugnance, or the strict but just nurse against whom it so strongly rebels, are often nothing more than scapegoats for its mother whom it would otherwise want to get rid of or destroy.

But the persons upon whom the small child thus displaces its feelings of hatred are also persons whom it loves—though not to the same degree as its mother—and it may not be prepared to hate them with such great intensity either. A further distribution of ambivalence accordingly takes place, whereby more distant and indifferent objects become the target of its hostility. A perfectly well-disposed visitor may, to his dismay, find himself rejected at sight by the youngest member of the family and greeted by it with shrieks of rage and terror, simply because he happens momentarily to have assumed the dreaded and abhorred aspect of its 'bad' and harming mother, or father, or nurse or aunt, as the case may be.

*   *   *

In addition to its need for nourishment the baby has other bodily needs as well which begin at birth, and these, too, give rise to specific component instincts, some of which are markedly erotic. But in the earliest period of its life they play a minor role and are overshadowed by the strength of its oral instincts. Some time in its second year, however—partly perhaps owing to the extensive frustration which those instincts suffer at weaning as well as to the spontaneous process of instinctual development—the small child leaves the oral stage and enters what is known as the *anal*, or *anal-erotic*, stage. In this stage the so-called *anal instinct* is the dominant one. The primary objects of this component instinct are the child's own faeces, anal passage and buttocks, and the same products and parts of the body in other persons. The child obtains instinctual gratification from defecating and from other activities connected with his objects, such as touching or being touched by them, or smelling them; and his buttocks and anal passage are the instinct's erotogenic zone.

During this stage the small child's destructive instincts remain to the fore. It regards its objects with hostility as well as love. This hostility is once more reinforced by the frustration which its leading instinct experiences at their hands. For its upbringers do not allow it to defecate when, how or where it chooses. It is made to evacuate its bowels at a stated hour and in a stated place and manner, and to refrain from doing so at any other time and place or in any other fashion. The child is often unwilling to obey these rules or unable to do so, and harbours much resentment against the persons who enforce them. Moreover, it often uses its own part-objects as instruments of its hostile intentions towards such persons. It is not always by accident that a little child makes a mess in its bed or defecates upon its mother's lap.

But the child also loves its whole objects very much, and accordingly its anal behaviour towards them also expresses a desire to please and benefit them. It not only defecates, or retains its stool, when, how and where they wish because it dreads to see them frown, but because it longs to see them smile; and it often defecates upon them as the only present which it can make. And, indeed, this gift, being the part-object of its leading instinct, seems, in its libidinal aspect, to be highly desirable. Thus this action may express both sides of its ambivalence alternately, or even at the same time.

In so far as the libidinal and the destructive elements of the child's ambivalence are fused, it once more adopts a sadistic attitude to its objects. Such a fusion is as prevalent in the anal instincts as it is in the oral-biting ones, if not more so. For this reason the anal instinct and stage are sometimes referred to as the 'anal-sadistic instinct' and 'anal-sadistic' stage respectively.

The small child, too, attributes great power to its anal behaviour since it is at a period of its ego-development at which it believes in the omnipotence of its actions, if not its thoughts and utterances. Thus it thinks that it can do great things by means of its faeces and flatus—can kill or cure, heal or destroy. And, since these objects are products of its own body, they participate in its importance. Similarly, the child ascribes almost as much power and importance, for good or ill, to other people's faeces, as it does to its own.

The anal instinct has a strong passive aim as well as an active one. In this it differs from the oral-biting instinct whose aim is pre-eminently active, though not so much from the oral-sucking instinct in which passive aims obviously exist alongside of active ones. One of the regular passive anal pleasures the child experiences is the daily passage of stool through its lower bowel. Another is having its anal orifice and buttocks washed and wiped in the ordinary routine of nursery care. Drawn on by the strength of its passive anal-erotic desires, it often responds to such perfectly innocent attentions, as though they were an attempted seduction of it. Nevertheless, this view of them is not always so very far out as it appears to be. For the person who is doing the supposed seduction or assault may, in fact, be putting a certain amount of erotic impulse into his or her behaviour to it—quite unconsciously, of course. A nurse or a mother who themselves have an excess of active anal erotism may show too much pleasure in washing and wiping its buttocks and may spend too much time and care in fingering those parts of its body. Again, a young brother or sister with a similar disposition may proceed in a more undisguisedly erotic manner. Nor is the child on its part slow to accede to or even invite such real or supposed advances, highly pleasurable as they are to it.

Owing to the large amount of destrudo present in the id at this stage, however, such advances are likely to be responded to with a great deal of hostility on the part of the child; and they are also likely, thanks to its projective activities, to be regarded by it as hostile attacks upon it and so to frighten it. Yet in so far as the child's passive destructive instincts are fused with its passive libidinal ones, this produces the passive form of a sadistic attitude, viz. a masochistic attitude, so that the experiencing of these attacks provide it with a high degree of erotic gratification of an anal-masochistic sort, and a corresponding pleasure, in spite of, or because of, their danger and pain.

The experience of being seduced, whether real or not, is a very common event in the life of young children and it often has an important influence upon their future development. Freud classes this event among a set of regularly occurring infantile experiences of great emotional, and sometimes even traumatic, importance which he calls *Primal Scenes*.

Another primal scene is the witnessing by the small child of sexual intercourse or other acts of sensual love between his parents (or other parental figures). Although he takes no direct part in the scene and although his observation of it may be very partial—may be no more than sounds heard in the night or movements seen in semi-darkness—the sexual instincts that come into play between the protagonists communicate themselves to him and stimulate his own erotic impulses. Moreover, such a scene involves strong passions and emotions between two persons towards one of whom at least, if not both, he has similar passions and emotions. Thus it arouses in him intense feelings of jealousy and rage as well. If, however, the child is at an anal stage, the genital excitations which he observes in his parents are apt to arouse anal,

*

rather than genital excitations in him; and he interprets their
behaviour in that sense. He supposes that one of them—
usually the man—is copulating with the other *per anum*, and
that he is assaulting and raping her with intent to hurt.
According as the child's active or passive aims are stimulated,
he is filled, now with sadistic impulses, now with masochistic
ones; and he identifies himself either with the attacking male,
or with the attacked female or both, with corresponding
excitement and terror.[1]

This type of primal scene occurs very frequently at the anal
stage because the small child is now coming into increasing
mental contact with the outside world and is able to perceive what is going on between objects in it. Nevertheless, the
scene can occur earlier. The child may experience it at the
oral stage, at any rate the later half of it. In that case it will
arouse his oral-erotic instincts, especially his sadistic (and
masochistic) ones, and he will interpret it in the light of them.
He will regard it as an eating up of his mother by his father,
or *vice versa*, or an eating up of each by the other. In so far, too,
as the small child already possesses a genital instinct at the
oral and anal stages, though it is not as yet his leading one,
the primal scene of parental copulation stimulates that
instinct in him; and he views the act—more correctly—as one
in which the genitals of both partners are principally engaged.
Similarly, he will be excited by nursery handling of his genitals
rather than of his buttocks; and he tends to regard both
actions as an attempt at a genital seduction.

As the child grows older the destructive energy of his
instincts becomes less great and their libidinal energy greater.
He is less desirous of paining and injuring them than he was
before. Moreover, he begins to combat his obnoxious impulses
by an extensive use of reactive formation. From having
yielded to impulses of hostility and destructiveness against

---

[1] In his *History of an Infantile Neurosis*—more familiarly known as the case of the
Wolf Man—Freud has described a primal scene of this kind, which in this instance
had a pathogenic effect upon the small observer.

his parents and other loved persons—or having, at best, dealt with them by projection and introjection—he is now full of solicitude for them and of anxiety lest any ill should befall them; from having taken great delight and interest in faeces and faecal activities he now tends to become averse to them and to want to be clean; and from having desires to expel his stool in an unregulated and aggressive way, he desires to produce it in a careful and regular fashion. Abraham, who was the first to discover these changes in the child's attitude in connection with its anal instinct, lays great stress upon the reversal of aim which they entail. In its original form the aim of the instinct was to get the faeces out of the body, but in its later form it is to keep them in. On the strength of this, Abraham has differentiated the instinct into an *anal-expulsive* instinct and an *anal-retentive* one; and he divides the anal stage into two successive sub-stages—an earlier 'anal-expulsive' stage and a later 'anal-retentive' one, in each of which the corresponding instinct is in the ascendant. It was Abraham who also pointed out what immense strides the ego makes in its development from the first sub-stage to the second. The child not only comes to adopt a much more loving attitude to his objects, and strives to overcome his ambivalence towards them more energetically than ever; he is able to have a far more realistic attitude to them and to know them more as they really are. His introjective and projective mechanisms are no longer operating so freely or with so little correction from reality, and his growing contacts with the world about him give him a more objective view of the facts. A disliked person is no longer an evil person; nor does a liked one possess every virtue under the sun.

Nowhere is the child's growing recognition of reality more clearly seen than in the modifications which his sense of omnipotence undergoes. We have seen at the beginning of this chapter how the small child comes to have an exaggerated belief in the power of its wishes, first merely as *thought* wishes and later as wishes expressed in gestures and cries, and, finally, in articulate words. But its wishes often go unfulfilled even when they are spoken. This is sometimes because its mastery of language is as yet inadequate to make those wants known. But more often it is because they are becoming increasingly complicated and difficult to fulfil, and, most of all, perhaps, because there is no necessity from any person's point of view, except his own, to fulfil them. One cannot refuse to feed a hungry baby or dry a wet infant, but one can refuse to give a small child a teddy-bear. In this way the small child's sense of its own omnipotence gradually yields to a recognition of the fact that it is surrounded by bigger and superior persons who are even more powerful than it. As it grows older it comes to realize that it is only at their good pleasure that its wishes are fulfilled, even when they are fulfilled, and that it is they who have the power to shield it from harm. And, besides this, they obviously know a great many things which it does not.[1]

But gradually, as the child's faculties of observation grow, he begins to see that his elders cannot in fact do and have everything they want and that they are often worsted by the common world. His mother cries because she has lost her necklace, or his father sulks when his breakfast is cold. He also discovers that his elders sometimes omit to gratify a wish of his, not because they intend to thwart it, but because they are unable to indulge it. Moreover, their power over him and their knowledge about him is diminishing all the time, and of this, too, he is increasingly aware. His newly-acquired ability to walk and speak, for instance, not only adds to his power to do and to know, but adds to it relatively to theirs. He can get away from them, can put himself in a position in which he can observe them without being himself

---

[1] Nevertheless, the child's growing belief in the omnipotence of its elders does not detract as seriously from its primitive belief in its own omnipotence as might be expected. Apart from the fact that its ego is as yet not a very cohesive entity, so that it is still able to entertain contradictory notions, we must remember that although it is contradictory to believe that both oneself and someone else possess *absolute* power, it is not contradictory to believe that both possess far greater power than they in fact do. To believe, for instance, that one's parents can kill one with a frown does not imply that one cannot oneself kill *them* with a frown, or that one cannot parry their death-dealing frown by biting one's thumb or frowning back at them.

observed, can deceive them by telling lies, and so on. Thus his growing apperception of their comparative impotence and ignorance is not merely due to his growing perception of reality. It is also due to a change in that reality.

It is at this stage, too, that the small child's super-ego begins to assume a recognizable aspect and an adequate stature. It no longer consists of some rudimentary and scattered portions of the mind, modelled upon highly distorted presentations of his parental objects, but of a fairly extensive and coherent field of more elaborate and true presentations of them. But, of course, this agency possesses all the extra power and knowledge which the child now attributes to those authoritative objects and it is the one in relation to which he is always trying to suppress his still very strong hostile wishes against them, and whose consequent wrath he must constantly strive to placate by penance and especially good behaviour and thoughts.

This stern super-ego—together with his rapidly growing ego—not only enrich the small child's endopsychic relationships, but greatly affect his attitude to the outside world. From having been a wild and irrational little creature, he begins to turn into a thoughtful and responsible individual.

Chapter VIII

LATER INFANTILE STAGES AND THEIR PROLONGATIONS

IN addition to the two pregenital instincts already described there exists yet a third. This is known as the *urethral* instinct. The part objects of this instinct are the urine and the organ from which it flows; its aim is to empty the bladder and emit urine; and its erotogenic zone is the bladder, and the urethral passage and orifice. In this instinct the child obtains pleasure from urinating and from playing with his urine and wetting himself and others with it. He also obtains pleasure from gratifying the opposite aim of retaining his urine. This instinct can be very strong in some children and may even at times dominate the field; but it has not, as far as I know, been accorded the status of forming a regular 'urethal' stage.

The urethral instinct is distinguished from the rest of the pregenital instincts by the fact that part of its erotogenic zone includes part of the genital region. In consequence, the child's urethral impulses are largely implicated in his genital ones and serve as a kind of introduction to them.

In considering the instinctual stages through which the child passes, we have so far made no distinction between the two sexes. This has been possible where the oral and anal stages are concerned, since the leading instinct of each is the same for the boy and the girl, having the same part-object, erotogenic zone and aim. Where the urethral instinct is concerned, however, the situation is not identical. One of its erotogenic zones is, as we know, the genitals (or part of them) and these have a different conformation in the male and female child. This entails a difference of behaviour between the sexes in gratifying that instinct. The boy possesses quite an imposing organ with which to micturate. He does so standing up; and he produces the stream of urine with a certain amount of force and can send it to a certain distance and in any direction he pleases. (Older boys in whom the urethral instinct has persisted strongly often indulge in competitions among themselves to see who can send his urine farthest out or highest up or hit a target most accurately.) This gives him a sense of power and control in connection with his main instinctual activity. The girl, on the other hand, has a much less impressive organ of micturition. She must squat down for her purposes, and the urine runs out in a shapeless, undirected and less forceful flow. She cannot even always prevent some of it from wetting her legs and soiling her clothes. Thus, for her, micturition, though a pleasurable activity, is hardly a matter of pride.

At the succeeding infantile genital stage the instinctually-based mental divergence between the sexes becomes much more marked. For the genital instinct which dominates it is very different in the boy and the girl.[1]

To begin with the boy. The part-object of his genital instinct is the female sexual organ and its aim is to penetrate that organ with his penis. Thus he is sexually attracted by female persons, and his attitude to them is (libidinally) aggressive.

In this instinct, by far the most important part obviously falls to the penis; and its importance in the boy's eyes is correspondingly great. In the first place, it is the sole erotogenic zone of his dominant instinct, and, moreover, of an instinct which is extremely powerful and extremely libidinal, so that a gratification of that instinct is accompanied by intense pleasure in that organ. In the second place, it is the executive instrument of his instinctual aim and as such has a high value in his eyes. In addition, it has another accomplishment. He

---

[1] Since, however, the genital instinct exists in some degree from birth on, the different psychological attitudes which it entails in male and female children are, of course, to that degree present in them—many of them manifestly—all along.

hardly fails to observe, sooner or later, in other boys or men or in himself, that it is able on occasion to become rigid and erect of itself. This ability heightens his ideas of its power and lends it a magic quality. Thus the small boy is extremely proud of possessing a penis, and this pride maintains and increases the pride which he already felt in it on the basis of his urethral instincts. Nor does his admiration of the male sexual organ stop at himself. He is enormously impressed by its bigness in older boys and men, as soon as he comes to observe them, and he wants and hopes to have one like it himself. He also longs to outdo, as he hates to be outdone by, boys of his own age in these respects of size and behaviour of the penis.

But this pride brings with it its own penalty. The small boy is very much afraid of having his precious organ damaged or even removed from him—a fear which its somewhat exposed position and tenuous attachment to his body do little to allay. Moreover, he is afraid of this fate overtaking him, not by accident but intentionally, and this from several quarters. In the first place he suspects his rivals in the sexual field who have obvious motives for wanting to deprive him of that organ. Then, too, the infantile genital instinct, though much more libidinal than its predecessors, is by no means devoid of destructive energy. In consequence, his penis is not only the executant of his *libidinal* aggressiveness. It is also the executant of his *destructive* aggressiveness, if in a much lesser degree. He wants to penetrate the female genital forcibly with it, not merely for sexually pleasurable purposes, but in order to do damage. This makes him afraid of having his penis taken away or injured by the very object of his sexual wishes, from revenge. Most important of all, however, is his fear of this happening to him as an inevitable consequence of, or as a fitting punishment—and generally at his parents' hands—for the forbidden sexual desires, pleasures and activities which are centred round his genital organ.

So strong, indeed, is the small boy's conviction that his penis is in constant danger that he is apt to interpret in this sense any punishment or scolding or admonition he receives, especially in connection with his sexual activities, or even any unfriendly motion towards or remark about that organ, or any accidental mishap or near-mishap to it or to some region of his body which he associates with it. Such experiences constitute in Freud's view the third type of primal scene—viz. castration, or the threat of castration.[1]

The small boy's fear for his penis—or *castration anxiety*, as it is called—receives added force and realism from certain observations which he makes at this time and which now begin to engage his interest. This is that some children do in fact lack a penis. He has no idea of the existence of the female genital organ, because it is not visible; and so he concludes that they are deprived of all sexual pleasure or means of discharge, as well as of an instrument of power and offence. Nor can he for long entertain the fiction that they are too young as yet to have a penis and that it will appear when they are older; for they may be as old as he, or older. Moreover, sooner or later he also makes the discovery that some grown-up persons, too, are without it. He watches his mother or his nurse undressing; and the evidence is plain. Now the small boy has hitherto regarded all persons as possessing a penis—partly because they are all like him in most other respects, partly through projection and partly, too, because he cannot imagine the non-existence in anyone of so important and valuable a thing—and he finds it exceedingly difficult to adjust his mind to the idea that some persons have not got one; even when he does so it seems to him more likely that they once had one but have since been deprived of it, rather than that they have never had it. But more realistic factors, too, help to confirm this view. In his observation of sexual intercourse he sees that the man plays an active role and the woman a passive one. His destructive instincts lead him to interpret this scene not only as an aggressive act on the part of the man towards the woman but as a hostile one; and, in accordance with the genital stage at which he is, he regards it as a destruction or

[1] The other two being, as the reader will remember, seduction by an older person and the witnessing of parental intercourse.

removal of her penis—or some form of castration. In addition, the boy may have had occasion to see traces of menstrual blood upon the underclothes or night-gown of some of his women-folk, and he regards the blood as coming from a wound made by their castration. The discovery that some people are in fact without a penis—i.e. to his mind castrated —greatly increases his fears of his own castration, for what has happened to them can happen to him. When, later on, he begins to generalize from his observations and to suspect that many persons whose genitals he has not inspected are also castrated, his fears are augmented in proportion to the supposed frequency of that calamity; and when, still later, it turns out that at least half the human race—viz. all females— lack a penis, the danger is indeed great.

On the other hand the boy's discovery that females are without a penis gives him a great sense of superiority over the sex. They seem to him to be a very inferior and unlucky sort of creature whom he can only pity and look down upon. But these are not the only feelings which their deplorable condition arouses in him. Since he expects to be castrated principally as a punishment for his reprehensible sexual wishes and actions he is inclined to regard their castration, too, as being due not so much to accidental causes or the malice of others but to a punishment for the same crimes on their part. Thus they seem to him to be depraved and dangerous characters who desire to lead him into temptation or harm him, and he both scorns and fears them. Moreover, whether their castration was due to the hostile action of others or to their own wickedness, they may well be seeking to revenge themselves for it, and if they cannot be revenged upon their actual castrator they may pick on him as a scapegoat. Finally, he suspects that they may seek to make up for the loss of their penis by seizing his from him—a suspicion which, as we shall presently see, is not altogether without foundation.

The boy's fear of castration, however, is fed from another, very important source as well. This is none other than his *wish* for it. From what we already know about the human mind we can understand some of the possible motives of such a seemingly paradoxical wish. One is his need for castration as a fitting punishment for his forbidden libidinal and destructive impulses on the genital level. Here we detect the hand of the super-ego which has by no means shed all its pristine ferocity and unrealism. Another motive may be certain masochistic impulses which promise him pleasure from the pain of castration and the humiliation and inferiority of being a castrated thing. A third is derived from the passive aspect of his genital instinct, which makes him want to have his sexual organs penetrated instead of to penetrate with them. We shall return to this motive later on in the chapter.

Pride in his penis and fears of its loss exert a very great influence on the small boy at this period of his life. They give rise to what is known as the *phallic phase*.[1] In this phase his happiness and *morale* are based upon the assurance that he possesses and will continue to possess a sound and effective penis. In accordance with this his behaviour inclines to overboldness on the one hand and undue timidity on the other. He tends to be aggressive, self-assertive and exhibitionistic, because he believes in the grandness and irresistibility of that organ; but he also tends to be apprehensive and self-effacing, because he dare not do anything that might attract unfavourable attention to it. In especial, his castration anxiety makes him afraid of obtaining any erotic gratification from his penis, and this may lead to marked inhibitions of his sexual life. He may no longer dare to play sexual games with other children, or to touch his penis or even to be attracted by persons of the other sex. On the other hand, that very anxiety may make him overbold, or aggressive or over-sexed, as a reaction to it, or as a defence against being castrated. He may try to overcome his fears by emphasizing the fact that he has no such fears, or that there is no such danger, or by attacking the people who threaten him before they can strike at him.

[1] For this, see in especial Ernest Jones' paper, 'The Phallic Phase'.

He may, too, exhibit his penis too often or masturbate too frequently or too openly or be too much or too obviously attracted by persons of the opposite sex, in order to convince himself and others of the continued existence and potency of his penis and to assure himself that he is not afraid of having it cut off by an angry parent.

But by and large he generally triumphs over his fears and hostility sufficiently to be able to establish a satisfactory infantile genital position, in which his sexual impulses find an adequate outlet that is neither too assertive and disagreeable on the one hand, nor too anxiety-ridden and self-condemnatory on the other.

*   *   *

And now for the girl. The establishment of a normal genital stage in her is a much more complicated and difficult business than it is in the boy. For it necessitates an extensive re-orientation of her sexual and emotional life. At first, however, no such re-orientation occurs. In Freud's view, the small girl's genital instinct is to begin with very much the same as that of the boy. Its erotogenic zone is the clitoris, which may be regarded as a kind of rudimentary penis and which resembles it in a small way as to shape and behaviour, being a part of her genitals which is protuberant and erectile; its part-object is the female genital and its aim is to penetrate that organ with the clitoris. This aspect of her genital instinct, which as we see is essentially male in character, may be called the 'clitoridal instinct' in continuance of the principle of naming the erotic instincts according to their main erotogenic zone. This instinct gives the girl an active and aggressive libidinal attitude to her whole objects, who are female persons, chief among these being still, as with the boy, the one she has had all along, i.e. her mother. The dominance of this instinct, moreover, affects not only the girl's sexual position but her emotional position in general. At the clitoridal stage she is active, aggressive and boyish.

The clitoridal instinct, however, brings great disappointments for the little girl. Her clitoris, though a source of sexual pleasure for her when stimulated, is useless as an instrument of penetration. She soon discovers, too, that boys possess in the penis an organ which is much better suited for that purpose, besides being far bigger and more imposing in performance. She admires it greatly and greatly envies him the possession of it, and she feels very inferior to him, because she has not got one. She often comes to the conclusion, too, that normally she should have a penis and that her lack of it means that something has gone wrong with her body, whether by accident or design. She may believe that her parents have withheld it from her or have not allowed it to grow properly, as a punishment for her forbidden sexual desires and activities, or that they, or someone else, have done so out of sheer malice. In the first case she feels doubly ashamed of her lack of it, and in the second she adds to her sense of inferiority feelings of hatred and revenge against those whom she supposes to have thus wronged her. She may believe, moreover, that she once had a full-blown penis of her own, but that it was taken away from her. This view is supported by her discovery of a hole where that organ should be. She regards the hole as a wound made by the removal of her penis.— Thus, as we see, she concurs in the boy's view that she is an incomplete being and, in all probability, a castrated one.

The little girl feels frightened, too, about her lack of a penis, because it means to her, as it does to the small boy, being powerless to attack or to defend herself against dangerous persons; furthermore, having a hole in place of it lays her open to attack from without upon the inside of her body. In addition, the hole arouses fear and horror in her, because it means to her that she has undergone castration. This imaginary event in the past appears to her as a most painful, violent and dangerous experience, and any revival of the idea of it evokes feelings appropriate to that event.[1]

[1] This imaginary event is generally attached in her mind to some real past occurrence which can subsequently (that is, at the infantile genital stage) be associated with castration, such as some bodily injury or threat of it. Such an occurrence would thus in retrospect constitute a primal scene of castration, as with the boy.

Furthermore, she has in all probability gone in for clitoridal masturbation just as the small boy has masturbated his penis, and the feeling of guilt which she has had about it, and the admonitions she has received from her elders, may well have been translated by her, too, into threats of its removal as a punishment. Thus, to her also, being without a penis is a mark of shame.

The little girl attempts to remedy this unhappy situation. She tries to provide herself with a penis of her own, either by taking especial care of her clitoris so that it shall grow into a penis, or by propitiating her parents through good behaviour or blandishments so that they shall give her one; or she may want to take a penis from its possessor by force or fraud. These hopes, however, receive a severe blow when she, too, like the boy, finds out that some older girls and even grown women, notably her mother, have not succeeded in keeping or getting a penis for themselves. Sometimes her anger at having been deprived of it is so great that she is more bent upon revenge than acquisition. She is willing to go without a penis so long as she can deprive another of it. Her envy and hatred, too, are often concentrated upon that organ itself, so that she thirsts to injure or destroy it. Thus it is that the boy's fear of the other sex as despoilers of his penis is not altogether baseless.

The girl may also meet the situation by *denying* her lack of a penis. She may overcompensate for its absence by pretending to herself that she is a little boy or by exaggerated boyish behaviour in herself and by seeking to outrival boys on their own ground. She rejects all girlish pleasures and pursuits, will not play with dolls or wear girl's clothes, is rough and noisy, tears her dresses, and so on. She often insists on micturating in an upright position, usually with disastrous consequences. Such an attitude in the girl corresponds, as we see, to the phallic phase in the boy, and for that reason it often goes by the same name in her.

Another thing that the frustrated clitoridal instinct may do is to reverse its aim from active to passive. Now the girl, instead of wanting to use the clitoris in a penetrative and aggressive way towards her object wants to be treated in that way by it. She adopts a sexually passive and submissive attitude towards her object. In addition any sadistic impulses that are present in her clitoridal instinct, in virtue of the fusion of libidinal and destructive energy there, will be reversed into masochistic ones, so that she may now want to be sexually assaulted in a painful and dangerous way, and perhaps even castrated.

These reversed aims of the clitoridal instinct are, of course, not able to be translated into reality either, seeing that its erotogenic zone is even less made to be penetrated than to penetrate and its part-object is totally unfitted for the latter purpose. But they assist the emergence of another aspect of the little girl's genital instinct, which is much better suited to the conformation of her sexual organs and for which direct gratification is possible. In it, the erotogenic zone moves on to the vagina; the part-object becomes the penis; and the aim is to receive that organ into the vagina.

This aspect of her genital instinct or the 'infantile vaginal instinct', as it might more specifically be called—is as obviously female as the clitoridal instinct is male and its ascendancy involves a corresponding change in her from a masculine to a feminine position. She becomes much less active and aggressive towards her libidinal objects, and she is attracted by male persons instead of female ones. In addition, her maternal instincts come strongly into play, and she very much wants to have a baby of her own. It is possible that her breasts, though as yet undeveloped, already begin to furnish her with an erotogenic zone for her desire to nurse it.

The change-over from a female to a male object which this new instinct entails obliges the girl to detach her libido from the person who has been the principal object of it all her life so far, viz. her mother. This requires a great deal of effort and involves her in severe mental conflicts which the small boy is spared, since *he* can continue to love her as before. Then again, her attitude to her part-object is somewhat mixed. At this stage she naturally relinquishes her wish to have a penis of her own, as a physical attribute. Instead, she desires it as an *object*. Nevertheless, she cannot but see that it is a far grander organ than hers and capable of a more impressive performance. She thus still mingles some envy with the admiration and pleasure with which she views it. The feelings of guilt, shame and fear too, with which she regards her vagina as a hole due to a castration, may drive her to want to have a penis of her own in spite of her now dominant female instinct. For both these sets of reasons, therefore, she often continues to harbour a lurking wish to deprive the male of his penis or damage it. She is not, as we see, quite out of the phallic phase.

In addition, her purely erotic desire to receive the penis into her vagina supplies her with a new motive for castrating its possessor (though not for harming him or it thereby). For she would like to have that pleasure-giving object at her service all the time; and what better way is there of doing this than by taking it away from him and having it by her all the time?

Again, the infantile vaginal instinct has much less destructive energy compared to libidinal energy than has the clitoridal instinct, so that at this stage the girl is much more inclined to love and cherish her instinctual objects, whether part or whole, than to hate them and hurt them. Nevertheless, the instinct is not totally devoid of destrudo, so that she has *some* impulses to harm her objects. Moreover, she is not entirely free from fears of an aggressive or hostile sexual attack on the part of her objects, and she shrinks from the penis as the main instrument of it. Here, too, her own lack of a penis is a cause for anxiety to her, since it means being without a weapon of defence; and the presence of a hole there alarms her still, because it makes her highly vulnerable to such an attack. In this way, her vaginal instinct continues to supply her with motives, though not so strongly and not all of the same kind, as did her clitoridal instinct, for wanting to injure the penis or remove it from its possessor, even though these are now her sexual objects.

With the advent of the vaginal stage, the small girl not only gives up her masculine aims for feminine ones in the sexual field, but adopts a corresponding attitude in general. She becomes much quieter and gentler, and likes to play with dolls or at keeping house rather than to rush about noisily or pretend to be a Red Indian.

Sometimes, however, in defending herself against a phallic phase which she has not altogether left behind, the small girl may exaggerate the feminine attitudes which her vaginal position normally produces, and may lay undue stress on the value of her female attributes, by way of overcompensation for her sense of inferiority about them. Such a child loves to dress up and look at herself in the looking glass and be admired by others. Her vanity is, *au fond*, a displaced overcompensatory vanity about her sexual organ; and her thirst for admiration betrays her secret disbelief in the attractive powers of that organ. Again, she may overcompensate for her envy of the penis by scorning, or professing to scorn, all masculine attributes and activities. She makes it abundantly clear that girls' games are alone enjoyable and that boys' games are horridly rough, dirty and dangerous. In her opinion—an opinion which is sometimes too loudly protested to carry complete conviction—boys are nasty, ugly creatures. They are made of 'frogs and snails and puppy-dogs' tails', while little girls are made of 'sugar and spice and all that is nice'.—Such an attitude of 'sour grapes' may, however, defeat its own ends if it is carried too far, or, more important, if it is too deeply entrenched. For it impedes the attainment by the small girl of a satisfactory female sexual position towards her objects, owing to the contempt and aversion to the penis and its possessor which it engenders in her. But normally it is more a matter of show than reality, and the gratifications which those objects promise her usually gain the day.

Sometimes, however, the little girl is not able to get the

better of her clitoridal position. Her male sexual instinct continues to be dominant, so that she keeps her libidinal attachment to her mother in full force, and has a masculine attitude. Nevertheless, she need not totally abjure that instinct in order to overcome it. She can adapt and modify a great deal of it, and employ it in legitimate and profitable ways. She sublimates her sexual impulses towards her mother and other female persons so that she has a more friendly relation to them than her unadulterated heterosexual impulses would procure; and she turns her masculine position to good account by gaining from it a more sympathetic understanding of the opposite sex than would otherwise be possible. Her interests are enlarged and her personality enriched. Without surrendering her feminine occupations, pursuits and pleasures, and without becoming aggressively tomboyish, she yet enjoys playing boyish games and taking part in hardy activities on many occasions. She shows more initiative in her character, too, and her mind is of a more adventurous and enquiring turn than would otherwise be the case.[1]

We see then that the steps which the girl must take before she attains a female genital position are that she gives up her original object for another, surmounts her repugnance to castration and her fears of internal damage and leaves behind most of her masculine aims.

The boy, on the other hand, makes no such sweeping changes. He retains his original object, continues to be averse to castration and does not give up his masculinity. In this way he is much more easily able to attain—or maintain—a

---

[1] It must be said that Freud inclined to the opinion that the small girl's feminine position is based on the reversal, mentioned above, of her masculine and aggressive clitoridal aims into passive and masochistic ones, rather than on an infantile female instinct in its own right. He did not believe that the vagina became an erotogenic zone until she reached sexual maturity at the age of puberty. He thought that before that period her wish to have a baby was a substitute for her frustrated wish to have a penis, and that she turned her love from female to male persons because she discovered that only the latter were able to give her a baby. More recent psycho-analytic investigation has shown, however, that although the female genital instinct does not come fully into its own till the advent of puberty—any more, for the matter of that, than does the male genital instinct—it undoubtedly makes its appearance in early childhood.

boyish attitude in every field, than she is to attain a girlish one.

Nevertheless, in maintaining these attitudes he is not altogether exempt either from having to make war against opposite attitudes. For he, too, like the small girl, has a certain amount of bisexuality in his mental make-up—is *ambisexual*, as it is sometimes called. Indeed, just as she possesses a regular male genital instinct (in the form of the clitoridal instinct), so may he possess a female one. The part-object of this instinct is the penis and its aim is to receive that object into an organ of the body which is its leading erotogenic zone. This is the perineum, an area which corresponds developmentally to the vagina in the female.[1] This 'perineal instinct' as it might be called, which is a kind of counterpart to the girl's clitoridal instinct, moves the boy to be sexually attracted by male persons and to want to be copulated with by them. Furthermore, it, or the more general female attitude which goes along with it, activates a maternal instinct in him so that he wants to give birth to children and nurse them and look after them like any little girl.

The leading zone of this instinct, however, is totally unfit, from its physical conformation, to satisfy any receptive aims, since it presents no cavity for the entrance of an object. The instinct is therefore obliged to fall back upon a near-by erotogenic zone more suited to this purpose, which is none other than the anal zone with its convenient passage. It is probable that the use of this zone adds an extra tinge of passivity and masochism to his instinct in virtue of the role it plays in the reversed aims of his aggressive and sadistic anal impulses.

The boy's female genital impulses, being far less strong than his male genital ones, hardly come to the fore at all in an open form, especially as they are so opposite to the latter. Then, too, his phallic ego acts against them very energetically; for to his way of thinking their gratification would involve a situation which is altogether abhorrent to it, viz. being

[1] Cf. Abraham, 'Ejaculatio Praecox', p. 285.

castrated. Thus he takes strong defensive measures against his feminine self. Among them, reactive formation and over-compensation play a major part. The boy makes himself extra manly, or makes himself out to be more manly than he is, and he puts away all girlish things with high and noisy contempt. In this way we see that the phallic boy's excessive masculinity is nearly always not only a protest against the possibility of castration and internal injury, but against his own desire for them or what entails them. Here we have a Nazi type in the making.

This being so, it is natural that the boy's ambisexuality should be much less apparent than that of the girl, who, like him, has more motive for resisting her female sexuality than her male sexuality. It can happen, nevertheless, that in him, as in her, the opposite-sexed instinct gains the upper hand. In that case he adopts a manifestly feminine position. He behaves like a little girl and is openly attracted by male objects.

As a rule, however, he, too, like the girl, is able to adapt and sublimate a considerable portion of his opposite-sexed impulses, to his great advantage. His sexual love for persons of his own sex is transformed into an affectionate and sociable attitude to them, and his feminine disposition forms a favour-able background for an intuitive understanding of the feminine mind. He can enjoy many girlish pleasures as well as boyish ones and can share many of the interests and pursuits of the other sex, instead of rejecting them with scorn or being at best tolerant of them in a superior sort of way. The small boy, for instance, whose masculine protest against his feminine impulses is very strong, will absolutely refuse to amuse his little sister by playing with dolls with her or to help his mother to lay the table or wash up; the little boy who has no, or next to no, feminine impulses will not mind doing those things occasionally to please his little sister or his mother, though he gets no direct pleasure from them; but the little boy who has a respectable amount of modified and well-tolerated feminine impulses will play at dolls with his little sister and help his mother in her household chores quite freely, and will like it. Nor will his doing so in any way detract from his manliness. When he has finished playing dolls with his sister or folding up the table-napkins for his mother, he will turn to playing at brigands or imitating a train, wrestling with the dog or whatever other active pursuit suggests itself to him, like any other small boy.

* * *

The infantile genital instinct continues to dominate the child's instinctual life until he reaches the age of puberty, so that it and the way in which it is dealt with in infancy decide his attitude throughout the rest of his childhood. Furthermore, the adult genital instinct which gains the supremacy at puberty is, as we shall presently see, very similar to it and amplifies rather than supersedes it. Thus the position which the child attains at the infantile genital stage is in many respects decisive not only for the rest of his childhood but for the rest of his life. The small boy who has dealt pretty successfully with his phallic phase, is, as a grown man, confident in himself without being unduly conceited, and he is able to be fond of women and respect them as well as being sexually attracted by them. But the boy whose pride in his penis is only equalled by his fear of losing it cannot, as an adult, establish this favourable attitude any more than he could as a child. If, at that time, he sought to overcome his castration anxiety by being self-assertive and over-aggressive, he will be self-assertive and aggressive in later life, and will be apt to resent any slights to his manliness with undue vigour. He is tender of his 'point of honour'. The boy who defies his anxiety by making more use than ever of his penis in prohibited sexual ways often becomes a notorious seducer of women—a regular Don Juan.[1] The boy who gives way to it and is timid and cowardly will be timid and cowardly as a man. The boy who responds to his discovery that women have no penis by despising them will not necessarily become a

[1] Though here another important factor comes into play, as we shall see in the next chapter.

woman-hater, but he will think poorly of their capacities and keep them in their place. The boy who responds to it by fearing them may become a woman-hater; or he may become sexually impotent.

In the same way his female instinct, being part and parcel of his genital life, remains in being from his childhood onwards (though, as we shall see in the next chapter, it is submerged, and perhaps even positively weakened, by the fresh onset of male sexuality which occurs at puberty), and so do the defences which the ego puts up against them and the modifications which it makes of them at that period. The boy who has dealt with those instincts successfully can, as a grown man, not only love and desire women; he can understand and sym- pathize with their feelings and views. He is not above indulging in some of their occupations and sharing a part of their lives. Brave soldiers often knit in their spare time and good husbands enjoy doing a little dusting round the house. Nor is the man who gets on best with his fellow-men always the most mas- culine type. The 'clubbable' man is one whose feelings of rivalry with his own sex, which are based on his hetero-sexual instinct, have been subdued by feelings of friendliness. These, as we know, are a sublimation of his libidinal instinct. Thus in this case they are based upon homosexual impulses in him, and many of these proceed from his female sexuality.

Similarly, the position of the grown woman is largely determined by what her position was at the infantile genital stage. If she did not get over her (active) clitoridal impulses then, or deal with them satisfactorily, she will still be com- peting with men on their own ground, instead of leading the kind of life for which her capacities fit her. She is often unsuc- cessful in these activities, or successful only at great expense to herself; partly, perhaps, owing to a lack of natural talent for them, but also owing to the great amount of hostility involved in her attitude, which is likely to make her spoil whatever she does, and to the sense of guilt, with its self- stultifying consequences, which that hostility arouses; not to mention the answering hostility which it calls out in her male rivals—a hostility which is greatly reinforced by their resentment, based upon their phallic position, against her for poaching upon their preserves.[1]

If she did attain a feminine position at that time but did not adequately surmount her phallic phase she will still be envious of the male sex and their achievements, which she is prone to overestimate, and she will still, unconsciously, be out to deprive them of their penis. Such a design takes the displaced form of depriving them of their masculine attributes, whether mental or physical, as, for example, Delilah did to Samson, when she cut off his hair, on which his strength depended. If, again, she has, as a small girl, adopted the method of enhancing the value of her secondary sexual characteristics so as to conceal the short-comings of her primary one, she will grow up into a person who is inordinately vain of her own appearance; and she is apt to decry the muscular strength of the male body in comparison with the softness of female curves. On a higher plane she may extol feminine virtues at the expense of masculine ones, and maintain that what women lack in intellectual capacity and physical daring they more than make up for in intuitive understanding and loving endurance. She depreciates all masculine occupations and interests. Thus, while not stepping outside the female role, she manages to put herself in a superior position to him. Indeed, she often prefers to regard him as nothing but a big baby who requires feeding, humouring and petting, and thus she denies not only the value but the existence of his adult masculinity. Such a woman can often love and cherish a man only if he is ill or incapacitated; for then he represents to her a castrated person of whom she is no longer envious.

Or if she took up an ultra-passive position in early childhood and one in which masochism plays a large part, she may

[1] The man's tendency to prevent women from excelling in fields of activity outside the sphere of the home is, however, also derived from sexual prohibitions, which make the working with her taboo to him. Nor is it only a question of preventing her from developing her masculine trends. It is often a question of preventing her from developing her feminine ones, as we see, for instance, in the opposition which was shown to the training of women as professional nurses. Here his envy of the female sex is at work, and this, of course, springs from his own frustrated feminine impulses.

renounce all activities, even of the kind which normally feminine women of her age and standing carry out. She will regard herself and her sex as physically weak and mentally incapable, and her admiration of, and trust in, the male sex as clever and strong is correspondingly extravagant. She restricts her interests to the home circle of husband and children, and even here she is often singularly inefficient in the more responsible aspects of it. She cannot keep house, or cook, or look after her own children properly. The Dora of *David Copperfield*—that *ne plus ultra* of helpless femininity—is perhaps the most outstanding example of this type of character. But even here the underlying cause of her helplessness—her original sadism and envy of the penis—is seen still to be at work in its unreversed form. For she often succeeds by her very helplessness, if not in accaparating the man's penis and power outright, at least in employing them almost exclusively for her own uses. She cannot look up a time-table, she cannot travel unescorted, or be in an empty house alone, or go out in public by herself; she cannot walk more than a quarter of a mile without a supporting arm or cross a field of cows without masculine protection. He must be dancing attendance on her all the time, doing things with her or for her that she ought to be able to do for herself, instead of going about his own business. Finally, if she failed, as a small child, to detach her sexual libido from her mother in sufficient quantity, she will, as an adult, be unable to be attracted by men, even if she has attained a feminine position and overcome her phallic phase in every other respect, and she will either have an unsatisfactory married life or remain a spinster.

But if, on the other hand, as is the general rule, she did manage to attain a feminine position at the infantile stage, did surmount her phallic phase and did reorientate her libido towards a male object, then her position in adult life will, other things being equal, be a satisfactory one. And if, in addition, she was able to modify and sublimate in early childhood what remained of her clitoridal instinct and her phallic phase and bring it into harmony with the rest of her per-

sonality she can later on make the most of opportunities for
a wider life from which she might have otherwise been
debarred, without having to sacrifice her dominant feminine
trends. She can become a doctor or a scientist, an artist, a
writer, a politician, not to mention an explorer, a member
of the police force or even, in time of emergency, take up
arms in her country's defence, without losing her woman-
hood. It may be that the highest reaches of physical prowess
are closed to her, and even that she cannot, as a general thing,
equal men in the intellectual sphere. Nor will she shine in the
more purely destructive fields of activity, useful and necessary
as some of them are, but rather in those where the libido is
mostly involved; for her mental constitution is coloured
through and through by her maternal instincts upon which
the existence of the race depends; and these lead her—for
better or for worse—to love and cherish things, whether bad
or good, rather than to hate or attack them. Women butchers
and soldiers and surgeons will never, I think, be very plenti-
ful, any more than are women burglars or homicides, be the
doors of those callings never so open to their sex.

E

Chapter IX

THE OEDIPUS PHASE AND AFTER

THE achievement of the infantile genital position brings with it a situation which is not only very important at the time, but which is fraught with consequences for the future.

In this position the child's genital impulses are directed to his or her parent of the opposite sex. The boy not only loves his mother dearly but has sexual longings for her; and the girl feels the same about her father. Each, too, wants to supplant the parent of the same sex in the affections of the parent of the other. The boy wants to oust his father at his mother's side; and the girl wants to take her mother's place with her father. This highly emotional situation is called the *Oedipus situation*, from the Greek story of Oedipus who unwittingly slew his father and married his mother. (In the case of the girl, it is also sometimes called the *Electra situation*, from another Greek story, in which Electra's mother is killed to avenge the murder of her father, King Agamemnon.)

But the small child soon sees that it has little chance of carrying its Oedipus wishes into effect. For the parent of the same sex forbids it to have sexual intercourse with the parent of the opposite sex, and the latter rejects its advances with reprobation and obviously prefers his or her grown-up sexual partner to it for such purposes. Then, too, it is aware of the inadequacy of its sexual organs to meet the requirements of adult sexuality. The boy suspects that his penis is neither large enough nor potent enough to excite and satisfy his mother's vaginal desires, and the little girl feels that her vagina is not sufficiently capacious or vigorous in its receptive activities to do the same for her father's big and powerful penis. Moreover, the child does not altogether want to put those wishes into effect. To begin with, they are filled with great anxiety for it, because it dreads the retaliatory vengeance of the parent whose rival it is. The little boy is terrified of being killed or castrated by his father or turned out of his home and abandoned to die, for wanting to put him out of the way, and the little girl is afraid of the same fate at her mother's hands for wanting to step into her shoes. Furthermore, those wishes are highly conflictual. For the child is also very fond of the parent whom it hates as its deadliest rival, so that it wants both to spare and destroy him. And, of course, its feelings of guilt and remorse are strongly mobilized. Then, too, the awe and veneration in which it holds its parents makes the idea of having sexual relations with either of them very shocking to it. Finally, it dreads the actual act of sexual intercourse with an adult person. The boy is afraid that his mother's huge vagina will engulf his penis or destroy it from the violence of its behaviour when excited, and the girl is equally terrified at the idea of having her small vagina stretched and torn and the inside of her body damaged by her father's out-size and super-potent penis.

For all these reasons the young child makes great efforts to master its Oedipal impulses. This it does partly by inhibiting and repressing them, partly by finding alternative outlets for them through masturbation or through displacement onto less prohibited and dangerous objects and partly by modifying their aims in a suitable way. The boy is more than ever attracted by his sisters or other girls of his own age, with whom he often carries on sexual or semi-sexual practices, and he sublimates his lust for his mother into an added fondness and devotion for her. He subdues his death-wishes against his father to milder feelings of hostility and rebellion, and he displaces much of them onto other authoritative male persons and vents them in quarrels and rivalries with his brothers, or other boy companions. The girl deals with her Oedipus wishes along the same lines. She directs the sensual side of her love of her father to other male objects, usually to boys

of her own age—her brothers, if any, in the first instance—
and she sublimates her love of him into pure affection. She
turns her feelings of hostility towards her mother onto other
female objects, engaging in quarrels and rivalries with a sister
or a girl acquaintance to take the place of the quarrels and
rivalries which she would otherwise have with her own
mother; and her fits of naughtiness and rebellion against her
father, as well as against her nurses, aunts and governesses,
are a substitute for even more savage attacks upon her mother.

These various methods of dealing with the Oedipus situation
are usually sufficient to enable the child to arrive at a reasonably satisfactory *modus vivendi* within the family circle. Nevertheless, the impulses concerned are so powerful that they
often threaten to break through those defences. The small
boy may refuse to leave his mother's side for a single second
so as to have her all to himself and keep his father from her,
or he may even make some undisguised sexual advances to
her; whilst at the same time he shows strong hostility to his
father and may even attempt to injure him. The small girl
may attach herself with all her feelings to her father and
make rudimentary attempts to seduce him. She may even
try to prevent her mother from ever coming near him and
be extremely hateful to her and attack her in all sorts of ways.
The child's ego, on the other hand, fearful of the strength
of these forbidden impulses, redoubles the vigour of its
defensive effort against them, and its repressions and inhibitions of them may not only be intensified but extended to
cover what should be quite innocent derivatives of them. As
a result, the child may become incapable of expressing or
even being conscious of emotional attitudes towards its
parent which are in themselves perfectly permissible and
often highly desirable. A small boy may be unable not only
to show, but to be aware of, any affection at all towards his
mother because that affection falls under the ban imposed
upon his lust for her; or he may be unable to express, or
consciously to have, any opinion which differs from his
father's opinions since to do so is associated in his mind with

opposing him in a much more deadly way.[1] This collection of repressed Oedipal attitudes becomes disassociated from the conscious system, and thus impervious to any further modification by it, and it continues to operate in its original form and force in the unconscious and to influence the conscious from there. Such a nexus of unresolved Oedipal attitudes forms the nucleus of what is known as the Oedipus complex.

The child's ego uses other methods for dealing with its Oedipal impulses besides repression and sublimation. In the first place, it may initiate a turning back of the libido from its external object to the self. The boy gives up his love for his mother and loves himself instead; and the girl gives up her love for her father and loves herself in his place. In this way the child finds a way out of the situation by adopting a narcissistic position. Reactive formation, too, is often extensively employed to combat its Oedipal impulses. In that case the child becomes hostile to its own opposite-sexed parent and over-fond of its same-sexed one. The boy turns away from his mother and is devoted to his father; and the girl is on bad terms with her father but adores her mother. These reactive attitudes are greatly facilitated by the child's ambisexuality. For the homosexual components of its sexual instinct lead it to desire persons of the same sex as itself and to be indifferent to persons of the opposite sex. Indeed, within the framework of its family relationships, these homosexual impulses cause the child not only to love its same-sexed parent but to hate its opposite-sexed one as a rival. The little boy is erotically attracted to his father and is jealous of his mother and wants her out of the way, and the little girl is attracted to her mother

[1] Indeed the situation can be still more serious. The child may not only be incapable of expressing or being conscious of those permissible derivatives of his Oedipal impulses along with the impulses themselves; he may be incapable of having them at all. For since the mental elements which are under repression are cut off from any further modification, the milder feelings and more rational ideas which should have been derived from them may never have been able to come into being. The child may thus remain truly unaffectionate to one parent, and truly subservient to the other.

and does her best to oust her father from her side. The position which the child attains on this basis is thus the reverse of the normal Oedipal position. This is called the *negative* or *inverted* Oedipal position, to distinguish it from the normal (or *positive*) Oedipal position which we have just described. The adoption of this negative position is often further facilitated by processes of introjection. As we know, the subject is often enabled to give up his object by assigning its properties to himself. Thus the boy assigns to himself the qualities belonging to his adored and desired mother, and the girl does the same with her father. But this, of course, means—in so far as the introjection is real—that each takes over characteristics belonging to a member of the opposite sex; and if the introjected properties should include sexual attitudes, both the boy and the girl will become homosexual.

All children have a negative Oedipal position as well as a positive one. But normally it is much less strong than the latter, and mostly performs the useful function of mitigating it. It is only in rarer instances that the negative position becomes a dominant. But the degree to which it is *manifest* is, of course, not always a measure of the degree to which it is *operative*.

*   *   *

The small child's efforts to cope with his Oedipal situation are never entirely successful at this early age, owing to internal as well as external causes. On the one hand, the violence of his impulses is too great, and the power of his ego still too slight for him to be able to master them adequately; and on the other, it is not as yet possible for him to leave the circle of the family, in which that situation is produced. But the march of events now comes to his assistance. Round about the age of six there sets in a period during which his genital instincts, and indeed all his instincts, undergo a marked decline and his impulses and affects become correspondingly milder. This time of diminished impulsional life is called the *latency period*. During the latency period children lose much of their early originality of thought and feeling and spontaneity of expression, and their creative powers suffer great and often permanent eclipse. It is at this period that the infant prodigy turns into a commonplace being and that the artistically-gifted child ceases to produce his vivid and imaginative pictures, and perhaps paints no more. Much of this loss is no doubt due to the increased repression of impulses which accompanies the Oedipal period; but much is due to the actual decline of them which marks its close. To make up for this falling off of id-energy the child's intellectual capacities and interests—its ego-functions—undergo a marked expansion. It wants to learn and to know about real rather than imaginary things. It develops a thirst for facts as opposed to phantasies and it likes to be told 'true' stories instead of fairy-tales. It also begins to have an interest in impersonal and even abstract topics. The girl, for example, gives up trying to attract her father's love away from her mother by acts of exhibitionism and wants to know how clothes are cut out and sewn or to learn a poem and recite it nicely before an interested audience. The boy is no longer consumed with jealousy and curiosity about what his father's strength and potency can accomplish. Instead, he watches trains or motor-cars or aeroplanes, and notes speed, power and make of each kind and speculates on their comparative performances. At this period, too, the child extends its parental attachments outside the family. Its teachers and other more remote grown-ups now claim a large share of its love, devotion, fear and hatred, as the case may be. Its ordinary non-parental objects as well are less confined to the home circle. It takes a larger interest in outside playmates and small friends and is less dependent on the company of its brothers and sisters. Its super-ego, too, continues to gain in amplitude and realism. Children in the latency period tend to be extremely conscientious and anxious to behave in the right way. They are deeply concerned with questions of right and wrong and want to know whether this or that person or this or that action are 'good' or 'bad'. They are very critical, too, about the moral behaviour of others—not excluding those in authority over them—and they are prone to view their conduct with a censorious eye.

The latency period lasts for a considerable time. The child's libidinal instincts remain in comparative abeyance up to about the age of nine or ten, during which time its mind continues to develop on the moral and intellectual plane. Freud attached great importance to this period of instinctual quiescence, which, as he points out, is unique to the human species. For all other animals, even the higher apes, pursue an unbroken course of sexual activity from the first appearance of the genital instinct. Freud even regarded this as a possible cause of man's superior intelligence over brute creation. He believed, too, that the higher level of intellectual and cultural development achieved by civilized peoples, as compared to primitive ones, was to be explained by the fact that in the latter the sexual impulses are less in abeyance during this period.

*   *   *

Round about the age of nine or ten, the genital instincts begin to assert themselves more strongly once more. From now on they continue to increase until, with the advent of physical sexual maturity at the age of puberty, they set in with full force. At this stage the genital instinct is completely developed. It can fulfil its procreative functions as well as provide sexual gratification. The adolescent boy has seminal emissions and the adolescent girl is able to conceive children. The adult genital instinct of the pubertal stage is not only stronger in itself than the infantile genital instinct; it is stronger in relation to the pregenital instincts. The latter, too, are reduced in actual strength and, moreover, they lose much of their independence of the genital instinct. They become organized into it as subsidiary parts of it, and are no more than an introductory step to its gratification. Their own gratification is no longer an *end-pleasure* but a *fore-pleasure*, which serves as an incentive to the gratification of the genital instinct. Kissing, sucking and biting are common preliminaries of the sexual act, and even faecal pleasures may open the way to it.[1] In addition, the genital instinct is less ambisexual at puberty than it was in infancy. The adolescent boy is more exclusively masculine in his attitude, and the adolescent girl more exclusively feminine; and each is less attracted to persons of the same sex. Owing to the considerable detachment from its parental objects which the instinct has undergone towards the close of the Oedipal phase and after it, in the latency period, and owing to the displacement it has made on to other figures during that time, its objects at the pubertal stage are no longer the old, incestuous ones. Mother and father are replaced by teacher, elder school-friend or even some more remote person.

The mature genital instinct is, moreover, less ambivalent than is the infantile genital instinct—though the latter, as we know, is less so than its predecessors, all except the oral-sucking instinct. This is doubtless due in the first instance to the increase of libido in the sexual instinct which takes place at this time, as well as to the aforesaid lessening of ambi-sexuality which allows the adolescent's love of his object to be undisturbed by his hatred of it as a rival; but it may also proceed from the increased association which the instinct now has, in virtue of its procreative element, with the parental instinct, which as we know, is the most purely libidinal one of all.

The adolescent's relative non-ambivalence towards his object is also to some extent determined by external factors. In the oral-sucking stage the infant is non-ambivalent not only because its biting instinct has not yet come to the fore, but because it has not yet been seriously frustrated by its object; at the infantile genital stage the child is once again less ambivalent in part because its frustrations no longer proceed mainly from the object of its love; and at the pubertal stage he is still less so, because his sexual object is now—in as much as he has detached his sexual libido from his parent— no longer one of its necessary frustrators at all.

[1] Cf. Freud, *Three Essays on the Theory of Sexuality*, pp. 68–71.

*

But the onset of puberty confronts the girl with a psychological task which she did not have to face at the infantile genital stage and from which the adolescent boy is exempt. This is the setting in of her menstrual periods. This event can be a very trying one for her psychologically, especially if she is still suffering from a strong infantile castration-complex. The pain and the feeling of unwellness, the partial incapacitation and the flow of blood which characterize the menstrual period all combine to make her re-experience her old feelings of disgrace, guilt and inferiority when she first discovered the fact that boys had a penis but she had none. In her unconscious she connects the blood and the pain with having had her penis cut off, and she regards this as a punishment for wrong-doing and, in especial, for sexual wrong-doing or as a result of her father's assaults or her mother's spite. Worse still, she takes it as a sign that not only has she been deprived of a penis but that serious damage has been done to the inside of her body as a result of forcible attacks upon it or forbidden sexual handling of it, so that her anxiety is acutely aroused. Nevertheless, if the girl's mental development has been reasonably normal and satisfactory up till now, she soon becomes reconciled to this physical disability and gets over her feelings of guilt and anxiety about it, the more so in that she can regard it, not as a mark of inferiority, but on the contrary as an earnest that she is now for the first time a mature female, able not only to have sexual intercourse but to bear children.[1] But, of course, if her infantile fears and guilt about her sexual wishes have been abnormally strong, these very signs of her sexual maturity will upset her, as will other signs of it, such as the development of her breasts and the growth of her pubic hair.

The adolescent is not yet out of the wood, however. For

[1] Incidentally, the physical suffering which menstruation causes her and the various disorders to which it is so easily subject, such as too much flow of blood or too frequent or infrequent occurrence of the period or an irregular occurrence of it, or none at all—are not seldom determined, in part or altogether, by the unfavourable psychological attitude which she has adopted towards it on account of its unconscious significance to her.

the recrudescence of his sexual instincts brings with it a recrudescence of his Oedipus situation. It is true that he has, to some extent, undone his original incestuous attachments and found substitutive objects for his sexual impulses. But such a detachment is far from complete. A large portion of his sexual libido still adheres to his parental imagos. These attachments have succumbed to repression at the end of the Oedipal phase and have lain dormant during the latency period. But they now become re-activated and once more press for satisfaction. The most the youth can do is to increase his displacement of them on to substitutive objects. But even so, the quality of his love and the kind of love-object he chooses often betray their continuing infantile source. He falls in love with women much older than himself or who are in a superior situation to him or who are already married— with women, that is, who stand to him for his mother or his father's wife. This age swarms with Cherubinos, Octavians and Young Woodleys. Similarly, the growing girl is attracted by older men, and often married ones. Schoolgirls fall in love with their schoolmasters or with the fathers of their girl friends, and boys of their own age are small beer to them.

Such infatuations, however, are usually of short duration, precisely because the adolescent's love-object is still to a great extent a surrogate one and his choice of it is largely determined by associative considerations—by factors which link it with his original object. These factors are often comparatively few, and many of them are of an accidental or extraneous sort and not an inherent property of his new object. Thus they are not likely to be very permanent. When they, or some of them, cease to exist, he ceases to be in love with his object, and he is liable to be attracted by some other person in respect of whom those associative links (or another set of them, it may be) are for the time being established. If, for instance, the married woman whom a youth loves ardently is widowed or gets a divorce he will more likely than not suddenly stop loving her, because now she no longer fulfils the role of his mother who belongs to his father. Then, too, the ambivalence which attaches to the Oedipal impulses has not entirely disappeared, so that the adolescent's love is liable to be neutralized by its opposite (if not reversed). Moreover, in so far as the adolescent's love is still fixed upon his parent in his unconscious mind the representative of that parent in his *conscious* mind only receives a portion of his love, so that for all its apparent intensity, it is superficial; and, in the face of any difficulty, it is likely to return to its original object or move on to another.

Another trouble is mostly of an external sort. Although adolescent boys and girls are fully capable of carrying out the sexual act, they are nearly everywhere forbidden to do so by social custom. But the mature genital instinct is exceedingly powerful and hard to subdue. Some of it can be sublimated into feelings of affection and tenderness towards the opposite sex and into platonic friendships with them, some can be deflected into interests and pursuits of a social, aesthetic or intellectual sort, and some can be discharged in non-sexual physical activities, such as games and sports and feats of endurance; but although these measures provide a certain amount of outlet for the instinct, they are rarely sufficient to carry it off altogether. A certain quantity of it still seeks gratification in its crude sexual form. Since the youth is not allowed to have an external object in regard to whom he can gratify it, he almost invariably makes use of himself for that purpose, and takes to regular masturbation.

In masturbation the genital instinct becomes auto-erotic, since it obtains gratification from parts of the subject's own body and nowhere else. But it does not therefore become narcissistic, for the subject's libido is attached to external objects. While he is masturbating, he imagines situations in which he is having an erotic relation with them. Yet the fact that it is his body alone which supplies him with sexual pleasure tends to make him, as the possessor of it, a valuable person to himself and so to give his attitude a narcissistic colouring. As we know, too, he may adopt a true narcissistic position by taking himself as a love-object in place of the prohibited non-self object, which he gives up mentally.

Solitary masturbation, masturbatory phantasies and self-love are not always enough, however, to satisfy the adolescent's libidinal needs. Some boys, driven on by their craving for heterosexual object-relationships, defy the ban upon them and do have sexual intercourse with girls or women. But the relationship which they enter into in this way is usually too sporadic and too chancy to gratify their instinctual impulses adequately, or to form the basis of ties of love and affection. Moreover, it is too uncertain and too much burdened with a sense of guilt and fear of discovery and of dangerous consequences to bring real ease of mind and happiness to the boy. Nor is he free to choose the kind of girl or woman who suits his inclinations, since scarcity of opportunity obliges him to take whatever offers. Indeed, she nearly always has to be someone whom he not only does not truly love but someone whom he either despises as a loose person or even as a bought one. In addition, the natural outcome of such a relationship is the birth of a child, and this is not desirable, since the youth is not as yet equal to taking on the responsibilities of parenthood. And the same applies to the adolescent girl.

But if the youth cannot have adequate sexual relationships with members of the opposite sex, he may be able to have them with members of his own. Such homosexual relationships possess many advantages over the heterosexual ones that are open to him. To begin with, his objects are more accessible to him. He can be together with other youths and men as much as he likes, so that he can indulge his impulses as often as he likes and with the kind of person who attracts him, and he can form erotic ties of a more constant, though yet not permanent, sort, and ties which involve his affections as well as his impulses. And since his objects are on an equal footing with him as to social standing, character and intellectual capacity, he can enjoy a free interchange of thought and feeling with them. Such a relationship has great possibilities of sublimation. Indeed, if the boy enters into a partnership of this kind with some male person who is somewhat older than himself he may derive much spiritual benefit from it. The ancient Greeks were well aware of this, and it was a regular part of a boy's education that he should be loved and taught by an older man. Such homosexual relationships, incidentally, do not involve a feminine attitude on both sides. One partner —usually the elder one—is only homosexual as regards his object, but not as regards his aim. Nor, indeed, if the relationship does not proceed beyond, say, mutual masturbation need either partner abandon his masculine position.

In the same way, the adolescent girl feels the stress of the years of instinctual frustration between her attainment of sexual maturity and the time when she is permitted to put her genital instincts into practice. Indeed, in her case, the external prohibitions—and the internal ones, too—are even stronger than in the youth. Yet in her the stress may not be as great as in him, for it would appear that the female genital instinct is more quiescent than the male one and that its arousal depends to a large extent upon sexual advances by the male. Nevertheless, she, too, has spontaneous urges with which she must deal as best she may—through modifications and sublimations of them, by engaging in flirtations of a more or less serious kind with boys and men, by indulging in masturbatory phantasies, by assuming a narcissistic position or by having intense, if passing, emotional attachments, whether sublimated or not, to persons of her own sex. Who is not acquainted with the passionate friendships which growing girls develop for one another, the 'crushes' they have for their friend's elder sister or their wild adoration of a popular mistress at school?

Gradually, however, as adolescents grow up, they leave behind the childish character of their sexual libido and detach it altogether from parental images. They choose as their love-object a person of the opposite sex towards whom they no longer have a dependent attitude and who no longer stands in lieu of a mother or father to them. Octavian gives up his adored, but not so young, protectress for the charming young *ingénue*, Cherubino leaves off sighing for the Countess and marries the youthful Barbarina, and it is to be surmised that young Woodley would presently have exchanged his headmaster's wife for someone nearer his own age. The young adult is now regarded by society as a responsible person, sexually, morally and intellectually, and he or she is considered to be fit not only to have sexual intercourse but to marry and bring up a family. His genital instinct finds full employment in real life, and he is no longer burdened with the problem of finding indirect outlets for it.

But in many individuals the Oedipus phase is slow to die and it stretches a long, if lessening, shadow over their lives, even after they have left adolescence behind. Many young men of twenty-five are still attracted by older, married women, and we are all familiar with the young governess who falls in love with her pupils' father and the budding hospital nurse who conceives a passion for the senior surgeon. Even the young typist who succumbs to the advances of her middle-aged business employer does not always do so from mercenary motives alone. Some persons, indeed, in whom the Oedipal position has become complexive, never overcome it adequately and remain bound to it for the remainder of their life. A middle-aged governess may fall in love with the father of her pupils because, although he is in fact no older than herself, he represents her father as he appeared to her when she was a child and because, in teaching them, she seems to herself to have taken her mother's place with them and him.

This adult Oedipal position has many variants, in accordance with the various aspects of the infantile and pubertal Oedipus positions which it perpetuates. The boy who has too completely separated his sexual desire for his mother from his sublimated love of her, may never again be able to join the two together, so that he must forever have a 'sacred' and a 'profane' love—admiring one woman whom he is not sexually attracted by, and being sexually attracted by another, whom he does not admire. Or the displacements which, as a boy, he had to make before he could find anyone who was far enough removed from his mother to be admissible as a sexual object, may have been so extensive that, as a grown man, he can only love women who are totally outside his sphere of life, and thus inaccessible to him or unsuited to him on other counts. Or the inhibitions and repressions of his love for his mother may have been so strong and so extensive as to include every female object in his boyhood. Such a man may never be able to love a woman all his life long. To him the whole sex is taboo. Or the strength of his attachment to his mother as a child may have been so intense that he has never given her up as his sexual object. In that case he once more shuns every woman because his mother is the only one he wants, or else he is constantly exchanging one mistress for another since each, in so far as she is *not* his mother is unsatisfying, and, in so far as she is, is forbidden.[1] Then, too, the boy's love for his mother may have turned into hatred of her because she rejected his advances. This boy may well become a woman-hater in later life. Or he may have been deeply shocked to discover that she whom he has idealized and who restrained him from indulging in sexual activities, is herself not free from sexual love for another, i.e. for his father. He may despise her for this and become ever after a despiser of women as low and lustful creatures. His complexive Oedipal attitude to his father and brothers is prolonged into adult life too. If he has not been able to repress his hatred and jealousy of his father he may, as a grown man, be unable to brook a rival, and he will be rebellious and critical towards his superiors. On the other hand, if he has repressed those feelings too much, he will never venture to compete with another man or to question his orders; and if he has reacted against them too strongly he will even be unnecessarily friendly towards him and ready to accept all his views.

Similarly the grown woman who has not adequately dealt with her Oedipal impulses in early childhood and at puberty will continue to be plagued by them and to respond to them in the same way now as she did then. If she has not detached

[1] This motivation is generally an added determinant in the Don Juan type of attitude mentioned in the previous chapter.

her libido sufficiently from her father she will be apt to fall in love with men who are much older than herself, or with men who are already married. If she has separated her sensual from her non-sensual love too widely she will have two sorts of objects—those for whom she has platonic love and those for whom she has sensual love—and will not be able to combine the two so as to love one man fully. If she has had to make a very extensive displacement from her original object she will only be able to love men who are not of her sort, and if no displacement is distant enough to be acceptable, she too will be unable to fall in love with any man at all; and the same effect follows if she has never given up her father as her love-object. Again, if her love for him has turned into hatred because he has not responded to her advances, she will become a hater of men in later life and reject their advances with scorn; and if she has been shocked by observing that he is sexually excited by her mother, she will regard all men as gross and carnal. Then, too, an insufficiently mastered hatred of, and rivalry with, her mother and sisters in childhood leads her to be hostile towards the women she knows as a grown-up and to dislike them and try to harm them in every possible way, especially, of course, in their relations with men; whereas an over-inhibited hatred of, and rivalry with, them prevents her from trying even to hold her own with them. And a reaction against such feelings may lead her to be more amiable to women than she need be, and to give way to them in every respect; and if they are her rivals for the same man, she may actually court defeat at their hands.

Finally, if the individual of either sex has adopted a very strong negative Oedipus attitude in childhood, neither may be able to recover from that attitude and adopt a positive one. Each will, in consequence, continue to love persons of his or her own sex in adult life, and they will be confirmed homosexuals for the rest of their days.

As we see, an unfavourable Oedipal position in the childhood of the individual has wide repercussions in his social as

Chapter X

DREAMS AND THE PHENOMENON OF REGRESSION

The first part of our enquiry is now drawing to a close. As will be remembered, it set out to discover what the unconscious mental factors are which colour the conscious outlook and affect the behaviour of the individual in his private life and personal relationships, with a view to showing that many of these factors engender states of mind in him that conduce to war. Such factors are, we believe, largely to be found in the primitive and infantile psychical attitudes which we have been describing in the preceding chapters, in so far as those attitudes have not been adequately surmounted by the individual in the course of his development and persist into his adult state.

As can be seen, some of the persisting attitudes—for instance, an undue amount of early hostility, or overstrong phallic self-assertion—tend in themselves to be disturbers of the peace, whilst others—say, too much mental dependence on parental figures, or an excess of anal-retentive impulses—do not as yet carry any such threat; and it will be the aim of the next part of our thesis to show how certain social relationships into which the subject finds himself not only increase the dangerousness of the first kind of attitudes, but cause the second kind to become dangerous as well.

But before we can do this we must direct our attention in the next two chapters to yet another underlying psychical factor, which has a very important part to play in what follows. This consists in a tendency, not merely for primitive and infantile positions of mind to persist in the adult, but for fully-developed positions that have been reached by him to disappear or to return to earlier and less developed ones from which they have emerged.

The operation of such a tendency is most clearly visible in two phenomena of the subject's private life—in dreams and in mental illness.

To begin with the first and commonest of them. Early on in his psycho-analytic work Freud discovered the unique value of dreams in these respects. Not only were they an almost universal phenomenon; they enabled ideas and modes of thought which would otherwise have remained unconscious to emerge, and thus threw a great deal of light on the deeper regions of the mind. They were, to use his own words, the Royal Road to the unconscious.

Freud subjected a large number of his own and his patients' dreams to a detailed analysis, and it was on the basis of the data obtained from this that he not only extended his theory of the unconscious to cover normal as well as abnormal minds, but worked it out in its fullest reach. His major work, *The Interpretation of Dreams*, is an exhaustive study of the subject; and the last part of it contains what he himself always considered to be his most fundamental and elaborate account of the structure and functioning of the unconscious mind. What will be said in this chapter is mostly based upon this book.[1]

During sleep the mind is in a state of comparative quiescence, and is unconscious. Moreover, the intending sleeper insures that as few physical stimuli as possible shall reach his senses from without, so as to avoid as far as possible any excitations arising from this source that might keep him wakeful. He shuts his eyes, draws the blinds and seeks a quiet and comfortable place to lie down in. Nevertheless, some external stimuli do from time to time reach him; and some of them may evoke mental presentations in him; and so may stimuli

[1] *The Interpretation of Dreams*, however, being a comparatively early work (though it has undergone several later revisions), does not include some of Freud's later postulations. These are to be found in his 'Metapsychological Supplement to The Theory of Dreams', in Part II of his *Introductory Lectures*, and, in a very clear and succinct form, in his last, unfinished essay, *An Outline of Psycho-Analysis*.

arising from his own body. Such presentations can become conscious, in which case they appear as a dream or as elements of a dream.

Another set of excitations which may evoke mental presentations in the sleeper come from ideas and feelings which he has had during his waking state and which he has not adequately dealt with before going to sleep. A smoker who has lost his favourite pipe after tea and has not had time sufficiently to lament his loss or to become reconciled to it before he goes to bed continues to repine about it as he sleeps; and a housewife who has been sold a rotten cauliflower that morning and was too lady-like to give full vent to her indignation with her greengrocer and yet too angry with him to forgive him, retires to rest in a vengeful mood. These undischarged cathexes of waking life are called the *mental residues of the day before*, or, more shortly, the *day's residues*.

The day's residues, however, are as a rule not forcible enough to become conscious in sleep unless they have become associated with other mental presentations, which are very highly cathected. These, needless to say, mostly belong to the unconscious and are based on instinctual impulses. Thus, the man who lost his pipe during the day might not be enough upset by this to dream about it, if losing his pipe did not also mean to him losing his penis, and thus arouse his castration anxiety; and the housewife might not dream about having been sold a rotten cauliflower, unless it also represented to her being given an ugly and sickly baby instead of the beautiful and healthy one she longs for, and thus excited immense rage and hostility in her.

Indeed, the underlying unconscious presentation contributes not only to the force of the sleeper's thoughts but to their form. It to a large extent shapes them according to its own ideas. The man who dreams of his pipe may dream of a pipe which has a flesh-and-blood texture, and the woman who dreams of throwing the cauliflower at the greengrocer's head may hear it emit a wailing sound as it flies through the air.

Thus the alliance between the day's residues and unconscious presentations benefits both by enabling each to find an outlet which would otherwise be denied it. The man who has lost his pipe dreams about it not only because his concern about it has gained added strength by also being a concern for his penis, but because his concern for his penis has found in his laments over his pipe an acceptable vehicle for becoming conscious; and the woman who has been sold an inferior cauliflower dreams about it not only because her anger at this is reinforced by her anger at having been given an inferior baby, but because her anger about not having been given the baby she hoped for can find a veiled expression in her anger at being given a rotten vegetable.[1]

In so far as ucs. presentations are so largely built up on instinctual impulses and are thus conative in character, we shall not be surprised to find that they introduce a strong wishful element into the dream, and that, in view of the weakness of the preconscious, such wishes are able to appear —though in a disguised form—as fulfilled. Nor, of course, are the day's residues wanting in wishful ideas, among others; and they, too, tend to appear as fulfilled. In his dream a man not only mourns his lost pipe, but sometimes finds it; and the housewife, instead of venting her anger at the greengrocer by throwing the bad cauliflower at his head, may come into possession of a prize vegetable.

Knowing what we do about the strength of infantile instincts and attitudes and their persistence in the unconscious throughout adult life, we shall not be surprised either to find that many of the unconscious presentations which motivate dreams go back to early childhood. The castration anxiety which was aroused in the sleeper by his lost pipe will, in all probability, turn out to date from his phallic phase, and the housewife's anger at not being given a baby is very likely to have originated from the rebuffs which her Electra wishes received when she was a little girl. The infantile nature of

[1] But it must be remembered that the day's residues also *excite* the ucs. presentations, so that they increase its need for discharge as well as facilitating the discharge.

these impulses and attitudes, too, often shimmers through in the dream. The man who dreams about his lost pipe may, for instance, dream that it was reft from him by a giantess, and this giantess turns out to be none other than a nurse by whom he had feared to be castrated as a child and who, being a grown woman, had naturally seemed very big to him. The greengrocer who sold the rotten cauliflower may appear wearing side-whiskers, though in reality he is clean-shaven; this is because he stands for the dreamer's father who wore side-whiskers when she was a little girl. (And he, of course, is the man who would not give her the baby.)

Sometimes, indeed, the power of the ancient ideas and feelings which the day's residues have conjured up is so great that they capture the scene. *Then*, the man who has lost his pipe dreams about infantile days, and of a giant nurse who is taking away his toys; and the angry housewife sees herself back in her old home, feverishly throwing cushions at her father's head.

But whether the events that are being dreamed about occurred on the day before or in the distant past, they tend to be dreamed of, not as having happened at those times, but as happening at the moment. The man who dreams about the loss of his toys forty years ago dreams that they are being taken *now*; and the housewife who was given a rotten cauliflower yesterday sees herself being given one at this very instant.

Such an intrusion of the past into the present is to a large extent due to the circumstance that the sleeper is having very few mental presentations arising from contemporary stimuli with which to compare and correlate his mental presentations arising from past stimuli and so place them in their proper perspective. Still more important is the fact that, in sleep, his preconscious ego, whose function it is to make such comparisons, is inadequate to its task. And the unconscious is never able to do it. It can retain experiences from the past—none better—but it is unable to recognize them as belonging there.[1]

---

[1] In this sense, as Freud observes, the unconscious is timeless.

Another very striking feature of dreams—and one which is also partly responsible for their depicting things as happening in the present—is that many of these elements appear in a sense-perceptual form[1]—as things being seen or heard or touched or smelt; and this, even when the things in question were not so apprehended by the subject in his mental residues. Thus if his sleeping thought is 'Mrs. So-and-So stole my pipe' and that thought is carried into a dream, it will probably appear there not as a *thought* of Mrs. So-and-So stealing his pipe but as an actual *sight* of her committing the theft.

Such a transformation of ideas into percepts is the result of a particular process in the mind to which it is time that we should turn our attention, especially as it plays an important part not only in sleep but in many aspects of waking life, and with much more far-reaching consequences.

Freud regards the mind as an apparatus consisting of a number of different psychic systems through which all the excitations which arise in it pass in a given order before being finally discharged or otherwise dealt with. The first of these is the sensory system. Here the nervous excitations coming from the various sense-organs are translated into corresponding sensations—into sights, sounds, smells, tastes, feelings of cold and warmth, sensations of softness and hardness, and so on.

From this system an imprint of the sensation is deposited in a set of psychic systems which store it up in the form of a memory-trace. These are known as the *mnemic* or *memory-systems* (or 'mem-systems' for short).[2] Such a depositing of facsimiles of the sensory elements in a special place is rendered

---

[1] The words 'sense-percept' and 'sense-perception' are used synonymously, nor are they differentiated from 'percepts' and 'sensations'. On the other hand 'perception' may sometimes mean more than a mental event on a purely sensory level. It may be used for a recognition of things, as when we perceive a chair, or someone else's annoyance (or even for abstract ideas, such as perceiving the difficulty of a situation—more in the sense, indeed, in which the word 'apperception' should be used).

[2] The mem-systems are differentiated from one another and placed in order of succession according to the various principles of association which link their elements together, the most primary one—the one regulated by the law of temporal contiguity—being placed next to the sensory system.

necessary in Freud's view by the fact that on the one hand such elements must not be allowed to disappear after their excitations have ceased, since they are an indispensable factor in enabling the individual to learn by experience and to adjust his behaviour in the light of what he has already perceived; and yet, on the other hand, they must not leave any trace of themselves in the sensory system itself, where they would interfere with the field of reception and prevent the production of new sensory elements in a clear and undistorted fashion. If they did remain there and happened to be re-excited, or not to have lost the whole of their original excitation, they would appear as sensations after their external stimuli had ceased. This time they would be unveridical and in the nature of hallucinations and yet they would seem to the subject to refer equally with his veridical percepts to things and events that were going on now, to the great detriment of his judgment. If, for instance, a man is walking beside the edge of a cliff and sees that the path which he took the day before no longer exists—because, say, there has been a landslide overnight—there is no harm in his *remembering* that the path was there yesterday; he will still see that it is no longer there now and will turn back. But if, instead of merely *remembering* his sight of the path yesterday, he actually re-sees it now, he will in all probability step forward confidently into empty space and fall to his death a hundred feet below.

The excitation next travels on to the unconscious system, where it evokes unconscious presentations; and it then proceeds to the preconscious system and evokes preconscious ones. From here it finally reaches the motor system and finds discharge in physical action.

This passage of excitation from the sensory to the motor end of the mental apparatus is called by Freud the *Psychic Process*.

A diagram of the psychic process, adapted from Freud's diagram in his *Interpretation of Dreams* (chapter VII, section B) is given overleaf.

The excitations which enter the psychic apparatus from without, can, of course, arise from the subject's own body, as well as from the world outside it. Excitations that arise within the apparatus (e.g. by association) also pursue the psychic process, from wherever they start.

Now in sleep, when much of the motor system is inoperative, scarcely any discharge of excitation in action is possible. The preconscious system, too, is pretty well incapacitated, so that it cannot take on more than a very small load of excitation. In consequence but few of the sleeper's thoughts can advance beyond the unconscious. Indeed, many thoughts which in his waking life belonged to the preconscious are given up by that system, and these tend to return to the ucs., finding no other way open. In other words, there takes place a backward

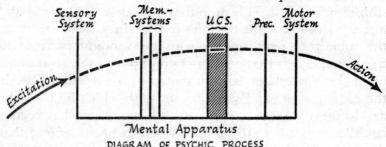

Mental Apparatus
DIAGRAM OF PSYCHIC PROCESS

movement of the psychic process. This reverse flow of excitation is termed by Freud *regression*. We have already come across examples of regression in waking life, in which the ucs. has not only overwhelmed the preconscious but has caused elements of the latter to be debased to its level. But in sleep, where the favouring factors are so strong, this regressive movement is a regular event and occurs on a grand scale. One interesting effect of it is, for instance, that doubts and denials in waking life often do not remain as such in sleep; for, as we know, the unconscious is incapable of anything but positive ideas, since the faculty of criticism and rejection belongs to the preconscious alone. Ideas which present themselves in the unconscious are accepted as true there—that is, what they are about is presumed to exist—and the only way in which the unconscious can disbelieve in something (if this can be called disbelief) is to have no ideas about it at all. Thus, for instance, if a boy's mental residue on going to bed at Christmas-time is 'I don't believe in Santa Claus', it may regress in sleep to the thought 'Santa Claus is dead' or 'is gone away', that being the nearest his unconscious can get to the idea of non-existence; and if his mental residue is 'I wonder whether Santa Claus exists', it may regress to the idea 'Santa Claus is ill' (this standing for his own weakened belief in him) or 'Santa Claus only comes every other year' (this meaning that he half believes, half disbelieves, in him).

But in sleep regression does not stop at the ucs. systems. Those systems are not able to hold the excitations, and many of them accordingly continue their regressive journey and invade the memory systems. There they not only revive the old memory traces of sensory elements but translate the ideas they have brought back with them from the preconscious and the unconscious into terms of those traces, lending the ideas all the concrete and imaginal properties that characterize the mem-systems, and removing from them all their other properties of which those systems are devoid. If, for instance, a man goes to sleep with the idea that Professor X is a learned man, this thought may turn in his sleep into a visual image of Professor X with a very big head or poring over a pile of books, these images being what best expresses in concrete terms the idea of learning. (The depiction of abstract notions in concrete images is not absent in waking life either. It is one of the most, if not the most, marked features of symbolism. There, for instance, innocence is designated by the colour white, happiness by a smiling mouth, justice by a pair of scales and so on.)[1]

[1] In the unconscious, as we know, things that are associated together seem the same, so that whatever stands for something else *is* it; and in so far as the subject's preconscious has not entirely triumphed over his unconscious, he is prone, in part at least, to adopt this view. Thus, for example, if a white dress which symbolizes innocence is splashed with dirt he feels in some way as though innocence itself had suffered; and if his country's flag is accidentally torn down he often cannot help feeling a dreadful pang, as though his country had come to harm, although his reason tells him that this is nonsense. (Cf. in this connection Dr. Ernest Jones' paper 'The Theory of Symbolism', which throws much light on symbolic thinking as distinguished from what he calls 'representational' thinking.) The inability of the unconscious to entertain the notion of meaning applies to

Regression to these sense-imaginal levels causes the mental residues to undergo still further debasement and distortion. Causal relationships, for instance, can no longer be depicted here and can at best be replaced by temporal sequence. If, for instance, a hunting man goes to sleep with the idea 'I fell off my horse this morning because I was too keen to be in at the kill', all he can do in the way of expressing the idea on those levels is to picture the two scenes of being in at the kill (the content of his wish) and falling off his horse, one after the other, either way round—the one order standing for 'I fell off my horse *because* I wanted to be in at the kill' and the other 'I wanted to be in at the kill, *and so* I fell off my horse'.

Lastly, regression can proceed still further. The excitation goes back to the sensory system itself so that the thoughts and pictures concerned take on the properties of actual sensations and perceptions. These elements are the sensations and perceptions of real things; and if they enter consciousness, they appear there as hallucinations. The person, for instance, whose mental residue was that Professor X was a learned man, may not be content to picture the Professor's large head in his mind's eye; he may actually *see* it as though it were before him in fact. In dreams, as we can see, a very large quantity of psychic elements belonging to this final stage of regression are created.

These last two stages of regression—to the sense-imaginal and to the sense-perceptual, hallucinatory stage—are often called by Freud 'formal regression'.

ideas and images in themselves in their capacity of denoting things. It cannot understand their relation to what they denote. To it they *are* the thing which they denote, in virtue of their association with it. The same is true of words; in his sleep, for instance, a person may believe that it is the word 'poison' on the label of a bottle which constitutes the poisonous nature of its contents; and accordingly if he wants to render its contents innocuous he thinks it enough to efface the word 'poison' on the label; or if he wants to commit suicide he imagines that swallowing the label will do the trick. Thus, if you want to kill your enemy, you can do it just as well by crossing out his name as by slashing his portrait.

On the concrete imaginal levels, moreover, verbal presentations themselves take on a concrete quality. They are things, and often human ones. If you want to make an object longer, you can do it just as well by calling it 'lo-o-o-ng' as by calling it 'longer'—except that it might be painful for the word to stretch it out.

Chapter XI

THE PERILS OF REGRESSION

LET us now turn to the second field of psychical events in which regression plays an important part in the private life of the individual—the field of mental illness.

As we know, Freud's earliest discoveries concerned hysteria. He found that hysterical persons are persons who have repressed a strong sexual impulse at some time in their early life; and this initial act of repression furnishes a nucleus of repressed material round which more material is continually built through associative accretion, and also because, having once used repression on a grand scale, the mind tends to continue to do so whenever it is confronted with unpleasurable mental presentations. In this way there exists in the unconscious a mass of highly libidinal interconnected psychic presentations which is ready on the first favourable occasion to break through the repression in the form of a symptom. Thus although hysterical illness may not set in till later life, the *predisposition* to it has been formed in early childhood at some time during the infantile genital stage, and in connection with a repression of Oedipal impulses. This infantile predisposition to hysteria is, in Freud's opinion, formed by two sets of factors. The first is innate or *constitutional*. The person may have been born with an id which possesses too much genital libido, or with an ego which is too prone to repress. The second set of factors is *accidental*. This may consist in an undue degree of external frustrations of the child's sexual instincts—in such things as a stern parental prohibition against masturbation or sexual games with other children or curiosity about sexual matters, or in threats, or supposed threats, of castration for such behaviour; or it may consist in the arousal of more sexual excitement in the child than its ego can cope with, in such things as witnessing what it takes to be sexual intercourse between parental figures, or feeling that it is being seduced or even sexually assaulted by someone, or in connection with any other of the primal scenes.

As Freud continued his psycho-analytic investigations he discovered that other mental disturbances besides hysteria had their origins in pathological predispositions that had been established in early life—predispositions which were, once more, determined by an interplay of constitutional and accidental factors—and that each of these illnesses proceeded from a different predisposition, which was specific for it and which was formed at, and coloured by, one or other of the stages of infantile development. He finally came to the conclusion that this was the case with almost all mental illness. He supposed that the actual outbreak depended, as in hysteria, not only upon a summation of pathogenic experiences ending with a final, precipitating occasion, which might occur any time in later childhood and adult life, but upon an underlying infantile predispositional factor as well, and that it was this factor which inclined the individual to respond to those experiences in a pathological way and in a certain *kind* of pathological way. These infantile predispositions are sometimes overcome in the course of the child's subsequent mental development. But often they are not overcome, or not entirely so. Part of the mind remains stationary there, as is to be expected in view of the difficulty which warded-off psychic material and the warding-off forces have in accompanying the rest of the mind on its forward march. Such an arrestation is known as a *fixation*.[1]

If the fixations are very strong or very extensive they exert

[1] The word 'fixation' is also used to mean the attachment of undue quantities of cathexis to an idea or set of ideas. A person is not only said to have a fixation, or to be fixated, at certain developmental stages, but to have a fixation upon or be fixated to, certain objects or beliefs or situations. The existence in a person of a fixation in the second sense often implies its existence in him in the first sense, and its existence in the first sense *always* implies its existence in the second.

a backward pull upon the rest of the mind, which has progressed to a normal adult position; and should the impulses and attitudes belonging to that position meet with serious obstacles, it is liable to revert to the earlier one, to which the fixations belong. Such a reversion to an earlier stage of mental development obviously tends to involve a certain amount of regression from the later to the earlier systems of the psychical apparatus, as described at the end of the preceding chapter; for, as we know, the strength of the unconscious as compared to the preconscious is greater in children, and still more in infants, than it is in older persons. Nevertheless, the two processes are not identical, and whenever a distinction has to be made between them, the one may be called 'developmental regression' and the other 'systematic regression'.[1]

Given a sufficient fixation at one or other of the infantile predispositions, the probability is that some occasion or series of occasions will occur which will bring on a regression to that place, and that the subject will develop a mental illness and pathological symptoms corresponding to it. Where the fixation is at a very early stage and, in especial, where it involves the faculties of the ego, the disorder is of a very grave kind (though the degree of its gravity in each individual varies with the amount of his mind which is involved in the regression). Illnesses of this kind are classed as psychoses.

In the psychosis known as *Dementia Praecox* or *Schizophrenia*[2] regression has gone farthest of all. The id has strong pregenital impulses of every kind and these are mostly autoerotic. What is more important, the affected part of the ego is unable to synthesize these or any of the other component instincts of the individual or to control their motor discharge; nor does it have proper emotional contact with his objects or, indeed, any proper notion of the existence, or at any rate the nature, of whole objects, even of the self. Accord-

---

[1] There is also such a thing as 'historical regression' by which is meant no more than a return to past attitudes and objects. These may be adult ones, so that regression to them entails no relinquishment of the developmental position achieved.

[2] In enumerating the various psychoses I follow the classification and nomenclature accepted by Freud, Abraham, Ferenczi and others.

ingly, the schizophrenic—at least the full blown one in whom most of the mind is at this stage—is loving, hostile or aggressive in an excessive degree by fits and starts, is greedy and exhibitionistic, plays with his food and faeces, which stand for all sorts of magical objects for him, indulges freely in auto-erotic activities and is often 'wet and dirty'. Moreover, in so far as he has any conception of himself as a whole object he is highly narcissistic, since his id-impulses are still largely directed towards himself rather than towards external objects; and he is equally megalomanic, since the fixated part of his ego is largely at the infantile stage of self-omnipotence. He has all sorts of notions of being the cleverest, most attractive or richest man in the world, or of being the Emperor of Europe or even God Almighty.

Schizophrenia does not lend itself to direct psycho-analytic investigation, at any rate if it has reached any appreciable proportions, since in it the affected ego is too fragmentary and too much out of contact with the analyst, and often too hostile to him, either to be able or to want to communicate its ideas to him. Nevertheless a certain amount of material has been gleaned in this way in recent years; and Freud himself was able to make a detailed study at second hand of a very outspoken case of it. Not many years before, a certain Dr. Schreber, a man of high standing and a judge of the high Court at Leipzig, was overtaken by a somewhat superior variant of this illness, known as *Dementia Paranoides*. In this the patient's delusions and hallucinations are rather more systematized; but they take the form of perceptions and beliefs that evil designs, plots and conspiracies are being practised against him by others—they take the form, that is, of what is commonly called 'persecution mania'. Dr. Schreber, having great intellectual power and moral courage, was able to observe and write down many of his nerve-racking experiences during his illness. These writings came to Freud's notice and formed the basis of one of his most illuminating studies.[1]

---

[1] Cf. his 'Psycho-Analytic Notes upon an Autobiographical Account of a case of Paranoia ("Dementia Paranoides")'.

While still at the height of his successful career, Dr. Schreber, to his horror, felt himself beginning to be assailed by irresistible feminine and passive sexual impulses, and by exhibitionistic desires. He also had strange and violent sensations inside his body, and tactile and auditory hallucinations of many sorts. These led him to the conviction that his nerves were somehow attached to God and that they had an influence over him, but, on the other hand, that the movements of his bowels were being controlled by evil and frivolous spirits who observed and jeered at all his thoughts. He believed, too, that the Universe had been annihilated and that all he saw about him was nothing but a hastily contrived sham. Finally he became convinced that it was his painful but solemn mission to repopulate the world with a new and superior race of men, by allowing himself to be emasculated, turned into a woman and impregnated with the 'divine rays of God'. The progress of his madness shows how, having struggled to keep down his homosexual, destructive and faecal impulses and having failed to do so, he projected the active side of them on to other persons, so that it was they who forced him into a feminine and masochistic-anal attitude, not he who desired it, and now he elevated the passive side of these impulses into a grandiose scheme in which they acquired merit and dignity by enabling him to play the principal, sacrificial part as the saviour of the world. All this is of the highest interest to the psychologist; and, fantastic and ludicrous as many of the events described are, Schreber's account of his experiences is a moving human document of spiritual fortitude under almost intolerable trial.

Another psychosis, known as *Paranoia*, is characterized, as the name implies, by the same sort of symptoms as those which distinguish the paranoid variety of Dementia Praecox from the ordinary sort. For these, too, consist chiefly in delusions of a persecutory kind. The victim of this mental illness believes that another person or persons are out to do him harm and that he is the object of all

F

sorts of evil-intentioned plots and conspiracies on their part.

A good deal more is known about Paranoia than about Schizophrenia, since in it the affected portion of the mind has attained a more advanced stage of development and is more accessible to direct psycho-analytic observation. Here the fixated id has reached the early anal stage and is no longer so auto-erotic and the fixated ego is capable of having whole objects. But the paranoic has highly destructive impulses, and his libidinal impulses are preponderatingly homosexual and to a great extent passive. His ego counters these impulses, which are obnoxious to it, chiefly by projection, and that often in the sense that he not only attributes them to the person towards whom he has them, but believes that that person has them towards him. Moreover, he tends to reverse his homosexual impulses—especially his feminine-passive ones, and these, when projected, make him feel that his objects are doubly inimical to him.

The fact that the paranoic feels not only that he is being persecuted by other persons but that those persons are conspiring together to do so seems to require explanation. It may be that his belief goes back to the time of his fixation in early childhood, when his parents and upbringers did combine together in their treatment of him and when, owing to his ignorance of their motives and to the projection of his own hatred on to them, he took this combination as unfriendly to him, especially when its purpose, as must so often have been the case, was to frustrate one or other of his deleterious desires. In addition, paranoic persons, and persons with paranoic traits, seem to take great pleasure in themselves weaving plots and complicated combinations of ideas—these being in part a defensive and retaliatory answer to the machinations to which they feel exposed.

The delusional systems of paranoia, however, are not always persecutory. They are not invariably concerned with ideas of being plotted against by enemies and plotting against them in self-defence. The paranoic may work out a complicated and more or less plausible theory about some abstract subject, or he may design an elaborate but quite impossible contrivance for practical use. He is the stuff out of which a host of unsuccessful innovators and inventors are made; and, indeed, he is the kind of person who, with happier distribution of mental forces or a more favourable early life, might have become a really creative thinker or a successful inventor. Nevertheless even so the hostile and suspicious elements in his character are very near the surface, as can be seen from the way in which, if his theory or his inventions are a failure, he attributes this not to any fault in them or to unlucky circumstances but to the spite and wicked machinations of a rival in the field or to malice or corruption rather than to the ignorance or prejudice of those to whose judgment they have been submitted.

The narcissism and self-grandeur of the paranoic ego are very great, in accordance with the early stage of development from which the illness proceeds. It sets high store by the subject's ideas and doings and considers him to be an object of interest to many, even if the interest is generally hostile. Nevertheless, its self-regard is not so high as is that of the schizophrenic ego, which knows no bounds. The fixated id, too, is much more allo-erotic and the ego is capable of relations to whole objects. As a result the paranoic no longer fills the stage of his own imagination so amply, nor do his imagos depict part-objects to nearly the same extent. His supposed persecutors are usually human beings at least, and the evil that they do to him is not as a rule more than human beings can encompass. In milder degrees of the illness he may content himself with believing that some person or persons are spying upon him to annoy, or from officiousness, or are saying nasty things about him behind his back, whilst in severe forms of it he may believe that they intend to ruin him financially or even to murder him. But he is not so likely to believe that fiends with forked tails are after him to carry him off to hell or that phantom shapes pass through his body, with fatal effects upon it, or that a giant hand is preparing to turn him inside out. Neither, owing to the lesser degree of formal regressions, are his delusions so apt to appear in the form of outright hallucinations (though auditory hallucinations are not infrequent).

Moreover his ego is usually in sufficiently good contact with external reality to realize that he cannot make his delusions believed by other people, so that he is often sensible and clever enough to conceal them. Another motive for concealing them, however, is less realistic. It is that his sick ego thinks the outside world hostile to all his ideas and out to spoil all his plans. For these reasons his delusions often appear much less wild than they really are, or much more lightly held; or they do not appear at all, and he passes for a perfectly sane person.

On the other hand, the paranoic believes as unconditionally in the truth of his ideas as does the schizophrenic. The reality-testing functions of his ego seem to be suspended in regard to them. Like most psychotics, he has no insight into his illness—no realization that it is in any way abnormal or pathological. This often has serious practical consequences. If, for instance, a paranoic has a delusion that his life is threatened by a supposed enemy he may, in all good faith, proceed to kill that enemy out of self-defence. And, indeed, not a few undetected paranoics have been wrongly executed as common murderers. In less serious delusions of persecution, such an implicit belief in their truth may urge the subject to commit all sorts of minor offences and unpleasant actions against his supposed persecutors, about which he feels absolutely in the right and absolutely innocent. So sane indeed is the ordinary demeanour of many a paranoic, so plausible his delusion, so strong and genuine his belief in it that not only can he not be dissuaded from it by any proof to the contrary, however convincing, but he often succeeds in persuading sane people—who are as a rule less strongly convinced of the truth of their true ideas than he is of the truth of his false ones— that he is in the right, and getting them to adopt his ideas and to act upon them. A countryman, for instance, may have a delusion—based let us say, on the projection of an infantile wish to poison his brother—that his next-door neighbour is putting arsenic into the village well. The patent sincerity of his conviction and the insistence and ingenuity with which he puts it forward may induce the more simple or weak-minded among the villagers to accept it and to accuse the supposed poisoner and drive him out of the village or push him down the well. Thus it is evident that paranoia is a form of lunacy which is very dangerous to society. The schizo-phrenic finds no imitators, and in any case he is soon detected and, if necessary, shut up in an asylum. But the paranoic is not only often allowed to go free but often becomes a deluder of others, who, left to themselves, would do no harm to anyone.

* * *

In the mental disorder known as *Melancholia* or *Depression*, the subject is afflicted by feelings of intense misery and gloom and these are accompanied by a deep sense of guilt and unworthiness and an inclination to accuse himself of all sorts of sins, known and unknown, which in fact, he has not committed, or to blame himself far too strongly for quite trivial faults which he has committed.

Psycho-analytical investigation, to which this illness is amenable, has shown that in it the affected portion of the mind has regressed to the oral-biting stage, in which the sadistic impulses are very strong and there is an intense wish to devour the desired object. This gives rise to corresponding ideas and phantasies which, at that early age of ego develop-ment, may well have been believed by the subject to be true, and which still continue to exercise his unconscious mind. He is thus horrified at what he has done to his object, which is presumably inside him, and what it may do to him in return, and he is filled with self-reproach. He also makes massive identificatory introjections with his object, and thus reproaches himself for many things for which he originally reproached it.[1]

[1] For this, cf. Freud's paper, 'Mourning and Melancholia'.

A counterpart to this disorder, and one which will turn out to be more interesting from our point of view, is to be found in *mania*. Here the subject is in a perpetual state of elation, exaggerated self-confidence and excessive activity. Far from shunning the society of his fellows, he seeks it eagerly and is ready to start new relationships with anyone at any moment. He feels no fatigue or illness, is up to anything, often talks incessantly and eats voraciously. He takes a rosy view of the world and believes that he is a good fellow, that everyone likes him and that he can do everything he wants to better than anyone. Mania, like melancholia, can appear spontaneously or as the result of some actual event, but this time it is generally an event of joy, relief or success, instead of one of danger, failure or loss. Like melancholia, too, it can be chronic or intermittent, or it can appear once only in the person's life.

If a person has only a mild form of mania he may indeed pass as a good fellow, be liked by many people and achieve social success. But in more serious cases his boisterous spirits are alarming and he is a menace to others and to himself. For his enterprising nature, his complete belief in his powers to carry out his enterprises, which are often quite unrealistic or quite beyond his capacity, make him liable to lead others as well as himself into dangerous situations. He may, for instance, persuade a gullible acquaintance that he possesses the power to tame wild animals; and the two may enter a lion's den, never to emerge from it alive.

It is more difficult to obtain direct psycho-analytic data about the mental processes which underlie mania than about those which underlie melancholia; for the excited state of the manic patient, and his belief in his mental health, not to say super-health, make it difficult to induce him to come for psycho-analysis, or, if he does, to obey the rules of the treatment which call for quiet and relaxation. Nevertheless something has been done in this line by analysing cases during their intermissions of sanity, and enough material has been gathered to get some sort of idea of what is going on in the manic mind.[1]

Although the manic presents such a complete contrast to the melancholic, his underlying state of mind has much in common with a depressive state and is based upon a closely allied predisposition. As with the melancholic, his oral-biting instincts predominate, so that he wants to eat and incorporate his objects, or the to him important parts of them—once more primarily the breast and penis—and he, too, introjects them or some of their properties, real or supposed; and he furthermore has a highly ambivalent attitude to them. But one important difference is that he incorporates them as good and desirable things instead of (mainly) bad or undesirable ones and he feels pleasure and triumph in having done so and perhaps thereby destroyed his objects, instead of fear and remorse. And the introjections he makes of his good and grand objects lead him to feel good and grand himself instead of bad and contemptible. Moreover, in so far as his incorporated objects are bad and hostile, he seems to be able to master them inside himself or else to expel them out of himself. This last capacity is largely based on the fact that the point at which his affected id is fixated is a little in advance of the point at which those of the melancholic are fixated. It is situated midway between the second oral and the first anal stage and includes impulses belonging to both. As a result, the manic subject has powerful desires and phantasies relating not only to the incorporation of his object by eating it, but to its expulsion by evacuating it through the bowels after it has been incorporated. By this means, too, he can freely extraject[2] real or supposed properties belonging to himself (many of which, incidentally, he may have introjected from his incorporated object). Thus if he is burdened with an object or

[1] Cf. in especial Abraham's papers 'Notes on the Psycho-Analytical Investigation and Treatment of Manic-Depressive Insanity' and 'A Short Study of the Development of the Libido', chapter IV ('Mania').

[2] I.e. divest himself in fact or fancy of properties belonging to him in reality or imagination, without necessarily attributing them to any other object or place, as he does in the case of projection.

plagued by an attitude which he does not like or is frightened of or guilty about, he can easily get rid of them. The elation of the manic patient is certainly as much based upon the removal of bad properties and objects as upon the acquisition of good ones. Lastly, and most important of all, the super-ego of the manic patient, in contradiction to that of the melancholic, seems to offer no opposition to his id-impulses or ego-trends and to make no criticism of them whatsoever. He feels no sense of guilt about his cannibalistic desires, nor any remorse about seizing the object he wants and throwing it away as soon as he has done with it.

Such a carefree and reckless attitude, however, is not the same as the confident and cheerful attitude, when raised to a high degree, of the mentally healthy person, and it is based upon a different disposition of psychic forces. The normal person, it is true, owes his good spirits to a great extent to his comparative freedom from a sense of guilt, derived from an approving super-ego. But since the super-ego of the normal person is reasonably realistic, its approval can only be won so long as he behaves in a reasonably ethical way. If he does not it soon comes down on him and spoils his happiness. The manic person, on the contrary, has no qualms of conscience whatever he does. Either, therefore, his super-ego is blindly and constantly favourable to him, or it is not functioning to capacity. Now, as we know, the super-ego of the manic is still quite unrealistic, so that it need not be deterred from approving of his actions because they shock a realistic code of ethics; but as we also know, it is not a very friendly one, since it is based on identifications made at a highly ambivalent instinctual stage when its prototypes in real life are almost as much hated by him as they are loved and consequently seem almost as hateful and hating as they seem lovable and loving. Thus there is no reason why the super-ego of the manic should be so much on the side of his ego. It looks, therefore, as though the second possibility was correct and his super-ego was out of action, or that his ego had repressed it or reacted against the sense of guilt which it was producing in him.

Nevertheless, it is doubtful whether the ego would be strong enough to do these things all by itself. Moreover, there is a quality of self-complacency in the manic's high spirits which seems to indicate that he is not merely unburdened by a disapproving super-ego or warding it off but is endowed with an actively approving one. And so he may be. Since the identifications which he makes take place at a stage when his attitude to his object is not only highly ambivalent but when his imago of it is not as yet firmly synthesized, that imago is liable to remain or become split into two halves, a loveworthy and loving one and a hate-worthy and hating one. This, when it relates to his parental objects, has the effect of erecting in his mind a super-ego which is similarly divided into a kind and friendly part which is on the side of his ego, and an unkind and unfriendly part which is against it. What has happened in the case of the manic person is that, unlike the normal super-ego in which both parts are fused (the favourable part predominating, of course, in consonance with the more libidinal position of its owner), the favourable part has gained the upper hand over the unfavourable one, and the ego is basking in the sunshine of its unstinted praise. The converse would naturally be true of the melancholic. He, too, would have a favourable and an unfavourable super-ego (both being unrealistic, too, of course),[1] since his identifications also take place at a highly ambivalent stage, when he is not yet very fully cognisant of whole objects; but in his case, the unfavourable super-ego has ousted the favourable one, and he is completely at the mercy of its cruel oppression.

The close connection that exists between mania and melancholia can also be seen from the fact that many persons alternate between them. So much is this the case that the two affections are generally regarded as complemental parts of the same illness, which is accordingly called a 'Manic-Depressive' psychosis. These alternations between depressive

---

[1] In the view of such a super-ego, for instance, eating a dead person is a worse crime than killing a live one, and many adults still consciously hold this view.

and manic states also appear in milder forms in the emotional life of more or less normal persons of a certain type. Such persons are liable to change from moods of optimism and confidence to moods of pessimism and despair and *vice versa* without any objective reason. What makes them gloomy one day will make them cheerful the next or the other way round. Such persons are sometimes called 'cyclo-thymic' types. This alternation would presumably be due to the existence in the subject of an almost even balance of forces between the over-friendly and the over-hostile aspects of his super-ego, so that each gets the upper hand in turn, as the side that is in the ascendant has had a long enough run and has played itself out for the time being and as the frustrated trends of the side that is being kept under have accumulated and reached a certain degree of strength. It often happens, too, that the manic and depressive phases do not succeed each other immediately but that there is a longer or shorter interval between them during which the patient seems to be in a normal state of mind. During these periods of remission the two sides of the super-ego may be regarded as being in a state of more or less unstable equilibrium, or they may have become temporarily merged. This latter view would fit in with Abraham's discovery that in between their attacks of mania or melancholia, when they enjoyed comparative mental health, his patients had advanced from the late oral or late-oral-cum-early-anal stage, as the case may be, to the late anal stage of development, at which stage, as we know, the synthe-sizing powers of the ego make a marked forward stride.

Moreover, a bout of melancholia is not infrequently wound up by a more or less noticeable manic phase, and this is in all probability due not only to a progression of the id to the oral-anal stage which facilitates the getting rid of the mourned and dreaded internal object but also marks the swing-over from the ascendancy of the hostile super-ego to that of the friendly one and the triumphant liberation of the ego from the tyranny of the former. Conversely, as has been pointed out by Abraham, many patients show signs of added energy and enterprise, which he likens to a mild form of mania, immediately before the onset of a depression, and he attributes this to an attempt of the ego—though an unsuccessful one— to stave off the oncoming depression, by an accentuation of its opposite state.

Certainly the pleasure ego must be interested in fighting on the side of mania—of the applauding super-ego—and against melancholia—the condemning super-ego—seeing how intensely pleasurable the former state is and how intensely unpleasurable the latter. Yet, just as mania may be a throwing off or suppression of the painful abasements of melancholia, so may melancholia be a nemesis for the wild triumphs of mania.

As regards the later anal stage, regression to it tends to produce a less formidable type of illness, as in the case of hysteria, with its point of regression at the infantile genital stage; for in both, the mind is already capable of strong relationships to whole-objects and of a respectable degree of reality-testing.

This illness, whose fixations are at the anal-retentive stage, is known as obsessional neurosis, and, once again like hysteria, it belongs to what are called the psychoneuroses rather than to the psychoses. It is characterized by everlasting doubts, obsessions and compulsions, based upon the unresolved ambivalence and the reactive formations which dominate the subject's mind, and by a burdensome sense of guilt emanating from an over-severe super-ego. This affection—whose workings, incidentally, are well exhibited, though not in an actually pathological form, in the hesitations and self-reproaches of Hamlet, no less than in his rash acts—has been exhaustively studied by Freud[1] and is full of interesting material; but as it will not be found to have any special bearing on our present enquiry, we shall not concern ourselves further with it.

[1] Cf. notably his case of the 'Rat Man' ('A Case of Obsessional Neurosis').

PART TWO

DANGER-POINTS IN
GROUP PSYCHOLOGY

Chapter XII

THE UNCONSCIOUS IN SOCIAL
BEHAVIOUR

AFTER this discussion of the processes of regression we are in a position to go on to the second part of our enquiry. We can now hope to understand by what means the subject's mental states not only influence, but are influenced by, his social life in such a way that many of them become more warlike or war-provoking than they were, or even become so for the first time.

Let us begin by showing how a person's unconscious attitudes find fuller expression through his conscious attitudes or behaviour in social life than they do in private life.

Take, for instance, the funeral customs of our day. The solemn *cortège* of mourners who slowly accompany the body to its last resting-place, the coffin under its black pall, the impressive burial service at the grave, the wearing of black clothes—all these things are obviously a public expression of sorrow on the part of the bereaved ones at the loss of a friend or a near relative, of their care for the safety of his soul, of their fond thoughts of him and, perhaps, of their hopes for an eventual reunion with him in the life beyond. Yet such sentiments might, one would have thought, find a more fitting expression in a less showy form and among a few intimate friends instead of being exhibited to the world at large. And, indeed, to many civilized persons, attending the funeral of a loved one is a very painful ordeal indeed. Nevertheless, nearly everyone feels obliged to do so and would suffer from feelings of remorse and shame if he did not. This is because these observances are, in fact, much more than an expression of the mourner's love and sorrow. They give utterance as well to far different sentiments in his heart—sentiments of which he is quite unaware, but which are none the less powerful for that. Convinced as his primitive ego is of the super-human powers of all human beings, he is inclined to attribute all death to the hostile action of some beings rather than to natural causes. Thus he believes unconsciously that some person has purposely killed the deceased by magical or secret means, or he may attribute his death to divine justice or the malign influence of evil spirits. Furthermore, in view of his own hostile impulses towards the deceased—impulses which are rarely wanting in the most devoted of mourners—he is more often than not persuaded that that person is none other than himself. This can easily happen since, believing unconsciously as he does in the omnipotence of thoughts, his mere wish for the deceased's death may in his view have brought it about. His feelings of guilt and remorse are, in consequence, immense. Besides, he not only feels guilt and remorse; he is afraid of being punished for his crime and of its being avenged upon him by the slain man's kin. Thus he hopes to escape punishment and retribution by declaring his love and innocence to all. This he does by lavishing money upon the funeral and by making an open display of his grief. And he also does it by having the corpse laid out so as to make it look as if it had not died a violent death.

Moreover, the mourners try to escape from their sorrow and remorse at the deceased's death and from the consequences of their supposed murder of him by pretending that he is not dead at all. The sleeping attitude in which the corpse is laid out is thus also an assertion by the mourner of the dead person's continued existence; and the pomp and circumstance with which it is surrounded serve, by insisting, through overcompensation, upon his power and glory, still further to deny the fact of his death.

Indeed, on a yet more primitive level of the unconscious, the mourner does in fact not believe that the deceased is dead. For his imago of him as a live person is still highly cathected in his mind, and it takes a long time for him to de-cathect it and to use the cathexes for other purposes and attach them to other imagos. (The first of these processes constitutes, in point of fact, the essential part of the painful and long task of mourning—of sorrowing for the loved dead one.)[1] So long as this imago is so highly cathected and so strongly before the mind of the mourner, not only is his unconscious unable to grasp the fact of the non-existence of the object which it represents; his conscious mind is not able altogether to do so either. Few people can bear to think of the dead body of someone they love being damaged, even if this is not done in a hostile way as, for instance, in a post-mortem; yet they very well know that he is past being hurt.

Nevertheless, it is obvious, even to the unconscious, that something terrible has happened to that body. It no longer moves, it grows stiff and cold and it presently begins to show unmistakable signs of dissolution and decay. If the soul which animates it is not extinguished, it must resent this damage to its body and exact vengeance for it. Such a vengeance may be worse than anything a living person can do; for although a dead body is in fact no longer capable of action, the unconscious mind of the survivors prompts them to endow it with occult and supernatural powers instead, which far transcend its natural ones, or else to believe that the soul of the deceased has left its mortal habitat and is now able to do things in a disembodied form which no substantial body can. It is a ghost that passes through key-holes and even through solid walls on its way back to punish the living who have destroyed its body. Or it assumes dreadful shapes with which to drive them mad with fear. Or it actually enters their body, unknown to them, and does terrible things to them inside. Small wonder that so much of the funeral rites are designed to placate the dead one and to prevent him from doing a mischief to the living. Nowadays we throw a handful of dust upon the coffin to keep the corpse from arising and coming back, and in other places stones are still piled upon a grave for this purpose. We

[1] Cf. Freud's paper, 'Mourning and Melancholia'.

wear black not only to express grief for our lost ones but to disguise ourselves so that they shall not recognize us if they should come back to do us harm. In some parts of Bohemia the mourners are still more thorough and put masks over their faces.

It is not only the major customs of society which minister to the unconscious mental trends of the individual. Even quite trivial conventions of behaviour, whose meaning, if any, seems to be perfectly simple and innocent, often turn out to be more complicated and more sinister on closer inspection. Saying 'How do you do' or 'Good-bye' on meeting or leaving a person for instance, does not merely express the addressor's natural good-will towards the addressee; it also serves to assure the latter that the addressor has overcome his contrary hostile impulses towards him, and does not wish him ill, and that he is a safe person to meet or to let out of sight—that meeting does not imply an attack or parting a wished-for removal or death. A great deal of social conversation too, is carried on not so much in order to entertain the listener, as to assure him that the talker is not concealing any hostile thoughts towards him. Opening doors for another is not done simply to spare the latter an exertion; it is—among many other things of course—a demonstration that he who opens the door has no intention of preventing him for whom he opens it from leaving his presence or the room at will.

* * *

In their aspect of providing outlet for the unconscious mental trends of the individual, the forms assumed by social customs resemble the forms assumed by his private expression of them, not excluding pathological symptoms. Ritual fasting for the dead, for instance, is paralleled by the abstention from food which is characteristic of so many depressed persons, and which has to do with not eating their dead object. Indeed, such social customs act as alternative outlets for the unconscious trends in question. If no funeral rites for the dead were allowed there would be more melancholics in the world. Thus although social customs can be regarded as public symptoms, they can also be regarded as preventers of private symptoms.

Nevertheless they are not on a par with the latter. There is a very great difference between using a recognized general and ready-made outlet for them and creating one of one's own. Doing the second argues a deviation from the average in the quality of the trends concerned, so that no generally-used channel suits them; and it also suggests that they possess a very large quantity of psychic energy, so that they are driven to cut channels of expression for themselves. To wear a hobble skirt when it was the fashion was no doubt an outlet, among other things, for masochistic tendencies, and was as such acceptable to many women, and even those who willingly wore them were not considered perverts or lunatics. But what should we have said of a woman who invented a hobble skirt for herself and wore it all on her own?

Public customs owe much of their existence and power to the value they possess for the average individual precisely from being a given and universal expression of his own unconscious attitudes. Being given, they not only relieve him of the exertion of inventing private customs for that purpose, but relieve him of any guilt or anxiety he would have about such self-made products, should he feel that they had not entirely disguised the unconscious attitude behind them; being universal, they assure him that everyone has the same unconscious attitudes as he, and they thus once more lighten his guilt and anxiety. (In this way, as we see, they act much as public phantasies do, in contrast to private ones.)

Then, too, it must not be forgotten that to depart from the usage of one's fellows would be to criticize the motives behind it and so to awaken anxiety and guilt in them and to incur their consequent hostility.

Finally, many customs impose themselves on the mind of the individual because they are long-standing—or rather, because they are known (or thought) by him to be so. They have been handed down from generation to generation and have thus acquired for him all the sanctity of ancestral tradition and have become securely embedded in his super-ego.[1]

So strong, for the matter of that, is the force of custom that the individual often falls in with and even gets satisfaction from customs which do not express his own unconscious needs and which, indeed, sometimes run counter to them. No woman, for instance, except an out-and-out masochist, would go in on her own for tight-lacing or wearing dangerously high-heeled shoes or a hat which obscures one eye; yet if fashion decrees, she will cheerfully do so.

Indeed, his social customs are as jealously regarded by the individual as if to put an end to them would be to put an end to him; and his days are filled with a constant round of them, both great and small, from the observance of public festivals and high ceremonies to the wearing of the right sort of tie or the avoidance of walking under ladders.

[1] Nevertheless, as we know, it is the parent, or the parental figure, which is the most important authority and model for the individual, and his ancestral figures obtain most of their influence over him only in so far as they are put before him in that role by his elders of the generation next above him. Thus a resolute and skilful ruler can often succeed in abolishing age-old and, as it seemed, eternal customs quite quickly, as we see in the case of Ataturk who modernized Turkey overnight. This, of course, happens all the more easily if the custom is so old that it has become obviously out of place and if another, equally satisfying but more expedient custom, is put in its place.

knows that a candidate for Parliamentary election must speak in very different accents to his prospective voters, according to whether he is addressing them from the hustings, or whether he is canvassing them singly or speaking to them in a small circle over the radio; and a man who has been at a mass-meeting often looks back with amazement at the thoughts and feelings that moved him at the time.

When an individual finds himself close together with a large number of other persons certain changes take place in his mind. In the first place this physical juxtaposition heightens his instinctual impulses and he becomes more excited. In the second place, he becomes more easily infected by the states of mind of those about him. This still further increases his excitations (since theirs, owing to their juxtaposition, are above the normal) as well as rendering him more easily excitable. It also implies an extensive identificatory intro-jection with his neighbours, so that he feels and thinks and wills as they do. Nor is an equal extension of identificatory projection lacking. The subject is not only inclined to feel (and be) like his fellows; he is inclined to feel and believe that they are like him. And the two processes between them help to give him an enormous sense of amplitude and assurance and of oneness with the rest of the crowd.

Furthermore, the inhibitory capacity of his ego is weakened, and he is much more liable to yield to his impulses. We see in Shakespeare's *Julius Caesar*, for instance, how readily the mob of angry Roman citizens take to violence and proceed to burn, loot and kill. Again, the ego's synthesizing powers are reduced, so that he lends himself more easily to his in any case heightened ambivalence. Once more we remember how the mob in *Julius Caesar* fluctuates violently between acclamation of Brutus as their country's liberator and condemnation of him as the murderer of its benefactor. A third effect is that the intellectual faculties of the ego undergo debasement and regress from the secondary processes to the primary ones. Here is a classical example in *Julius Caesar*. The crowd, thirsting for the blood of the conspirators, one of whom is called

Cinna, come across a poet who happens also to have that name:

> *3rd Citizen.* Your name, sir, truly?
> *Cinna.* Truly, my name is Cinna.
> *2nd Citizen.* Tear him to pieces; he is a conspirator.
> *Cinna.* I am Cinna the poet, I am Cinna the poet.
> *4th Citizen.* Tear him for his bad verses, tear him for his bad verses.
> *Cinna.* I am not Cinna the conspirator.
> *2nd Citizen.* It is no matter, his name's Cinna; pluck but his name out of his heart, and turn him going.
> *3rd Citizen.* Tear him, tear him . . . etc.
>
> (Act iii, Scene 3)

Having the same name is enough to make two quite different people the same in the eyes of the members of the mob.

Yet another effect is that the ego resumes a good deal of its ancient narcissism and sense of omnipotence, so that the subject's self-regard is very much enhanced and he feels grand and great and good; and this belief he projects onto his fellows, so that they also seem grand and great and good.

Nor does the super-ego escape regression. It, too, reverts once more to the earlier and more primitive stages through which it has passed in the course of its development. Indeed, it tends to shrink back into the nothingness from which it came. As we see, the mob in Julius Caesar has no compunction in looting and burning all it can lay hands on; and it tears its victims to pieces without a thought.

But the same regressive process which causes a person to lose his super-ego also causes him to feel the need once more for an external authority to take its place. If they are together for any length of time, the members of a crowd accordingly tend to look for someone who shall dominate and guide them in virtue of his superior intelligence, resolution and eloquence —a Brutus or a Mark Anthony on however small a scale. Or at any rate, they are very ready to accept such a person. They gladly turn to him and set him up, or allow him to set himself up, over them and direct their feelings, thoughts and actions. And now, too, it is not difficult to detect in the figure of the leader the lineaments of their childhood father-imago.

But his ascendancy is apt to be short-lived. In accordance with the primary process they make easy displacements from object to object so that the leader of the moment is always in danger of being superseded by another. Then, too, we have to consider their ambivalence which makes them liable to change their feelings from love to hatred (and *vice versa*) and to take up an opposite side from the one they have just espoused. The fickleness of crowds is proverbial. We see once more in *Julius Caesar* how the mob gives up its allegiance to Brutus in favour of Anthony as quickly and frivolously as it had abandoned Caesar for Brutus before. Nor is the crowd an enduring unit. It soon melts away; its leaders, if any, disappear, and the individual who has formed part of it returns to his ordinary frame of mind.

*   *   *

There are, however, other collections of people which are not changeable and short-lived like crowds, but which yet exercise a considerable degree of regressive effect upon the minds of their members. These owe their stability and permanence to the fact that the spontaneous ties of feeling which arise between their constituents are increased and secured by artificial means.[1]

Freud was specially interested in one type of artificially organized group as being the most successful of all. This group exhibits two main external features. One is that it has a leader who possesses autocratic power over its members. The other is that its members all belong to the male sex.

To begin with the first feature. The fact that the rank-and-file members are in their leader's power and must obey him in everything tends to make them submissive to him in mind as well as in outward behaviour. One reason for this is that

---

[1] For what follows in this section, cf. Freud's book *Group Psychology and an Analysis of the Ego.*

being in his power takes them back to a childhood situation in which they had to obey their father (or their father-figures) without question and in which they also felt mentally dependent on him. Thus physical and mental submission became linked together. In addition, they felt awe of him and love for him as an omnipotent and (mainly) benevolent being; and these attitudes, too, are revived by the contemporary situation, so that their wish to please and obey their leader is further reinforced. Furthermore, in virtue of the massive identificatory introjections they make in respect of him as their father-figure, each sets up a considerable portion of super-ego which is modelled on him and his commands. Thus they come to have a common or 'group' super-ego which represents him and whose word is law. Finally, such a common attitude to their leader promotes powerful ties or identification with one another. All this makes strongly for the stability and cohesion of the group.

As regards the second feature, that of the members being all males, this means in the first place that the libidinal ties which exist between them are of a homosexual kind, and this lends itself better to complete sublimation than does heterosexual libido (doubtless because it is necessary for the survival of the species that the latter should be resistant to complete de-sexualization). Unsublimated sexual love leads to one-to-one relationships of an exclusive kind and to situations of jealousy and anger between the members, which would tend to break up the group. In the second place, sameness of sex once more constitutes an important likeness between the members and thus furnishes a good soil for identificatory ties between them. Lastly, the sameness of sex between the rank and file and their leader assists them in making those identificatory introjections of him which are responsible for the setting up of a common super-ego in each. The reason why such monosexual groups should be composed of males rather than females is partly because, as we have seen, leaders are nearly always male persons, the properties of command and domination being for the most part masculine. In any case, in Freud's view women are less well fitted for making the necessary sublimation.[1]

We see then that the intra-group attachments thus set up in each member of the group are of three kinds: ties of mental dependence, ties of identification and libidinal ties.

Freud cites as the two most outstanding examples of organized groups of this kind the army and the (Roman Catholic) Church. Both have a supreme head invested with autocratic power: in the first case, the Commander-in-Chief, and in the second, Christ Himself, with the Pope as His earthly representative, and in both there is a rigid hierarchy of officers or priests, as the case may be, to consolidate the top leader's power and to bring it home to the rank and file. Both, too, consist only of men.

These two groups, moreover, strengthen their internal ties by many added means. To begin with, they increase the members' mental submissions to the leaders' will by repeated exactions of acts of external submission. This is seen in the many rituals and fixed hours and movements of devotion which the Church demands from its priesthood, and the constant drill and severe discipline to which soldiers are subjected—a discipline which is thus seen to have something more than the useful and necessary aim of making soldiers able to carry out orders promptly. In matters of external discipline, indeed, the army excels the Church; but to make up for this, the Church approaches the matter more directly as well and enjoins its members not only to obey their leader but to worship him. Such actions in common also directly strengthen the identificatory ties between the members, since it makes them alike in their demeanour (not to mention the fact that if it is carried out by large numbers of them close together, it increases those identificatory experiences which are more especially connected with crowd-mentality—and which perhaps belong to still earlier states of mind than those regressed to in group-mentality). Similarity of dress, too—the

[1] Cf. in this connection his *Civilization and its Discontents*, pp. 73 ff.

priest's cassock and the soldier's tunic—strengthen the identificatory ties between the members of each group, as well as
between them and their leaders of every rank, in so far as the
latter wear the same kind of uniform, though with suitable
differences to mark their varying degree of superiority.

As we can see, it is not only the Roman Catholic Church
and the Army which fulfil the necessary conditions for being
a regressive group of the kind we have in mind. Other
Churches, Christian or otherwise, also to a greater or lesser
extent satisfy those requirements; and so do the other branches
of the armed forces.

Moreover, there are collections of persons outside religious
or military bodies which also qualify to be regarded as arti-
ficially-organized groups of a regressive kind, even if in a
minor degree. We have only to think of our own Public
Schools, with their hierarchy of headmaster, assistant masters
and prefects under him, their quite considerable amount of
discipline, their games and other actions in common, their
distinctive dress and their exclusively male population; or of
secret male societies—e.g. the Freemasons—with their implicit
obedience to an often mysterious leader, their special rituals
and signs, and so on.

The regressive operation of organized groups, moreover, is
not limited to collections of people which exhibit the two
external features so far described, even if those which do are
the most marked type of them.

As regards the first feature, we find regressive groups in
which the leader does not wield autocratic power—in which
he must rule them according to law. Or the group may be
inspired and held together by a cause rather than a person.
Nevertheless, these differences are more seeming than real.
If the group is founded on law, then that law and the makers
of it are revered as the omnipotent father or at any rate the
omnipotent ancestors; and if it is inspired by a cause, the
cause assumes his place. (Yet those symbols of the great father
are rarely as potent as a living representative, and the group

is by that much less effective in its influence.) Lastly, if the group is democratic, it almost gains on the swings what it loses on the roundabouts. Whilst the parental authority in it is weakened, another ancient power is increased; for the members also admire in the leaders they have elected a projection of their own infantile sense of grandeur and omnipotence.[1]

As regards the second feature, certain groups which are not exclusively male are nevertheless regressive. Political parties such as the Fascist or Communist parties, with their iron discipline and autocratic rule, are clearly of this type, yet they contain women as well as men members. (Though here there is no doubt that it is the men who are not only the leaders but who constitute the backbone of the group.) On the other hand, we know that some secret societies are exclusively made up of women and the same cannot be said of *them*. Then, too, we have co-educational boarding schools and boarding schools for girls only; and both these exhibit nearly as much group-spirit as do their purely masculine counterparts.

Even groups which are much more loosely organized than those described above, tend to cause some degree of regressive group-mentality in their members. Boy Scout and Girl Guide movements, sporting clubs, ordinary clubs, trade unions, women's institutes and local bodies of all sorts, whose members are not regimented to anything like the same degree as are the members of the Church or the armed forces or even Public Schools, do nevertheless develop a strong common spirit in which regressive features are not wanting. Even societies which exist for the sole purpose of promoting intellectual and progressive thought and whose organization is as loose and liberal as is consonant with its proper functioning

---

[1] It must be said that Freud lays much more emphasis on the member's filial attitude to his leader than on his, perhaps earlier, narcissistic attitude to his group, as a characteristic of regressive groups. But, as will be seen later, the group itself takes on a parental aspect for its members, so that they do have a filial attitude to it as well as a narcissistic one.—On the other hand, in a democracy the members have more power of individual choice over their own fate, and this encourages their realistic and preconscious activities and so makes them less liable to regress. We shall return to this point later in the next chapter.

are not entirely free from traces of group-regression. The amateur botanists of a country district, for instance, may form a local society for the sole purpose of reading papers to one another and conducting discussions about plant life. But they will soon develop some kind of *esprit de corps*, on however modest a scale, from the mere fact that they meet together for their discussions under the auspices of a president or a chairman and undertake expeditions in common in order to collect rare flowers. As a result, each member is inclined to think a little more highly of himself, his fellow botanists and his society and to feel a little more strongly on their behalf than he would otherwise do and than the facts warrant. This mild group-mentality tends also to manifest itself in small outward and concrete signs—signs which in their turn fortify it—as befits the proneness to symbolization and sensory regression which are some of its accompaniments. The local botanists, for instance, may celebrate their existence as members of their botanical society by wearing a distinctive badge in their coat lapels and by instituting an annual dinner with self-congratulatory speeches and toasts to their president.

*   *   *

Hardly less remarkable than the extent to which the member loves and overestimates his group and its leaders, is the extent to which he identifies himself with it and his fellow-members. A soldier, for instance, is as proud of a victory which his army has gained or as humiliated by a defeat it has suffered when he has not been in the battle as when he has been in it and has helped to win or lose it; and according as his fellow-soldiers who fought in it behaved in a brave or cowardly fashion on that occasion, so does he feel that he has behaved in a brave or cowardly fashion, even though he was not there at all. A worthless member of a first-rate school feels far superior to a meritorious member of a third-rate one; and the latter may, in his turn, accept his own inferiority in virtue of the inferiority of his school (unless, of course—as is quite likely—he refuses to recognize that his school *is* inferior).

Moreover, on the mental level to which he has regressed, he is very prone to personify his group. He thinks of it as something that can be born or can die, be sick or well, happy or unhappy, hurt or not hurt, brave or cowardly, clever or stupid, well- or ill-intentioned, and so on and so forth, instead of being something whose *members* can be born or die, happy or unhappy, etc. And more than this. In so far as he identifies himself with his group, he thinks of himself as participating in its supposed human qualities and vicissitudes. Thus, e.g., if a boy's Public School is an old one he not only tends to think of it as mature and wise, as an old man is; he tends to think of his schoolfellows and himself as mature and wise—or as more mature and wise than the inmates of a new school.

These unrealistic views of groups are not only held by the members of them. The ordinary outsider, too, is inclined to have them, though perhaps not so strongly. For after all, even as a private individual, he is not exempt from anthropomorphic attitudes and other forms of primitive thought. Thus, for instance, when we look at a collection of persons moving in various directions—as say in Piccadilly Circus any day of the week—we often get the totally false impression that the collection as such is *feeling* undecided in what direction to move, and that consequently each individual in it is undecided, when in fact each is going steadily on his way with a single purpose in mind.[1]

Organized groups not only engender group-mentality in each of its members while he is together with the rest of the group. Unlike crowd-formations, whose effect on the individual vanishes as soon as he leaves them—and which are in any case short-lived—they continue to influence his mind even when he is going about his ordinary business. But then,

[1] Poets and imaginative writers, who are licensed to regress in phantasy, are, of course, entitled to speak of groups and crowds as a living entity—as a many-headed monster. But even the scientific approach to them is often distorted by such a view. Even the sociological term 'group mind' seems sometimes to cover the concept, not of individual minds as they have been changed by being in a group—changed among other things, it is true, in the direction of becoming more alike—but of a single 'collective' mind which informs the whole group.

of course, it continues to have its external holds on him, so that he still feels that he belongs to it. Yet it can go on influencing him even after he has ceased to be a member of it (as we see in the case of old Public School boys or ex-Army men). Nevertheless its influence is not as strong then as it is when he is still a member of it. The group has yet more effect when he is together with other members of it—and the more of them, the stronger the effect is. And it is most powerful of all when he and his fellow-members are together not by chance but as a group, especially if they are taking part in one or other of the activities which help to consolidate and symbolize its existence. An ex-college man, for instance, is apt to be more offended by adverse outside criticism of his college tie than he is by adverse criticism of a private tie of his own. But he is not so much put out by it as he would be if he were still at college. And his resentment is still greater if he is with his co-collegiates, and greatest of all if he and they are on their way to a college celebration.

For this reason every group sees to it that its members shall not only be together a great deal but shall from time to time convene in a more formal manner to mark its existence and exalt its worth. Church festivals and processions, military tattoos and trooping the colours, college commemoration days, Communist or Nazi rallies—all these occasions help in their varying degrees to strengthen and perpetuate the group spirit of those concerned.

An organized social unit of the kind we have described does not permit the minds of its members to regress as far as does such an unorganized social unit as a crowd. It obliges them to inhibit many of their instinctual impulses and to sublimate others, and it provides them with a super-ego. Nevertheless, it does cause their minds to regress to a point at which they are unable to take a realistic view of their own group or of objects outside it, especially in relation to their group, or to make independent ethical judgments about them. Moreover, since the regressions that take place in a group are much more lasting than those which take place in a crowd, their effect is more serious. A member of a crowd in a killing mood only wants to tear its enemy to pieces while he is in that crowd; a member of a group like the *Mafia* is *always* in a killing mood towards its enemies. When the organized group is of a high standing this regressive effect is, however, very much obscured. In the first place, certain progressive influences do take place as well in the minds of its members. An illiterate peasant, for instance, may learn to read and write for the first time because he is sent to a school for making priests. In the second place, the members of a group are bound to accept the views of the leader of their group, however little they understand or appreciate them. If a leader is in favour of beneficent and enlightened behaviour, so are they. But though the first fact may operate progressively, it only does so within a limited sphere; and the second fact, however useful from an external point of view, can scarcely be called a progressive phenomenon in itself. An ignorant savage who believes that the world is round just because his white master tells him that it is round, is no more capable of realistic thinking than is an ignorant savage who believes it is flat because his own medicine man tells him that it is flat.

The regressive attitude which such groups engender in its members is apt, moreover, to impair their capacity to grasp difficult ideas or ideas that are at all abstract. Thus the ideas which they are taught by their leaders tend to become debased and to assume concrete and personal forms in their minds. It is, for instance, easier to worship an idol of God than a concept of Him. Indeed, good leaders know this and take care that the ideas they want to put over to their followers shall be clothed in sense-perceptual forms. The Church abounds in painted images and symbolic signs.

Moreover, the aims and ideals which the leader promulgates tend to be regarded by the rank and file not only as being put forward *by* him and thus acquiring great authority, but as being personified *in* him, or being a part of him (for that, of course, is how associations work in the unconscious). To most Nazis in Germany, for instance, it was not the pure doctrine of Nazism or even Nazism as put over to them by Hitler that captured their imagination, but Nazism-cum-Hitler; and the average Communist gives his allegiance not simply to Communism or the Communist idea but to it plus his idea of Marx, Lenin and Stalin, or, in some cases, to them alone.

This adds still more to the value and importance of these aims and ideals in the eyes of the members of the group. The leader is not slow to take advantage of this, and he magnifies his personality not only in order to keep the group in being and to maintain his place at the head of it, but to give the cause it stands for added force and virtue for his followers. Nazis, Communists and Fascists alike decorated every available place with more than life-size portraits of Hitler, Stalin, Lenin, Tito and Mussolini, as the case may be. This was done not merely as a spontaneous expression of feeling on the part of the members but by orders from above. The same can happen in the field of religious beliefs, too, where the subject's idea of God is not only enhanced by his membership of a Church congregation under a priesthood, but may to a greater or lesser extent become attached to that priesthood. In comparatively recent times, for instance, the Pope has, as head of the Roman Catholic Church, officially taken on the attributes of Infallibility—an attribute which, one would have thought, could only belong to God.

The fact that group-mentality involves a strengthening of primitive attitudes of mind in the individual does not mean that it is altogether a bad thing. For such attitudes have great value in many respects. In the first place, they help to secure the happiness and well-being of the members of the group by encouraging in each feelings of pride in and devotion to his group which often alone may enable him to behave in an altruistic way in regard to his fellow members. It is only by believing rather more than is true in the value of his fellows, himself and his leader, in their oneness and in the immortal soul of his group, that he can summon up the necessary fortitude and self-sacrifice to put its interests before his own —and that he thinks it worth while. Furthermore, as has been

G

said, the receptiveness and docility of mind which group-mentality engenders in the rank-and-file towards their leaders (and fellows) undoubtedly open their minds, within limits, to instruction and betterment, should the group or its leader chance to be a progressive and enlightened one. Then, again, the mental relaxation produced by regression is not only pleasurable and perhaps even healthful in itself, but may even enable the subject's mind to function more realistically and preconsciously in spheres of thought not connected with the group, or at times when his group mentality is not being activated, since it rests his mind and so gives it renewed vigour to work on higher levels. Then, too, group-thinking, may, like phantasying, drain off much of his wishful and ucs. modes of thought into permissible channels of discharge, so that they do not impede his realistic thinking in other fields. Furthermore, the individual gets a great sense of power and security from being in a group, partly because he feels protected by his omnipotent father once more, partly because his own sense of power is vastly expanded and partly because there is safety in numbers, both as a means of sharing guilt and being protected from external danger. These things give him and his fellows the requisite confidence to carry out dangerous but necessary actions—such as, say, fighting a bad fire, where the fire-brigade depends not only on its combined force and organization to master the fire but upon the heroism of its men.

As we know, too, instant and full execution of orders is often absolutely requisite for effective action; and this is not only a matter of skill and practice but of unquestioning and automatic obedience to authority which is the hall-mark of the group.

The *dis*value of regressive group-mentality, on the other hand, is considerable. In the first place, it induces an unrealistic state of mind in the subject on all matters connected with it, so that the ends he aims at in regard to it are often bad, from being mistaken, and the means he adopts to attain them are inexpedient. In the second place, it makes him indifferent to persons outside his group, since his libidinal impulses are mostly directed to persons within it, and most of his identifications are made with them. Nor has he any sense of duty or compunction about outsiders, since his group super-ego is not concerned with them. Indeed, if he happens to dislike them there is nothing to prevent his wanting to injure them and trying to do so, if he thinks it possible and safe.

This brings us to the third and perhaps the most serious objection to group-mentality. Much of the large amount of libido which a group-member expends upon his attachment to his leader and his fellow-members is got by withdrawing it from non-members, and that makes him not only indifferent to their welfare and happiness but actually desirous of their destruction and unhappiness. For, since his attitude to them is in any case bound to be to some extent ambivalent, such a withdrawal of libido increases the relative proportion of his destructive and hostile impulses towards them and removes another check upon them. These destructive impulses, moreover, are *positively* increased by the fact that he also increases the relative strength of his libidinal attitude to his co-members and his leader by deflecting the destructive side of his ambivalent attitude to them on to persons outside his group. On top of this, it must be remembered that members of regressive groups have actually more destrudo in their mental composition than have individuals in their private capacity, from the very fact of having regressed to an earlier developmental stage.

Furthermore, the ties of mental dependence and of identification which the member forms as well with persons within his group detract from the strength of similar ties which he has formed with persons outside it. This, if it does not increase his *hostility* to the latter, does increase his *indifference*. And it decreases the efforts he makes to inhibit his hostility.

All this, it is obvious, makes groups that are powerful a serious potential danger to the outside world, and history is full of its struggles, sometimes successful sometimes not, to keep them in their place.

Chapter XIV

STATE-MENTALITY AND WAR

THE point mentioned at the end of the previous chapter, concerning the deflection of destrudo away from the group, seems to me to be a very important factor in the formation of regressive group-mentality, and it calls for the addition of yet another external feature to the group. This is that it should be self-contained—that its members should be cut off from intercourse with persons who do not belong to it. In this way the member has no libidinal ties with anyone outside his group, and he can concentrate all his libido upon those inside it. Moreover, since this isolation of the members from non-members also prevents him from forming ties of dependency or identification with them, it also removes these obstacles to his directing his hostility to them, and thus still further purifies and accentuates his libidinal ties within the group. This condition is satisfied to a considerable degree in the two notable groups cited by Freud. The Roman Catholic priest is not allowed to marry, so that he has not strong family ties to detract from his ties within the Church; and the soldier is not encouraged to have a full life outside the barracks. Even the Public Schools make their children live and board with them. Nevertheless, the barrier is by no means absolute. Not all priests are celibate; and even those that are have fathers and mothers and brothers in the outside world, whom they love or look up to or identify themselves with. A private soldier may walk out with his sweetheart. And Public School boys go home for holidays.

In addition to this there are, I think, two more features whose presence promotes regressive group-mentality. One is that the group should have power not only over its own members but over persons who are not members of it. Another is that it should be exempt from the power of anyone outside it. Both these features greatly increase its standing in its members' eyes.

These conditions are once more partially satisfied by the groups we have mentioned. As regards power outside itself, what the Church says has great weight in the country; the Army can requisition private land for its uses; and even the Public Schools oblige the middle-classes to conform to their standards. Nevertheless, these powers are severely restricted. The Church cannot punish people who are not members of it; the Army cannot order a civilian about, and though Public Schools can persuade Grammar Schools to copy their manners, they cannot force them to. As regards immunity from outside interference, the Church may be left, within reason, to appoint its own priests and air its views, the Army can build its barracks as it likes and school holidays are left to the school to decide; but in modern countries at least it is the Government which has the last say in directing Church policy, the Army is not allowed by the civil authorities to build insanitary camps, and schools cannot give themselves eternal holidays.

There is, however, one organized group about which we have not yet spoken, which does admirably satisfy these three conditions. That is no less a body than the sovereign State.

In the first place, the sovereign State is almost completely self-contained. Most of its members spend all their lives within it and have no attachments of feeling to any persons outside it. Thus they are free to hate, despise or ignore outsiders altogether and to love, admire and feel with one another the more.[1]

[1] A distribution of ambivalence on these lines is seen at its maximum in times of war when such intense hatred is directed to the outside enemy, and it is one of the reasons why, at such times, the members of a State feel the greatest and most unadulterated love for one another. People often wonder why, after the *camaraderie* of war-time and the sense of pulling together, we should in peace-time relapse into our old mutual hatreds and squabbles, when it would be so much pleasanter to be amicable and it is still so necessary to work together for the common good. The answer is that there is no one now outside our country for us to hate enough.

Secondly, there is no law to restrain a sovereign State from interfering with people outside it. If it is a colonial empire, for instance, it has power over people who are not members of it. Lastly, a sovereign State cannot legitimately be interfered with by any person or group from outside, and if such interference is threatened, it has the right, the duty and the means to defend itself. No one else may tell it who are to be its rulers, what sort of laws to make, how to direct its domestic economy or its foreign policy, and so on and so forth.

In these respects, then, the sovereign State seems eminently suited to function as a regressive group.

Let us now see how far it exhibits the two external features of such a group—the features described by Freud (p. 184).

As regards the leaders' power over the members, this is absolute in all totalitarian and autocratic States, so that that condition is completely satisfied. In democracies, on the other hand, or under constitutional rule, the leaders have much less power, being to a greater or lesser extent controlled by the people or by the written law. Here the condition is *not* fully satisfied. Nevertheless, even here the leaders still have very considerable powers. Moreover, as we know, the established law which controls them represents ancestral imagos, so that in bowing to it the people are bowing, if not to their fathers, at least to their forefathers. Again, even if it is the people who control their leaders, the group itself still represents to some extent a paternal imago, as well as a narcissistic one. Thus though this situation detracts from the *leader's* regressive authority over the people, it does not detract by that amount from the regressive authority over them of the *group*—except in so far as in a democracy the people are encouraged to exercise their reason in matters of government and are brought into proper contact with reality, so that the regressive influence in general of the group upon them is less.

In any case, the State itself, whether authoritarian or democratic, *has* absolute power over its subjects in every aspect of their lives; and this is something which no other group possesses. The power wielded by the State over its subjects has all the more effect on their minds, since it lasts throughout their lives and embraces the whole of it. With only a few exceptions, every individual is born, lives and dies as a citizen of the same country.

Then, too, its long tradition and material power and wealth and bigness exceed that of any other group, so that it is the object of especial awe.

On the other hand, this very bigness might seem to prevent it from acting as a group. The large area of land which it covers disperses its members widely, so that they do not all know one another, and the size of its population makes it impossible for them ever to meet together in a single body.

This drawback, however, is not unique to the State. There are other groups besides it which consist of too many persons and are too much extended in space to allow of such things. This is true, notably, of both the Church and the Army. It is not possible for all the clergymen of the Church of England, let alone all the priests of such a huge ramified body as the Roman Catholic Church, to know one another or to get together, in the way that the members of a Public School or a secret society can. Similarly, only a very small proportion of the soldiers of an army are directly acquainted with one another, nor can they be massed into a single, vast conglomeration.

Here it must rather be the individual's *idea* of the group as a whole, his realization of its bigness, greatness, wealth and strength—which, supplementing his more immediate personal experience of parts of it, makes it an instigator and a focus of his regressive attitudes. What also often happens is that big groups are subdivided into lesser ones which are subordinated to and integrated with them. Each member can thus experience the more direct sense of community with the small group to which he belongs, and this feeling as it were feeds his more abstract sense of community with the larger group of which it is a part. We see this well exemplified, for instance, in the armed forces. The group-mentality which a soldier or a sailor has about the army or navy in which he is serving is supported by the group-mentality which he has about his regiment or his ship. These sub-groups may be further divided into still smaller units, each of which, once more, is subordinated to, and integrated with, the larger sub-group, so that if the latter should still be too large to produce a great deal of group-mentality in its members, the former—the sub-subgroup—will add its quota. Regiments have companies, and companies, platoons; and a private—especially a private with a somewhat limited intellect—may be more moved by the group-spirit of his platoon or company than by that of his regiment, let alone the army as a whole.

The same kind of sub-grouping is found in the State, though generally the integration of the subordinate groups is not so close as it is in the case of the armed forces. The police, the civil service, possibly even State-run schools, can be regarded as more or less powerful 'feeders' for State-mentality. In most countries, too, the Church itself is put under the State; and in well-conducted ones the army owes allegiance to it.

States whose aim it is to exercise the maximum amount of power over the actions and minds of their subjects make great use of this device. In totalitarian States all the important groups contained in it are strictly sub-aligned to it in this way. Not for it the independent trade unions or the freely elected County Councils. Its structure is monolithic.

Regarding the condition that the group should be exclusively male, this is obviously not fulfilled by the State. True, its rulers are nearly always men (and when they are not they are nearly always not the real source of power); but the rank-and-file members are evenly mixed. This, in respect of its homosexual ties, is a weak point. And so is it in respect of its identificatory ties, since half the population is unlike the other half as to the very important and striking primary and secondary characteristics of sex. Nevertheless, on other points the members of most States exhibit very marked similarities. They have the same cultural and historical background, speak the same language, wear the same clothes, etc., and differ in

these matters from the members of other States. Most important of all, they usually come from the same race or stock, so
that they also have a similarity of innate characteristics, in
which they once more differ from the members of other
States. Thus they feel themselves to be part of a single, wide
family, inherently separate and distinct from all other families
of the kind—a true nation.

So strong indeed is the influence of a sense of common
nationality, that it induces a group-mentality on its own even
when the nation is not a sovereign State. Thus, as we know,
the Scotch, the Welsh and the English have a tremendous
sense of oneness among themselves and apartness from the
others, as a Scotch and Welsh and English people respectively,
even though there is no Scotch or Welsh or English State for
them to belong to but only Great Britain.

*   *   *

It is clear, I think, that in most important respects the
sovereign State, and in especial the national sovereign State,
is well qualified to figure as a regressive group. And certainly
the facts bear out this view. The differences between a man's
attitudes in his personal and domestic concerns, and in his
national and international ones, are indeed great; and they
do actually correspond to the differences we should expect to
find in him between his attitudes as private individual and as
a member of a regressive group. Mr. Briggs, who is a perfectly
honest man at home and who would not dream of keeping
what is not his by rights, strongly advocates a 'what we have
we hold' colonial policy for Britain; Mr. Smith, who feels
greatly for the sufferings of his countrymen, has no care for
the sufferings of foreigners, opining that that is none of his
business; Frau Schultz, a placid lady who is not touchy about
herself, sees red when Germany is disparaged and thirsts for
the blood of the disparager; Signor Cappello, who has no
wish to attack or oppress his neighbours at home, applauds
Italy's colonial expansion; M. Duval, a solid bourgeois of
France, with an eye to the main chance, gladly risks material

*

ruin for a war of glory; and Miss Jenkins, the soul of charity to her fellows, has no patience with the faults of foreigners and is blind to their virtues. Even the most peaceable citizen admires and supports his country's conquering heroes—its Napoleons, its Caesars, its Henry Vs, its Hitlers or its Mussolinis, and makes no enquiry into the harm their conquests have done to other countries, or, for that matter, to his own.

Apart, too, from ministering to their infantile piety and egotism in a general way, the State also enables its members to gratify many of their more specific instincts and attitudes —usually infantile ones—which have been repressed and inhibited in private life; and since these vary considerably from one person to another, they tend to produce a somewhat different brand of nationalism in each, as we have just seen in our examples. Mr. Briggs, in insisting on his country's holding on to its colonies, is no doubt obtaining a (psychologically, if not socially) sublimated gratification of his early anal-retentive instincts; Signor Cappello, in egging his country on to territorial conquests, is obeying the dictates of his own displaced instinct of acquisition; and Frau Schultz, in so strongly resenting any insult offered to her country, is perhaps seeking to combat her sense of inferiority due to her castration complex; and so on. The secret agent who spies for his country when he would not spy for himself is gratifying his ancient *voyeurism* in a legitimate way and without offence to his super-ego; and the politician who tells lies and spreads false propaganda to bolster up his own country, or undermine another, is not only prolonging his past belief in his and his parents' greatness, but is, at the same time, exercising and enjoying his first-found ability to take them in. Even the ruin which such behaviour sometimes brings upon a nation may not merely gratify concealed masochistic trends in many of its people once it has happened; it may in some measure have been brought about by those very trends.

Only a thoroughly anti-social adult says, 'Myself, right or wrong'; and even then, if he is wise, he says it to himself. And only a madman says 'I am always right'. Nor, nowadays, does any adult in his right senses feel those things—consciously at any rate—about his father or his mother or any other human being. But he still feels them consciously and self-approvingly about his own country. The national roundly asserts 'my country, right or wrong' and even 'my country is always right', without being deemed criminal or mad. Indeed, any man who thinks that his country *is* in the wrong, especially in its attitude to another country, is apt to be regarded by his fellows as wrong-headed or downright wicked; and any man who works against his country's interests abroad, because they are unethical or do great harm to another country, is not only punished for being a traitor—as, of course, he is—but regarded with loathing for being loyal to principles which he puts higher than the principle of patriotism. Unfortunately, too, the lowered level of intelligence to which their group mentality sinks often makes nationals believe that what is in fact *not* in the interest of their nation *is* in its interest; so that the few who try to open their eyes to the dangers to their country which their blind patriotism is conjuring up are likewise ignored or branded as traitors. If, for instance, the just and sensible idea of Home Rule for Ireland, as supported by some enlightened Englishmen—an idea which would have done England no harm and Ireland a great deal of good—had not from the beginning been met by howls of rage and indignation from the majority of Englishmen who were outraged at the idea of their country shrinking in size and losing its domination over another, much bloodshed and bitterness of feeling on either side, which did England as well as Ireland a lot of harm, would have been avoided. The '*sacro egoismo*' of the resurgent Italians was no mere figure of speech. Their new Italy was their old selves revived, and nothing was too good for it. Such a belief in the grandeur of his country has the further effect of making the subject believe that it, and he and his fellows as parts of it, are unconquerable and invulnerable, so that he does not hesitate to rush in where common sense would give him pause.

We can also see how it is that national fervour is so catching and that a nation can be swept by a kind of patriotic hysteria. It is not only that what one national feels strongly about his other co-nationals are likely as well to feel strongly about for the same reason. Each also feels strongly about it because he takes on the feelings of his fellows.

We can, furthermore, understand why the moral values which the national has in regard to his own and other nations are so different from the moral values which he has in regard to his private life. For they belong to his infantile view of things. Thus it is, for instance, that he admires his country for its power, grandeur and size more than he does for its virtues and fair dealing: what he understood and admired first and foremost as a small child was power and bigness.

Again, we can now account for the strange terms in which a national talks when he thinks of his country as a *land*. To him the land he and his people inhabit shares in their being; it is a person. Thus, if it is invaded he thinks of it as being 'violated' or 'raped' quite literally, as he thinks of a woman—in this case *his* woman and his great mother into the bargain, as well as his feminine self—being raped and desecrated, and he responds with frenzied rage. He even violently resists a peaceable partition of his country, however just and even advantageous, because it means a cutting up of the beloved land made up of its fields, trees, houses, streams, mountains, plains and seas which is at once his own great self and his still greater parents.

It is clear that such mental attitudes on the part of the members of a State towards outsiders is bound to make them adopt a hostile line of action against them or to provoke hostile feelings towards themselves in the minds of those outsiders and when these in turn are members of a State and equally inflammable and provocative in *their* attitudes to those who are outsiders, the situation is bound to be explosive.

In addition, there are two practical considerations which make sovereign States by far the most dangerous of all regressive groups, even if they are not the most regressive of them. One is that they are not only large groups, containing very many people; between them, they contain all the people in the world, so that no one is exempt from their influence. The other is that they, and they alone of all other groups, provide their members with the *means* as well as the *will* to carry out their dangerous wishes. For it is only they that possess the necessary weapons of mass-destruction.

PART THREE

RECOMMENDATIONS

Chapter XV

CHANGES IN THE STATE

OUR enquiry into the psychological causes of war is at last completed, and we have, I think, arrived at some new and valuable conclusions.

It now remains for us to approach the third and final part of our task, which is to consider what contributions our added knowledge can make to the practical question of putting an end to war.

So far, the chief villain of the piece seems to be the national State in its aspect as a regressive group. The first thing that suggests itself, therefore, is to aim at doing away with, or at least reducing, those features of it which make it a group of this kind.

To begin with the power of the leaders over its members. As we have seen, a democratic form of government is less intense in its regressive effects than an autocratic one. The first thing, therefore, is to foster democratic government in every country.

Many States are already non-authoritarian and need no further modification in this direction. But with others this is far from being the case and it should be our endeavour to free their people to the fullest possible extent. Such a change, however, is not easily made all at once. To begin with, the leaders of authoritarian States strenuously oppose it, because it entails the loss of what they most prize, viz. absolute power over their subjects; and since they have that power, they have every means of preventing the change. In the second place, the group-mentality which an authoritarian State engenders in its subjects makes them, on their side, unwilling to shake off the power of their leaders. They hug their chains and would feel lost without them. If the liberalization of an authoritarian State is effected at all speedily therefore, it is usually through a forcible uprising of the people against their leaders, and by a minority of them at that. Yet a change of this sort, made in this manner, is not likely to last, for many reasons. To begin with, the ousted leaders will leave no stone unturned to get back into power, and in this, too, they will have the support of the bulk of the majority who originally opposed the liberalizing revolution; for although a liberal régime may, in time, make them less regressively group-minded and therefore less desirous of a despotic leader than they were before, this cannot happen very rapidly. For we must remember that they have been under the influence of the authoritarian régime that preceded it all their lives from childhood up, so that their minds are completely habituated to it—perhaps irrevocably so. Thus it may take at least a generation—and more if we consider the influence of parental imagos and the unmodified super-ego—before the members of a former despotic State can be expected to become truly free in their minds. Till that distant time arrives there is plenty of opportunity for the old despotic leaders, or new aspirants to that position, to head them in a reactionary *coup d'état*.

A further trouble is that in order to prevent such a reactionary revolution, and the conspiracies which precede it, the non-despotic rulers of the newly liberated State must themselves adopt stern measures and take over a good deal of power and run a secret police, etc. Thus they themselves, against their own principles and their own wishes, become to a large extent despotic rulers; the State reverts to authoritarianism and its people continue in their subservient mentality, though to new rulers. This, one suspects, is what has happened in Russia, against the hopes and ideals of the original Bolsheviks.

An immediate change from an authoritarian to a liberal régime can, of course, be forcibly imposed and maintained in a State against the will of its people by a stronger foreign

Power. But such a régime would be still more hated and detested by them (and, indeed, would be disliked by many of the minority who were in favour of it on its own merits) precisely because it was forced upon their State by a foreign agency; and they would not rest till they had got rid of it. This was what happened to the ill-fated Weimar Constitution which was set up in Germany as a result of her defeat by the Allies, and which so many good Germans regarded with rage and humiliation as a badge of national servitude.

But even when the revolutionary change is made with the support of the majority of the members of the State, there is no guarantee that it has come to stay. For though their *conscious* motive for such a revolution is a desire for liberty, their *unconscious* motive is generally an intense hatred of their infantile father-imago, of which their despotic rulers are manifest representatives, and a wish to kill him. But such a hatred of him is, as we know, opposed by an equally strong love and awe of him. Thus, having accomplished their revolution and killed him by proxy—whether actually, by killing their rulers, or symbolically, by turning them out—they are overcome by remorse, guilt and fear and seek to reinstate him, either by bringing back those same rulers or by setting up new ones on the old terms.[1] After their popular revolution of 1789, the French gladly accepted the domination of Napoleon, and the English had to take two bites at a cherry before they finally threw off the Stuart yoke.

This displaced hatred of the father on to the leader, incidentally, is the most common cause of that recalcitrance to the influence of authoritarian groups, which is found in some individuals and which is in such striking contrast to the attitude of the majority. Such individuals loathe being reminded of the power of their father and they strive to deny it or undermine it in the person of their leader. They avoid belonging to any group of this kind, or, if they cannot do that, they take as little part in it as possible or they do their

[1] Cf. in this connection Ernest Jones' very interesting paper, 'Evolution and Revolution'.

best to bring down its leaders and either break it up or set up a democratic constitution in it—or, what not infrequently happens, they try to make themselves the autocratic leaders of it; i.e. they aim not only at killing their father but at taking his place.

In addition to all this, there is the following point to be considered. Although a non-despotic State may make its members less mentally subservient to their rulers than they would be if it were despotic, it does not make those of them who have an inclination to rule others despotically less so inclined; and some of these, if they possess the rest of the qualities required for being successful despots, may, by force or luck or cunning, set themselves up as such in the State and maintain themselves there long enough to reduce the majority of its subjects to a condition of mental subservience to them or those who succeed them.

Now every State, like every other large number of persons, contains some potential leaders, who thus constitute a standing menace to its internal freedom. A necessary precondition for abolishing State authoritarianism for good, therefore, might have to be to make sure that no one who possessed the attributes of leadership should ever be in a position to exercise power. These attributes are known to us, nor do they hide their light under a bushel, so that it should not be hard to detect a potential leader. In the first place such a person has very strong instincts of self-assertiveness and domination, and probably of aggression as well, and a high degree of self-love, self-sufficiency and ruthlessness towards others. At the same time, those instincts and attitudes are approved of by his super-ego and unopposed by his conscious ego, so that he can manifest them freely and without any sense of guilt, with its inhibitions and self-imposed failures. He also has a strong and uncritical belief in his own powers and in the goodness and rightness of all he thinks and does. And these qualities he must be able, and indeed wishful, to exhibit to other people. With all this, too, he can persuade them that he has their interests at heart and cares for them all equally (though this, in fact, is rarely the case, or not nearly so much the case as he makes out—as is inevitable, considering how self-loving he is, and how much filled with the sense of his own importance). In this way he puts across to them the picture of a strong, righteous personage and makes an excellent peg on which to hang their infantile father- (and self-) imagos, whom they are glad to obey and to identify themselves with. It is, of course, possible for a person who does not possess these attributes to maintain his position as the absolute ruler of a State and to be clothed with its authority once he has been put there, in virtue of his actual possession of absolute power, as is the case with hereditary despots, but he could not attain that position of himself unless he possessed those attributes. A Caesar, a Cromwell, a Hitler, a Mussolini—widely different as were their merits, their outlook and their characters in many respects—all had this in common, that they believed in themselves or their stars or their causes and that they were able to impose themselves and their beliefs upon their companions, who thus became their followers.[1]

Let all such persons, then, be kept down.

Unfortunately, however, their qualities are precisely those which make keeping down difficult. However much such a man is discouraged and put into inferior positions, he does not lose heart; he enlists the allegiance of those about him and makes his way to the fore. And in civilized countries at least humanitarian considerations forbid putting him out of the way altogether.

Besides, even the most democratic and liberal of States must have persons who exercise dictatorial powers in certain fields on however small a scale. Not everything can be best decided for the people by the people. The captain of a fire brigade must be able to order his men about as he thinks fit during a fire, and so must the captain of a ship during her voyage on the seas; doctors and psychiatrists must be authorized to restrain infectious patients or lunatics from roaming about

[1] Cf. Freud's description of the attributes of leadership in his *Group Psychology*, pp. 92, 93.

at will; Cabinet Ministers must have power to carry through certain decisions even if they know that those decisions do not at that moment please the majority of the electorate, and so on. The *Führer-Prinzip*, so odious to all democrats, can never be entirely abolished. Now the persons whose function it is to impose their will on the others in such matters, must possess some qualities of leadership in *some* degree, otherwise those whom they command will not respond properly to their orders and the business in hand will not go on well. Thus not only cannot they be done without; they inevitably occupy positions which give them added authority in the eyes of others and which, moreover, often make it especially easy for them to attain absolute leadership of the State. In this respect the armed forces present the greatest danger, since in order to function at all they must be organized on strictly authoritarian lines, and in order to function efficiently their officers must be capable of leadership in a high degree (not to mention, of course, the physical might of the group under their command). Certainly it has happened more than once in history that a liberal and democratic State has succumbed to a military dictatorship from within.

In view of this, it might, indeed, be better always to put unleaderlike persons in the positions of leaders, on the grounds that it is preferable for a concern to be inefficiently run than efficiently run by a potential dictator. But even so, the danger would not be entirely eliminated. For the mere fact of making decisions, accepting responsibility and giving orders which are obeyed would tend to evoke some degree of leader-mentality in the leader, however unleaderlike he was by nature, by giving him, if not self-confidence, at any rate the habit of commanding and being obeyed and deferred to; whilst on the other side, the mere fact of obeying him and paying him outward respect would evoke some measure of mental subservience to him on the part of his obeyers. And it is not inconceivable that the two things between them would take him to the top.

Another way of loosening the hold of the State over its

subjects is to strengthen the power of the non-aligned groups within it and weaken that of the aligned ones. The Church, for instance, is by nature a non-aligned group, since its members owe no ultimate moral allegiance to any being except God. It has often undermined the State loyalty of the individual in the past and sometimes still does so now. Rulers of States understand this well, and if they want their State (or themselves) to be powerful they try to deal with its influence in various ways. If they are themselves religious—or rather, pro-Church—or if they think that the pro-Church feeling of their subjects is too strong to be safely ignored, they take care to gain the goodwill of the Church; or if they are anti-Church and deem that their subjects are not too deeply imbued with belief in the Church to be able to be weaned from it, they weaken its power and make it subservient to the will of the State and integrate it into its system, or else they reject or oppress it. Our King Henry the Eighth followed this plan when he made himself the Head of the Church of England—a position which, incidentally, our sovereigns still occupy—and when he suppressed and despoiled the monasteries. Napoleon made terms with the Church but kept it well under control. The Nazis allowed their Churches no independent voice, and the Communist countries do the same.

There is thus a good deal to be said for increasing the power, independence and size of the Church, or Churches, within the State as a means of curbing its authority. (Other things being equal a single large Church is more effective than several smaller ones, since the power which members of the former attribute to their Church is greater than the power which the members of the latter can attribute to theirs, so that its influence over their minds will be more.) Much might be done by stiffening Church discipline and by giving the Church independent powers over its members—and perhaps over non-members too—and endowing it with riches, pomp and splendour, as in the olden days. And first and foremost, of course, comes the strengthening and spreading of belief in its Godhead, in order to make the group whose leader He is paramount in the minds of His flock. Unfortunately for these possibilities, religious faith, faced with people's growing knowledge of its many self-contradictions and its many contradictions with other religious faiths and with hard facts, seems decidedly on the wane, so that the establishment of a single, strong and independent Church within the State is scarcely possible.

To strengthen the power and independence of the army would clearly also weaken the power of the State. But this might only be jumping from the frying-pan into the fire. For powerful as the army already is, any addition to its power often results in an overthrow by it of the civil government and the establishment of a military dictatorship, which would probably be more despotic and therefore more regressive than its predecessor, besides being more favourable to war from its very profession.

The group-mentality engendered by local governments can also to some extent weaken the influence of the State—so long, of course, as they enjoy a high degree of autonomy and independence; otherwise their effect will be the opposite. Local self-government should therefore be strongly encouraged.

Another group which is able to counteract the influence of the State is the family, and since these social units include every individual in the State, their influence is great from extension as well as intensity. This being so, it might be advisable to strengthen the power of the family over the minds of its members by giving it more authority over their actions, making it more self-contained, independent and so on. Nevertheless, it must be remembered that what is a person's family group as a child is not the same as his family group as an adult, and that it must be possible, for the sake of his mental health—as well as the need for him to become attached, as a married person and a parent, to his 'adult' family—to move from the first to the second as he grows up. In order to avoid fixations to his 'infantile family' it may be desirable, therefore, that he should not have been too much dominated by it as a child. What is now such a fixation on an infantile group which no longer exists for him, may cause him to displace it onto a group which does exist for him and which is very like it—viz. none other than the autocratic State itself; in which case, instead of counteracting his State-mentality it would abet it.[1]

A State, too, which contains separate national or racial units tends to be weakened by their divided allegiance or mutual strife. This was the case up till the eighteenth century in the Scottish Highlands, where their clan and its feuds with another clan were more important to its inhabitants than was their country and its feuds with other countries, and made them by that much the less dangerous to their foreign neighbours. Even such anti-social groups as revolutionary bodies, secret societies, conspiratorial factions and criminal gangs may do their bit towards making the State less stream-lined. But whether that is a sufficient reason for encouraging them is another matter.

Coming to the homogeneity of the members of a State, this presents no problem as far as their sex is concerned; and as concerns their likeness as to race, language, customs, etc., something might be done towards encouraging large numbers of people of different origins and speech to become part of

[1] It will be understood that both in considering the effect, respectively, of local government and the family on State-mentality, I am regarding them here solely from the point of view of the group-mentality they arouse. Over and above this, of course, they affect the attitude of their members to the State through other influences which they exert on them. Free local bodies, for instance, enable their members to exercise responsibilities in real life, and so strengthen their preconscious and make them less liable to regress, and thus once again increase their resistance to State-mentality. Again, as Dr. Edward Glover has pointed out in his book, *War, Sadism and Pacifism*, if a family is a happy one, it creates large quantities of libido in the child, which, among other things, neutralizes his destrudo. On this count, though it does not make him less State-minded in later life, it does make him less hostile to persons outside the State, and by that much a less dangerous member of it. (This, incidentally, is an argument for *happy* families rather than *powerful* ones.) Similarly, religions which, like Christianity, preach forgiveness and pacifism, and which believe in the value of life on earth, have the same desirable effect of opposing bellicose or war-provoking attitudes of mind—this effect being greatly strengthened, of course, by proceeding from the Church as a regressive group to its congregation as members of it.

the State and diversify it. Yet, unless intermarriage between them and the rest of the population were discouraged, they would soon lose their identity and become merged in the whole. Some kind of local separation might be desirable, such as we see, for instance, in the Swiss State with its various German, French and Italian cantons. Certainly, no one can accuse the Swiss of exaggerated patriotism.—Failing this, individual differences of every sort between one member and another could well be encouraged instead of being frowned upon.

*   *   *

As regards the characteristic of self-containment, it is obviously a good thing for the members of every State to get to know all about foreign countries, to make the acquaintance of foreigners and to travel abroad and even stay there for some time; likewise to encourage foreigners to get to know all about their country and visit it and stay there.

There is much to be said for this idea; but it would have to be carried out on a very large scale so that most people of one country had first-hand experience of the people of at least one other country. And even so, it is doubtful whether anything short of strong libidinal and identificatory ties, such as are only got from a long stay in a country, or indeed from bonds of kinship and marriage, would be sufficient to counteract the members' group-ties at home. And this is hardly feasible for most.

Perhaps a more effective method would be for the subject to belong to some group outside his State so as once more to pit one group-allegiance against another. International groups like the Red Cross or the Boy Scouts or scientific bodies have not a very strong group spirit of their own with which to combat their members' State-mentality. On the other hand, international Churches, or Churches of other countries, have. Buddhism, Mohammedanism and, above all, Christianity as embodied in the Roman Catholic Church are powerful regressive organizations which can do much to counter the influence of the State upon their members. But here again, not everyone can reconcile his reason or his conscience to belonging to one or other of those religious bodies. Another external group-membership which greatly weakens the individual's allegiance to his State is one which is based on nationality or race. Before the 1914 war, for instance, if a man who belonged to, say, the German State was a Pole, his group-feeling about Germany was enormously lessened by the fact not only that he belonged to a Polish nation within it, but that he belonged to a Polish nation *outside* it—half of it owned by Russia and half by Austria —to which he was strongly drawn and of which he felt himself to be a part.

As regards the power of the State over people who are not members of it, it is desirable as soon as possible either to include them as members of it or to abolish its authority over them. They should be free whenever they are fit for it to become full citizens of the State that rules them, or of any other State they choose and which is agreeable; or they should be allowed to form a new State of their own. This is, in fact, gradually happening, as we see in the case of our own Empire; but the resistance to it on the part of members of the ruling State is tremendously strong, in no small measure on account of the loss of prestige which it involves for their country.

Similarly the independence of the State in relation to other States must be restricted. No one should be able to pride himself that his country has the right to do as it pleases, even if at its own risk, outside its own boundaries as well as inside. This second necessity is beginning to be recognized on practical grounds; but its psychological implications have not been understood; yet the opposition which steps in that direction encounter stems entirely from the psychological side; and the strength of that opposition is a measure of the strength of the group-mentality behind it.[1]

[1] Indeed, subjection of the State to outside interference is the only way in which a restriction of its power, whether autocratic or democratic, over its own subjects

Submission to external authority—which entails nothing less than loss of sovereignty—is a bitter pill to swallow. It can most easily be done where the members of the State are able to displace a substantial amount of their attitude to their leaders onto that authority, so as to form the nucleus of a new group-mentality side by side with the old—a super-State mentality. For this would also help them to form the necessary libidinal and identificatory ties with the members of the other States which came under the rule of that superior external body. It is necessary, therefore, that the persons who compose such a body should be capable of attracting their love as well as their awe and should seem to them to be equally well disposed to all, so that every member of every State can make the required libidinal, dependent and identificatory ties with them. This step has, in fact, been successfully achieved in various parts of the world. The United States of America combined the many independent sovereign States of which it was made up into a single Federal State—though only at the cost of a civil war—and today every American citizen is as proud of Uncle Sam as he is of Iowa or Missouri or wherever he hails from.

But for this it is important that the States so combined should not be too unlike one another. The inhabitants of each must be drawn together mentally not only through common allegiance to the same leaders but by the fact of inhabiting a single geographical area or of talking the same language or having the same laws, habits, traditions, code of morals, religion, physical characteristics and general level of civilization. Many States are very unlike one another in most of these respects, and it would be a difficult if not impossible task to overcome the numerous, striking and often deep-seated differences which distinguish the people of one from those of the others sufficiently to enable them to make the requisite inter-identifications for a successful union. Thus

can be assured. (Thus, paradoxically enough, a situation can arise in which they are most free, as individuals, precisely when, as members of their State, they may feel least free—viz., when an external Power assures them the enjoyment of fundamental civil rights over the head of their State.)

although it may be perfectly possible to form several large groups of federated or united States, each containing peoples with racial and cultural affinities, it does not seem likely that these Super-States would grow beyond a certain size. There might, for instance, be a North American-cum-European State, an African State, an Indian-cum-Asian State and even a Russo-Chinese one, if Communist ideology should prove a strong enough bond. Now whatever other advantages there are in having a few large sovereign States over having a lot of small ones, there is none as regards war. Quite the contrary. There is just as much motive, reasonable or not, for one giant State to hate and fear another giant State as there is for little States to hate and fear one another; and though wars might be less frequent, their effects would be far worse. Clearly, what is needed is nothing less than a single World State, or World Federation of States.

There is yet another reason, I think, why it is not likely that such a single State can be established. This is that in it one of the main ingredients of an organized group would be lacking —viz. the extrapolation of the destructive instincts of its members, which makes their mutual attachments so much more purely libidinal; for then there would be no external object onto which to deflect those instincts. In consequence, the State would tend to fall apart of itself.

Chapter XVI

CHANGES IN THE INDIVIDUAL

THE dangers of State-mentality in these days are so great that one is almost tempted to recommend that States should be altogether abolished and that people should co-operate freely as private individuals in attending to all matters that are necessary for their survival and well-being. But even if it were possible to do away with States in the first instance, in spite of the passion with which their members cling to them, the resultant situation would be calamitous. For, as we now know, the reign of peace and order which prevails within a State is by no means purely the product of the good sense and good feeling which each individual naturally has towards his fellows; it is to a great extent the product of that regressive group-mentality which his State, thanks to its organization, evokes in him and which makes him so egotistical and ruthless to everything outside it. Those very conditions which incline him to hate and distrust every other State and all its members and which weaken his sense of reality, justice and conscience about them are the same conditions which also incline him to admire, love and trust his fellow-citizens, to deal honestly by them, to feel for them and to have a sense of right and wrong about them. Thus, the dissolution of the State would soon be followed by mutual destruction and complete chaos.

This brings us to what is perhaps the most important point about regressive groups and what seems to make their abolition finally impossible. This is that even in his private capacity the individual has a need for them. They afford him great relief and pleasure by allowing his mind to regress to less exacting standards of thought and to older attitudes of feeling, and they allay his anxiety and sense of guilt by giving him back an omnipotent, protecting father and accomplices to aid and to share his dangers; and, finally, they give his ancient megalomania and narcissism room to expand. On this score alone, the establishment of an anarchical society—a society in which there is no ruler and no law imposed by force—such as is advocated by Ruskin, Tolstoy, and other political philosophers, would be an impossibility quite apart from its practical inexpediency. The human mind could not stand it.

Being in a crowd, too, is often no mere matter of chance. It is true that a person may find himself close together with a large number of other persons because he has to catch the same train as they, or because he wants to see the same football match or listen to the same public speaker. But he often chooses to join a crowd for its own sake. Many people enjoy holidays *en masse* more than singly or in small parties, as witness the beaches of Margate in August or the Butlin camps everywhere. People celebrate anniversaries and other great occasions in common rather than alone; football matches and public speeches would not be nearly as popular and as exciting to the onlooker if he was one among a few or quite alone. Even the higher forms of entertainment, such as concerts and theatres, are generally speaking more pleasurable to a large audience than to a small one. The excitations and regressions effected by being in a crowd afford the individual pleasure, and are things which he cannot forgo. Indeed, so strong and so universal is the tendency of all human beings to collect together, that it is considered by social psychologists to be innate and instinctual, and it has accordingly been variously termed 'the social instinct', 'the instinct of gregariousness', or 'the herd instinct'. Certainly there never was a time when people did not live in communities. Freud, moreover, regarded his autocratic, male groups as descendants and variants of what he calls 'the primal father-horde', which was the prototype of all later human societies.[1]

Thus we may perhaps be entitled to speak of a 'horde instinct'. At any rate, the tendency to form horde-like groups of the kind we have been discussing is, as we have seen, fed by certain instincts, even if it does not compose one.

*   *   *

A more promising angle of approach, therefore, is to go behind the regressive group itself and tackle the mental attitudes in the individual which creates them—or, more correctly, which cause him to respond to them. For what matters is not that he should be in a regressive group but that it should exert a regressive influence on him; and the two do not always coincide. Suppose that a civilized man has to live in a savage community and share its life. It is possible that, if he lives long enough in it, he will 'go native' and come to believe in the magical powers of the head chief before whom he must grovel three times a day, on pain of death; but it is more likely that he will continue to grovel before him without being reduced to believing in his magical powers as his fellow-grovellers do. (Conversely, a person with strong primitive attitudes is liable to respond in a regressive way to groups which are not markedly regressive. Thus, for instance, a savage may be obliged by a paramount civilized Power to elect his local rulers by vote; but once they have been elected he is likely to regard them with superstitious awe as omnipotent persons whose authority over him does not depend upon his will but theirs.)

As we know, the underlying attitudes of the individual which find outlet in his group-mentality are often in part due to his innate mental constitution. Much of his pugnaciousness

[1] Cf. Group Psychology, Chapter X. In this Freud bases himself on Darwin's conjecture that the primitive form of society was that of the Cyclopean family—a collection of males and females ruled over by the strongest male, who had exclusive sexual possession of all the females. In his book Totem and Taboo, Freud elaborates this theme; and he derives from the primal horde and its subsequent changes and vicissitudes many of the groups and institutions—notably that of exogamy—which characterize primitive societies of to-day.

towards other nations, for instance, may go back to an excess of aggressive and destructive instincts which, or the seeds of which, were brought into the world with him. To revert to our examples in Chapter XIV, we saw how Mr. Briggs' reluctance to give up an inch of England's empire was based on his exceptionally strong anal-retentive instincts, and how Signor Cappello's thirst for foreign conquest sprang from *his* exceptionally strong acquisitive ones. But those underlying attitudes are also in part due to the subject's early experiences and to their impact upon his innate instincts. Mr. Briggs' possessiveness about the Empire may owe much of its intensity to difficulties he met with as a small child in being trained in cleanliness—difficulties which may have been as much caused by an unsympathetic nurse as by his own anal impulses—so that he has never got over his dislike of parting with stool. Similarly, Signor Cappello's lust for foreign conquest may spring not only from his excessive instinct of acquisition but from experiences in infancy which increased that instinct. He may have had an elder brother who made it a habit to take all his toys away from him; or he may have felt, as a small child, rightly or wrongly, that his father and mother were not giving him enough to eat or were withholding from him other things that were his due. So now, in egging on his country to seize other people's possessions, he is only trying to get his own back.

The general mental disposition of the individual, also formed from a combination of constitutional and early accidental factors, furthermore largely determines the strength of his tendency to attach himself to regressive groups and to be influenced by them—to be what might be called 'group-prone'. For not all people are equally group-prone, by any means. Some are exceedingly so; others less; and a few not at all.

A person with a disposition which, if more accentuated, would amount to a regular schizophrenic predisposition, is distinctly not group-prone, since he cannot establish proper relations with any whole object. A person with a disposition

H

which similarly corresponds to a paranoic predisposition is more group-prone, so long as his relations to his objects are not too hostile to permit of a satisfactory distribution of his ambivalence. For he greatly needs an external object upon which he can vent his hatred with public approval, and group-aggression affords him a high degree of gratification. But, of course, if his destructive energy is too great, not even this outwardly directed hostility can save him from hating his fellow-members to such an extent that he cannot remain within his group. (And, indeed, he may have a disruptive effect upon the group itself by setting up hostile attitudes between one member and another.) The kind of group which such a person enters or makes is characterized by being very hostile and aggressive towards everyone outside it, and is usually exceedingly dangerous while it lasts.[1] The depressive kind of person is not prone to form groups or to lend himself to their influence, since he shrinks from the society of his fellows; nor is the maniacally disposed one, since he is too narcissistic and megalomanic to be affected by anyone else.[2] The obsessionally predisposed person is not particularly group-prone either, since he is apt to oppose any ideas and feelings which arise in him or are put before him, or to have eternal doubts and hesitations about them, so that he is not easily swayed, or swayed for long, by others, whether they are his leaders or his fellow-members.

The hysterically disposed person, on the other hand, is eminently group-prone, owing to his readiness to identify himself with his objects, his strongly libidinal but still ambivalent relationships with them, his intense infantile attachments to his parental imagos, the many repressions he has made and his somewhat insecurely established super-ego. This suggests that group-proneness begins to arise in the individual at the same time as his infantile genital instinct, which, as we

[1] Such a person, too, makes a very strong and dangerous leader of a group, seeing that he has no sense of guilt, and is convinced of the wickedness of people outside the group.

[2] But he, too, may make a good—if temporary—leader for that reason. For he is sure of himself and has no sense of guilt or fear of failure.

know, is the point of departure for the predisposition to hysteria. Observation has in fact shown that children start forming groups at about the age of four or five—when, that is, they are beginning to feel the frustrations of their Oedipal position.[1]

A person with an *averagely* normal disposition, based on the predominance of his adult genital instincts, is also appreciably group-prone. For while on the one hand he has real and preponderatingly libidinal relationships with whole objects and makes identifications with them, he is not without relics of his childish attitude to his father, nor without some repressed and infantile attitudes which clamour for expression and cause him to seek it in the regressive group. None but an *ideally* healthy-minded person, if any such exists, would be quite free from group-proneness—and then only, perhaps, if there is no such thing as a group, or horde, instinct.

In view of the fact that the determinants of the individual's group-proneness date from his early years, it is clear that measures for mitigating it should as far as possible be applied to him during his infancy and childhood.

To begin with, he should receive adequate gratification of his instincts as and when they first arise. This not only protects him from the immediate and direct ills of instinctual frustration, but promotes the normal progress of his mental development. For, other things being equal, the small child can move more easily from one developmental stage to the next if the paramount component instinct of the stage at

[1] Cf. Mrs. Isaacs, *The Social Development of Young Children*, p. 248—There are, however, some people who do not appear to wish to join groups, whose attitude is not based on their lack of need for them; nor, when they are in them, are they necessarily immune from their influence. On the contrary, they often enter into a state of group-mentality which is quite equal to that of their fellow-members. Such people have either repressed their desire to be members of a group or have reacted against it because they are too much afraid of, or guilty about, the removal of inhibitions which membership of a group will effect in them, or because groups have come to represent something bad or dangerous to them, or because they cannot abide their omnipotent father even in the guise of a leader. And the same may be true of some people's attitude to crowds. Such attitudes, however, are far from normal, and they can proceed from fixations on a still earlier level.

which he is has been given full play. He should not, for instance, be weaned too soon, or trained in cleanliness too early. He can move on more easily, too, if the instinct which is going to be paramount in the next stage is not thwarted on its first appearance; for this may cause him to fight shy of it and to cling too long to the earlier stage. Too complete a prohibition of genital masturbation often fixates him at the anal stage where he can find some permitted outlet at least for his anal instinct, even if only in the form of a daily visit to the lavatory. It is not wise, on the other hand, to encourage an instinct before its spontaneous emergence, since the child's ego is not yet ready to cope with it, and since to do so is probably to draw him on from his natural instinctual position before it has died down of its own accord.

Again, the child's instincts that have to be thwarted should not be thwarted too suddenly or too completely all at once, so as to give him time to adjust himself mentally to the change and to assimilate it with the rest of his mind and deal with it on a conscious level rather than oppose it or, what is worse, repress the forbidden instinct and thrust it into his unconscious. Moreover, as with adults, in so far as gratification of such instincts must be forbidden, it should be generously replaced by substitutive pleasures—the more so, since the small child is as yet incapable of making sublimations. Thumb-sucking should not be disallowed to the weaned baby; and later on sweets should be freely given to him if he is orally-minded, so that if he may no longer suck or bite the breast, he may at least suck or bite something else that is nice. And if he may not indulge his destructive instincts towards his father he must at least be allowed to smash his house of bricks.

The child's imaginative thought, which is potentially so rich, should be given full scope, too, as an alternative to the enactment of his wishes. Fairy-stories and games of make-believe should by no means be banned from the modern nursery but, on the contrary, encouraged in every way. But, of course, the child must not have phantasies thrust upon him which his mind is not able to tolerate; nor must he be required to believe in them more completely than his own preconscious warrants. But he is often quite content to know that a story is not true, so long as he has the story.

His rational thought should likewise be fostered—though not forced—and should have ample opportunity to unfold. He should be taught how to use his intellect so that he can make correct inferences from what he already knows and so that he has some notion how to set about finding out what he does not know, beyond merely asking questions. Factual information should be given for its own sake as well. In this way the child gets used early on to regard the world of reality as a familiar and interesting place and one with which he can to some extent deal adequately, and thus he is not so likely to retire from it to a world of unreality whenever he finds himself in difficulties. In especial, his desire for sexual knowledge should be satisfied. For much of his earliest and powerful epistemological drives are directed to matters of sex, since it has such intense impulsional and emotional importance for him. If these drives are thwarted at the very beginning it is highly probable that the whole development of his instincts of curiosity may be seriously arrested and the once bright and enquiring child may turn into a dull and uninterested one. In regard to the child's intellectual growth, the modern tendency to make infant education a responsibility of society as well as of the parents is an excellent thing. For early teaching no less than late is an expert art.

In addition, the young child's parental objects must be affectionate ones. He must feel that they love and prize him, and that his presence and physical nearness gives them much pleasure. This not only allows him to give free rein to his feelings of love for them but lays down a lasting sense of being liked, which adds much to his happiness throughout later life. Furthermore, such an attitude on his elders' part, by indulging his infantile narcissism and self-grandiosity, gives him a permanent feeling of self-confidence, which makes him able henceforward to bear hardship and frustration with a hopeful mind. (The lastingness of these attitudes and their independence of later events being, of course, to a great extent due to the fact that these authoritative objects become a permanent part of his mind in the shape of his super-ego.) Nothing, of course, can exceed the importance of the child's parents as loving objects; and here, naturally, the role of the mother is paramount. It is very important, too, that the child's elders should be on friendly terms with one another. For it is both painful and bewildering for him to notice that those people whom he loves and admires hate and despise each other; and the super-ego which such objects set up is bound to be a hostile and conflictual one.

Furthermore, the emotional conflicts which are peculiar to the small child should be mitigated as far as possible. Its early ambivalence, for instance, can be lessened by seeing to it that he has more than one parental object, so that he can distribute his love and his hatred on to separate persons. Again, the full impact of the Oedipus situation should be avoided. The child should have other, less important and less revered objects besides his parental ones, in the shape of brothers and sisters or playmates, upon whom he can vent some of his Oedipal love and hatred and with less anxiety. These small companions also help to decrease his anxiety by joining in his activities and imaginings and so sharing his guilt about them. A family of more than one child is, from this point of view, generally better than a family of only one; and nursery schools are, once again, greatly to be recommended.

Last but not least, the small child should be protected, as far as possible, from traumatic experiences. Witnessing sexual scenes, especially between grown-up persons—in particular his parents—having sexual advances made to himself, seeing dreadful sights, being attacked or abused or beaten, being present while angry quarrels are going on between its parents or while one of them is violently excited or drunk—things like these, impinging upon a mind which is not yet fit to deal with the intensity or the quality of the excitations which they arouse in it, may well set up repressions and fixations in the child which have their revenge later on.

Proneness to become the leader of a regressive group should be dealt with along these lines at an early age, too. In this respect, children should be given reasonable scope not only for their narcissism and self-grandeur, but for their instincts of domination and aggression, for their ambition to excel and for their need to assert themselves. These states of mind must also be allowed to play themselves out, so that the child can the more easily outgrow what is excessive about them and adapt them to reality later on. At the same time, other instincts and attitudes should be encouraged in him, so as to offer him alternative modes of outlet for his psychic energy.

*   *   *

In thus mitigating the subject's group-proneness by bringing his mental development up to date, we shall, furthermore, be killing two birds with one stone; for we shall not only help him overcome trends which conduce to regressive group-mentality; we shall also help him overcome trends—first and foremost, those based on his destructive instincts—which are much stronger during his infantile stages and which make him dangerous abroad as well as at home, apart from his group-mentality.

But to carry out these recommendations is by no means easy.

Take to begin with the recommendation of allowing the little child as much gratification as possible of his instincts. As we know, some of those instincts are extremely strong and his ego is only able to cope with a very small quantity of undischarged mental energy; yet it is precisely those instincts which undergo extensive frustration. His oral-sucking instincts are thwarted on a grand scale by the process of weaning; his anal-erotic and urethral instincts are similarly thwarted by his nursery training in cleanliness, and so are his infantile genital ones in regard to his masturbatory activities and his

Oedipal wishes. The best that can be done is to check those instincts gradually and fairly late, so as to give them time to run their course and to yield to natural processes of development, to do it in such a way that the child shall not become frightened and guilty about them and angry with or frightened of his upbringers, and to offer him every possible substitutive outlet for them. Nevertheless, even so, he is bound to feel their prohibition as a not inconsiderable frustration, and to respond to it with repressions and fixations of them and the obnoxious wishes which their prohibition arouses in him.

The only absolutely safe method would appear to be to gratify the small child's instincts immediately and completely and for as long as he wants. But this often clashes with the requirements of reality and with the claims of society, especially modern society. Take the case of his oral-sucking instincts. The ideal thing would be never to wean him at all, but to let him suck the breast whenever he wanted to, so that he could enjoy this pleasure, as primitive children sometimes do, long after he had learned to walk and talk and eat roast meat. In the same way, it might be best never to train him in cleanliness, to let him continue to urinate and defecate when, where and how he pleases. In good time, these component instincts would then die down of themselves, gradually giving way to, or becoming absorbed in, other, more advanced ones. To give free rein to such instincts and to allow them to be gratified as long as they persist would, however, make life very difficult for the adult members of the family, besides often endangering the physical well-being of all concerned, including the child himself. To have to suckle her children, even sporadically, for many years, would greatly handicap the other activities of a woman; and dirty habits spread disease everywhere. The oral-biting instinct is still more of a problem. For, even though time might of itself cure the small child of wanting to bite through his mother's nipples, he obviously cannot be allowed to indulge this wish even temporarily, but must be restrained from enacting it as soon as it makes its appearance. And so, for that matter, must he be in regard to many of his other impulses. He cannot, for instance, be permitted to swallow pins or grasp a red-hot coal or strangle his baby brother—aims which, at any moment, may be his principal ambition. Even his permissible desires cannot always be immediately satisfied or satisfied to the full. The infant's mother may happen to be away just when it begins to want its milk, or her milk may run out or not taste nice; and some time must pass before these faults are put right, during which it is exposed to the tension of unfulfilled desires.

Furthermore, many component instincts are incompatible with one another, so that a gratification of the one entails a frustration of the other. If a little girl wants to dash her doll to pieces on the ground, she can do it, and if she wants to nurse it she can do that; but if she wants to do both at the same time, she cannot. She must either inhibit her desire to dash it to pieces or her desire to nurse it. It is not the grown-ups who frustrate her instincts, but the instincts themselves.

It must be remembered, finally, that even if the child's up-bringers give it permission to enact its instinctual impulses freely, this is not enough. They must themselves enact them, too. Otherwise the child, as soon as it has reached the age when it observes what is going on around it, will see that such things are not done by them; and since its ideas of what is right and wrong are as much based on imitation of them as upon obedience to them, it will judge that it, too, should not do those things, and it will, under the guidance of its super-ego, itself undertake frustrations and repressions of those instincts in spite of its elders. Thus, for instance, in order to enable a small child to bite and attack others, to be wet and dirty, to practise masturbation, etc., to its heart's content, its elders must do likewise in its presence. And this is apt to go against the grain. Moreover, such behaviour on their part is often calculated to strike terror into the small child, giant figures with unlimited strength as they must appear to him. To see huge persons, in whose power one is, kicking and screaming with rage—a rage which might at any moment be directed to oneself—cannot but be appalling, and

*

it is likely to set up a super-ego which is far more ferocious than a super-ego founded upon well-behaved parents, however strict and prohibiting.

Emotional conflicts, too, are not possible to avoid or easy to resolve in the small child. Its ambivalence is based upon a conjunction of love and hatred which, owing to their strong oral and anal sadistic components are not easily separated out by being distributed over different objects. Again, however kind and tolerant to it the parent of the same sex as itself may be, there comes a time when its Oedipal attitude is bound to make it hate him or her in a way that clashes violently with its love of that same person.

Traumas are not things either from which small children can always be shielded. They are bound, sooner or later, to undergo some kind of shock. They fall down suddenly, or hurt themselves, or have a severe illness, or they see an accident. Nor can parents be absolutely certain of preventing other children from attacking it or making sexual advances to it (and even if they could and did do so, it might be at the cost of frustrating the aggressive or sexual instincts of the older children so that if *it* was saved, *they* would suffer). Other inevitable events can also constitute a trauma. The sudden loss by death of a loved mother may leave the little child unable to dispose of its libido elsewhere or give it a sense of being utterly unprotected from external and internal dangers, and thus fill it with an intolerable quantity of anxiety. And when all is said and done, every individual has to begin his life by being born; and the nervous upheaval and mental excitations set up by that event are, perhaps, the greatest trauma of all.

Moreover, owing doubtless to innate constitutional differences, infants seem to vary from the very beginning of their lives in the quantity and kind of stimulus which are traumatic for them. It is not possible to know exactly beforehand what stimulus will be traumatic and what will not for any given child. In order, therefore, to make certain that no child shall experience a trauma we shall have to protect every child from receiving all except the smallest degree of stimulus in any form. And this would be a practical impossibility.

Besides, it is probable that such a course would do more harm than good. Some amount of excitation is necessary to the mind in order to set it in motion at all. The stronger that excitation is, the more vigorously it activates the mind and, up to a certain limit—which again varies from child to child —the more it encourages the ego to exert itself and to expand its activities in its efforts to cope with the excitation and find a suitable discharge for it. Thus, in cutting off the child from any considerable stimulus of any kind, we should, in all likelihood, be stunting its mental development. This means, too, that the child becomes less able than it would otherwise be to deal with any future stimulus which may impinge upon it; and since one set of stimuli, namely its instinctual ones, are bound to do so in great force, regardless of external circumstances, it is more liable to experience them as a trauma and to respond to them by a pathological alteration of its mental disposition than it would be if it had already received and learned to master other stimuli.

Indeed, the absence of instinctual frustration might well be a disadvantage to the small child, too. A certain amount of non-gratification of instinct increases the activity of the mind in a practical as well as an imaginative and intellectual way, since it not only increases the excitations there but spurs the ego on to seek alternative channels of discharge for the instinct in substitutive actions, phantasies and derivative ideas. Complete and immediate gratification of every instinct might retard the development of the ego by giving it no motive to exert itself, and such unreserved gratification might also retard the development of the id by giving it no motive to move on from one stage to the next. Here it is a matter of finding the just mean. Too much frustration of an instinct makes the child loath to give it up, because that instinct is still clamouring for gratification; too little frustration of it makes him loath to leave it because of the intense pleasure he has experienced from it. It is a matter, too, of timing as well as of degree. The frustration should take place after the child has received both a good deal of gratification and gratification over a considerable period of time, so that it occurs not only when his id has been fully gratified but when it is ready to move on to the next stage of its own accord and in the natural course of its development. Children once again differ from one another very much in the amount of frustration they can tolerate at each stage of their instinctual development and in the rate at which they naturally pass from one stage to the next. It is possible to some extent to tell from ordinary psychological observation how the mind of each infant is constituted in these respects, so that the amount of gratification which it needs and the period of time over which it needs it, could be assessed in a rough and ready sort of way; but in default of a precise knowledge of its mental make-up it is better to avoid the greater evil of undergratification and to lean to the lesser one of overgratification. This means, however, that we should still have to indulge small children in their wishes to an extent which would be highly inconvenient for the rest of the world, and not always good for their own physical health. The same is true about the small child's conflicts of feeling. Provided they are not too strong, they may well be one of the factors which, by exercising the synthesizing and distributive functions of the ego, assist in its development. But the trouble, once more, is to know what, for each child, is the optimum amount of conflict, and, even if we knew it, to ensure that it shall have neither more nor less than this optimum.

Even offering the small child substitutive gratifications of his unpermissible impulses is beset with difficulties. It often happens that displaced aims and objects which seem to outsiders to be adequate to take over much of the cathexis of his original aims and objects are not so from his point of view. This may be due to a variety of reasons. He may distrust the motives of his elders who offer him this alternative mode of gratification and think that it will do him harm. Or else it may still be too closely associated with the original mode to be tolerable to his ego or super-ego; or it may not be closely associated enough to have any true value of this kind; or the original impulse may be so deeply repressed or so strongly fixated that no alternative path of discharge can allow it to come to light or can take its place. If, for instance, a small girl wants to tear her mother to pieces and is given a rag doll to tear to pieces instead, she may be unable to do so, either because the rag doll is not sufficiently remote from her original object to make the action allowable, or because what most makes her want to tear her mother to pieces is her harsh voice and dolls do not have voices, or because her rage against her mother is so great that nothing short of tearing a live person will satisfy her.

And, of course, there is always the danger of forcing the child to indulge in activities which seem harmless to us, but which are by no means so in its eyes.

For the same reasons it is not easy to mobilize the child's imaginative activities to help in discharging its impulses in phantasy instead of in action. Apart from the difficulty of knowing what its *unconscious* phantasies are, so that we cannot bring them out, we shall often not succeed in getting the child to elaborate and reinforce its *conscious* ones. Moreover, it is not always a good thing to encourage them actively. For, once more, they are often obnoxious to the child as being too closely connected with the desires which gave rise to them so that it cannot bear to have them expanded, and such an enforced expansion does more harm than good; or else they are already too remote from those desires to have an abreactive effect, so that although it can bear to have them expanded and this has no ill effects, there is no use in doing so—and, indeed, not much expansion will take place, as the child is not interested.

Then, too, the degree to which the child's realistic ego can be strengthened by extending its field of knowledge and by teaching it how to think correctly is often conditional upon deep emotional factors. Since its instinct of curiosity is largely founded upon curiosity about sexual matters, and since these arouse in it erotic impulses and affects of rage and jealousy which have to be extensively repressed, its sexual curiosity is often repressed along with them, so that it does not want to know anything about such matters and no amount of sexual enlightenment enlists its interest. In addition to this it often prefers its own imaginary explanation of such matters, based upon its pregenital impulses; and, moreover, it employs these imaginary explanations to prevent itself from knowing the true explanation, if that explanation is unpleasurable to it. As a result, the child may be interested in nothing or unable to learn anything; or it concocts wildly distorted versions of what it has been told.

Again, the adoption of a loving and reasonable attitude by the child's parents towards him does not do as much as might be hoped in the way of inspiring him with a lasting attitude of trust and goodwill towards others or giving him a super-ego which is friendly and concordant with the rest of his mind; for, as we have seen, his parents are bound to thwart many of his desires and so, in some part of his mind at least, he can hardly avoid regarding them as unkind. Moreover, convinced as he is of their omnipotence, he is apt to regard any check to his desires and any unpleasure which he experiences as due to their wish, rather than to the necessities of the case, so that the many misfortunes he meets with from chance and circumstance are laid at their door. If he falls ill, *they* have ordained his illness; if he is hurt in an accident, *they* have staged the accident; if he is turned away from the circus because the seats are full up, *they* have made this happen. And in so far as he does not regard these misfortunes as merited punishment for his own wickedness, he regards them as being due to their deliberate cruelty.

The love and care which the child's elders show him may to some extent help him to overcome these hostile and distrustful attitudes to them. But they often fail to come into contact with the underlying causes of that attitude, which are deep-seated and unconscious and so fail to affect it at all. Indeed if they do come into contact with that attitude without relating it back to its causes the results may be more unhappy than if they had made no contact at all. The child may regard his parents' professed love as a trap to gain his confidence in order that they may know more about his obnoxious thoughts and punish him with corresponding severity; or he may regard it as mere hypocrisy, designed to conceal from others their hatred of him. Or, since he loves as well as hates them, their very kindness to him may fill him with a dreadful sense of guilt and remorse for his hatred of them and make him feel that he merits their utmost displeasure, so that he shrinks away from them with fear and self-abhorrence. In addition, it must be remembered that, after a certain age, the child is all the time wrestling with his sexual instincts and that these, too, are primarily directed to his parental objects. Any marked demonstration of love from them may excite those imperfectly mastered instincts, so that he has to put up an extra strong defence against them. As a result he may have to renounce not only his crudely sexual impulses towards them, but the whole of his libidinal attitude, which rests upon those impulses, and to replace his feelings of affection, tenderness and trust by an attitude of coldness or indifference. He may even have to replace them by feelings of distrust and suspicion, since, as we know, he is apt to regard their demonstrations of love for him and their bodily care of him as attempts at sexual seduction.

There is one final difficulty in the situation. This is that it involves not only violent and complicated emotional attitudes on the part of the child towards his parents and upbringers, but almost equally violent and complicated emotional attitudes on their part towards him. To begin with, he is the prime object of his mother's and father's parental instincts. This instinct is charged with libido, seeing that it is designed to cherish and protect the child; and it is especially so in the case of the mother, at any rate during the earliest part of the child's life, on account of the important activities which she must carry out in the way of feeding, cleaning and generally looking after him while he is yet an infant-in-arms. Nevertheless, the parental instinct is not entirely libidinal. Certain quantities of destructive cathexis are present too. Parents—even mothers—cannot avoid hating their children as well as loving them, though the proportion of hatred to love may be very small. This ambivalence is, of course, greater towards the children of the same sex as the parent than it is towards the children of the opposite sex, owing to the powerful operation of the heterosexual instincts. A father loves his sons with a greater admixture of hatred than he does his daughters; and a mother is less exclusively fond of her daughters than she is of her sons. Moreover, parental ambivalence towards the child of the same sex is greatly increased during the time that the child is in the Oedipal position, since the father can scarcely avoid responding with hostility to his son's hatred of him and his desire to oust him from his mother's side, nor the mother avoid being angry with her daughter for wanting to supplant her with the father.

Furthermore, the child is not merely the *original* object of his parents' instincts and affects. He is also a vicarious object of them. His parents tend to displace on to him instincts and affects which were originally directed to other objects. In especial, they are inclined to revive in respect of him their own infantile family situation. They tend to reverse the situation and have the same attitude to him as one or other of their parents had to them (or as they thought that parent had). If the relationship between themselves and their parents was a happy one, well and good. But if it was not, they are liable to visit their sufferings on their child's head. If a woman, for instance, feels that, as a child, she had always been out-rivalled and put in the shade by her mother, she is apt always to be outrivalling and outshining her own daughter; and if the father felt as a child that he was despised by his own father for his feeble performances, he is apt to treat his own son with contempt, however undeservedly.

Needless to say, most of the hostility which parents entertain towards their children is not conscious. And, whether conscious or not, they naturally strive to counteract it, on account of their natural love of their children, their sense of responsibility to them, and the unpleasure which they feel at the idea of hating them. This they do by means of the usual defensive mechanisms of repression, inhibition, reactive formation, overcompensation, projection, etc. These mechanisms, however, do not always work in the most desirable way possible. If, for instance, a parent projects his hostility to his child on to it, he no longer hates it, but he believes that it hates him and is grieved and indignant at it for this, so that his attitude towards it, though changed, is not improved; or if he *reacts* against his hostility to it, he will have a great deal of love and care for it; but it is love and care of an anxious, overdone sort which is calculated to spoil and coddle the child rather than to make it care-free and self-reliant. Nor are these defensive mechanisms always altogether effective. The impulses which they strive to ward off are generally strong enough to infiltrate through them, at least partially, and to make themselves felt to a greater or lesser extent. The parent who does all he can to inhibit and repress his desire to injure his child does, nevertheless, often manage to hurt or injure it involuntarily. He forgets to get its shoes mended, so that it gets wet feet and catches a cold, or he slams the door by accident on its fingers, or he omits, out of absent-mindedness, to keep his promise to take it to the zoo or to show it a picture-book, or he makes a hasty and unjust criticism of it, and so on.

Nor can a parent always hide his unwished-for emotional attitudes to his child from it, however well he succeeds in hiding them from himself; for the intimate ties of love and dependence and long familiarity which bind the child to him make it extremely sensitive to every shade of feeling in him towards it and enable it to divine what is going on in him from the slightest external signs—a faint inflection of the voice, a tiny lift of the eyebrow, an almost imperceptible tightening of the lips—indications which are quite involuntary and of which he may be totally unaware; and if the signs are unfavourable, so, too, will be the child's response to them.

Chapter XVII

THE PSYCHO-ANALYTIC METHOD

so far, the recommendations we have been able to make on the strength of our psycho-analytic knowledge do not seem very promising.

There is, however, a more radical method of approach. When Freud first began practising as a nerve specialist he made considerable use, among other therapeutic techniques, of hypnosis and hypnotic suggestion. He met with a certain amount of success with it, but not enough to satisfy him. Far too often a symptom which had vanished at his command came back after a time, when his influence over the patient's mind had waned; and then the treatment had to be repeated, usually at shortening intervals, until it failed to work altogether. Or else the symptom would only be exchanged for another. Again, many patients objected to submitting to the treatment in the first instance and would not even try it; others, though they tried could not be hypnotized. Yet others did become hypnotized, but failed in that state to respond to his suggestions; they paid no heed to him whatever he said, or they obeyed him in everything except losing their symptoms. Occasionally they even responded negativistically, doing the opposite of what they were told; and their symptoms grew worse than before.[1]

[1] Psycho-analysis, incidentally, is able to throw some fresh light upon the nature and mode of operation of hypnosis and hypnotic suggestion. As can be seen, one of the things that happens in hypnosis is that, as in sleep, the mind has undergone systematic regression. Its critical and reality-testing faculties are in abeyance so that it accepts as true any idea that comes into it, and its inhibitory capacity is lowered so that it readily carries out its conative ideas in action; and, in the deeper states of hypnosis at any rate, regression to the sensory system can take place so that the mind translates its ideas into a corresponding hallucination. Furthermore, in the absence

But two interesting facts had begun to emerge. These were firstly, that the removal of symptoms was facilitated and their

of an effective ego or super-ego (for both these agencies have, of course, been greatly reduced by the regression) the subject obeys his hypnotist's commands involuntarily, indeed automatically. It is as though the hypnotist had stepped into their shoes and was constituting an auxiliary ego and super-ego in him. Freud considered that the mental attitude of the hypnotized person to his hypnotizer could be equated to the mental attitude of the rank-and-file member of a regressive group towards his leader. (Cf. his *Group Psychology*, pp. 78 and 100, where he describes the hypnotic situation as a group of two, a leader and a follower.) Developmental regression also takes place. The subject reverts to a period of childhood when he had exceedingly strong and almost exclusive attachments to certain external objects upon whom he felt completely dependent and whom he not only loved but looked up to in every way in the highest degree. These, needless to say, were his original parental figures. It is these imagos which the hypnotist revives and embodies, and in virtue of which he exercises much of his power over his patients.

The role of the hypnotizer as the representative of his subjects' infantile parental imagos has naturally received a good deal of attention from psycho-analytic quarters. It has been found that he can stand not only for the all-powerful and infallible father, but for the equally (though earlier) all-powerful and infallible mother, or for a mixture of both in varying proportions. Which it is to be depends on the one hand upon which of the two had most power over the subject's mind in the stage to which he has regressed and, on the other hand, upon whether the hypnotizer behaves in a paternal or a maternal fashion towards him. For, whilst some hypnotists proceed by issuing stern orders to their patients, and behaving in an impressive manner and exacting obedience from them through awe rather than love, as would a father, others play a mother's part, using gentler forms of approach and seeking to persuade rather than command. In his paper, 'Introjection and Transference', Ferenczi discusses these two kinds of hypnotic relationships, which he calls 'father-hypnosis' and 'mother-hypnosis' respectively. It is of course a fact that there are many more male hypnotists than female ones; and in so far as this is not merely the result of social prejudice, it points to a special aptitude of the former for the role. This, however, need not mean that the infantile parental imago which they embody is that of the father; it may well be that they are also best suited to embody the infantile mother-imago in all its ancient greatness and power.

Long before the days of Freud, too, it was well-known that women patients were apt to regard being hypnotized as a sexual procedure and to have all sorts of phantasies during hypnosis of having sexual relationships with their hypnotizer. Psycho-analysis has shown that *every* person unconsciously regards hypnotism as a sexual procedure and that male patients are not exempt. In this, they, like female patients, sustain a feminine role, and a specially passive one at that. Both feel themselves to be submitting to the sexual advances of their hypnotizer and even being sexually assaulted by him. This is no doubt partly due to the passive and quiescent attitude, both mental and physical, and often the recumbent position which they are required to adopt by their operator and to the mentally active and dominating part which he plays towards them, as also to some of the physical measures which he uses on them. But, of course, their own feminine and passive impulses have a great share in creating this imaginary situation and the stronger these are, the more will the subject respond to it and fall under the hypnotist's spell. The only exception to this is when, as sometimes happens, especially with men, the patient's passive-feminine impulses are so repugnant to him that they are strongly resisted by him even in hypnosis, or that they prevent him from allowing himself to be hypnotized at all.

[Continued on page 244

recurrence made less likely if the hypnotist, before suggesting that they should disappear, first found out what the occasions, or series of occasions, were which had precipitated them, and secondly, that though the occasions were often unknown to the patient in his normal waking state, they were frequently known to him in hypnosis, or could become so with a little persuasion and suggestion on the part of his operator.

This new procedure, moreover, introduced a fresh element into the picture. The hypnotized patient, instead of merely *remembering* the events which occurred in the pathogenic situation, would often *re-live* them as though they were actually happening at the moment, and would feel once again the emotions and impulses which they had aroused in him at the time; and it was this emotional re-experiencing of the scene in consciousness which seemed to have the main curative effect, largely in virtue of the discharge of excitation which it entailed.

This Cathartic Method or Method of Abreaction, as it was called, shed a flood of light upon the unconscious mind, and the discoveries which Freud made by means of it formed the basis of his psycho-analytic theory. But as a therapeutic instrument it, too, proved relatively disappointing. One weakness was that, as in the original method of suggestion, the patients had to be put into a hypnotic state before they could revive their pathogenic experience. Freud was thus still

Although ordinary influencibility is not the same in kind as hypnotic suggestibility, there is little doubt that the average mortal has enough of the unconscious in himself to add a certain amount of such suggestibility to his capacity to be influenced by others in his normal waking life—a capacity which, as we have seen, is itself usually greater than would be expected in an adult person, owing to his inadequately surmounted infantile and passive attitudes and the continuing operation of his unconscious system at the expense of his preconscious one. In this lies the strength of such things as advertisement, propaganda and smear-campaigns. If a thing is stated often enough and in loud enough tones or large enough letters, it will not only impress itself upon the minds of the receiver as something to be attended to, investigated and accepted or rejected according to its merits; it will be accepted without judgment. Hitler knew this well when he said 'The bigger the lie' (and the more thumpingly told and often repeated) 'the more it will be believed.' Often, too, the suggestive operation is reinforced and disguised by ordinary rational influence, so that the recipient swallows its absurdity more easily. It is easier, for instance, to make Aryans believe that all Jews are wicked if, as well as saying so very loudly and persistently, one adduces a real example of a wicked Jew.

faced with the old difficulty that so many patients were recalcitrant to hypnotic influence. As he himself complained, he was tired of saying to his patient 'Now you are asleep' and, upon receiving the all-too familiar answer 'But, Doctor, I'm *not* asleep', of having nothing better to reply than, 'Yes you are; you only imagine you are not', when it was perfectly obvious to both that his patient was as wide awake as ever.

The second difficulty was that even when a patient had been successfully hypnotized and induced to re-experience the pathogenic situation, he did not always lose his symptoms, or if he did it was not for long. True, the impulses and affects which had been denied discharge in his normal waking state found discharge in abreaction under hypnosis, so that when he came back to that waking state their pressure was relieved and the symptoms gone; but nothing had been changed in the position of his normal waking mind, and the excitations concerned could find no more adequate outlet or association with his preconscious after the abreaction than before, so that as the excitations once more mounted up the symptoms reappeared. Abreaction is only certain to be successful where the main pathogenic factor is a single, non-recurring stimulus —as, say, in the case of some trauma like a railway accident or a bad shock.

Freud had meanwhile become greatly interested in the work of Liébeault and Bernheim at Nancy. He went to Nancy and observed the great successes that were being scored by their methods of suggestion. He was especially impressed by Bernheim's experiments in effecting the reproduction of memories which could not be recalled at will. Without putting the subjects into a hypnotic state before suggesting to them that they should recall those memories, Bernheim contented himself with encouraging them to do so in their normal waking state, and with assuring them that if they made a real effort and concentrated their will and attention upon it, they would succeed. If the subjects did not respond to his urgings, the most he did in the way of giving them active assistance was to say, 'When I press your forehead with my hand the lost memory will come back to you', and then proceed to do so. This device was usually successful. When the patient felt the pressure of his operator's hand upon his forehead the relevant ideas, or some of them, would reappear in consciousness, either as a direct memory or as a set of new images or perceptions or ideas.

Freud was so much taken by the performance of this 'Pressure Technique' as he calls it, that he soon began to use it instead of hypnosis as an adjunct to the Cathartic method. And this he continued to do over a number of years.

The cathartic method, however, was often a somewhat lengthy business. For the patient's symptoms were usually the product of a *summation* of repressed affective experiences, each of which had to be restored to consciousness and abreacted before it ceased to have a pathogenic effect. As a rule, too, they were restored in the reverse order of their occurrence, so that the earliest of them was the last to appear; and it was precisely this one which was the most important from a curative point of view, and most likely to remove the patient's illness for good and all.

Freud found, too, that his patients were not always able to conjure up the required experience at his bidding, however much he drew their attention to it and they concentrated their thoughts on it. This was especially the case when the treatment was carried on with the sole use of pressure technique, as was now his practice. For then the patients remained in their normal waking state—or very nearly so—so that their ego and super-ego functions were practically unimpaired, and their resistance to the dystonic material was almost as strong as ever—certainly much stronger than in hypnosis. Nor were they so amenable to their operator's will. Thus it was by no means the first spontaneous idea which arose under his pressure that was the wanted one; the technique had often to be repeated over and over again before this happened. And sometimes nothing relevant emerged at all.

Nevertheless, Freud knew enough about the unconscious by now to realize how strongly and unceasingly the repressed emotional experience was seeking expression. He consequently felt sure that any conscious idea or image or memory, however seemingly irrelevant, which came into the patient's mind when he turned his attention to his repressed experience (or to his symptoms as its representative) and tried to recover it was likely to be in some way derived from it, however distant, devious and obscure the derivation might be and however much alloyed with contributions from other sources; and he was convinced that a way back from those conscious mental presentations to the unconscious one behind them could be found. Moreover, his study of dreams was beginning to teach him a great deal about symbolism and the unconscious meaning of conscious ideas. Thus he could now not only make sense of many of the apparently nonsensical thoughts which formed part of the ideational content of symptoms and dreams, but could satisfy himself that many of the apparently irrelevant ideas which arose in the patient's mind when he thought about his symptom or the occasion of it, or fixed his mind on the missing experience, were not irrelevant at all. Furthermore, dreams themselves, as containing highly cathected mental elements, could now be seen to provide a starting-point for the recovery by this means of unconscious material.

So eager, indeed, is the nexus of repressed ideas to come to light that it is not only by concentrating his mind on it or on his symptom or on his dreams that the patient can have spontaneous ideas that are derived from it and that may lead back to it. *Any* ideas which occur to him spontaneously, without any previous orientation of his attention, are likely to be in part descended from it, so that there will be some path of association, however circuitous, along which he may be able to retrace his steps.[1]

[1] Similarly ideas which are put before him from outside may furnish him with a way back to the repressed experience, provided they have some associative chain of connection with it which his mind can exploit. This fact is made use of for diagnosing possible complexes as well as for other purposes by the well-known modern psychological method of 'Word-Association', in which the subject is presented with a list of words chosen at random and betrays the nature of his complex by the emotional way in which he reacts to those of them which are significantly associated with it.

[Continued on page 248

It was not long, therefore, before Freud ceased to make his patients start their spontaneous conscious ideas from those or any other special points of departure and let them begin where they liked.

Furthermore, he gradually abandoned the pressure technique and came to rely for the eliciting of the material solely upon the method of free association—i.e., the spontaneous occurrence of one or more ideas in succession to a given idea.[1]

All he did now was to ask his patient to put himself into as relaxed a state of mind as possible, to adopt an uncritical attitude to all the ideas and images that passed through his consciousness, and, beginning anywhere he chose, to tell them to him without reservation. In order to facilitate this relaxed state Freud would get the patients to lie on a sofa, and in order not to disturb their train of thought he sat behind them out of their sight.

This procedure, however, had the disadvantage of being even longer than that of pressure technique, and at times very tedious; for the patient's thoughts, left to start where they liked and to proceed how they chose, were apt to wander off into many by-paths before they got near the pathogenic material. Besides this, they encountered many difficulties in their approach which they could not overcome without extraneous assistance. This greatly added to Freud's task. On the other hand, it was in encountering and learning to sur-

---

Indeed, almost any idea which is put before the subject, or which he thinks of spontaneously or not, offers him a road of return; for almost any idea is ultimately connected by some associative chain or other with almost any other idea. If the need is strong enough that chain will be found and followed. Furthermore, most ideas are associated with most other ideas along more than one associative chain. This, incidentally, is what makes it possible, as so often happens, for a spontaneous idea which has emerged from some repressed material along one path of association to be traced back to that material through free associations that proceed along a different path.

[1] The regular term, 'free associations' has, unfortunately, two different meanings. It can mean, as it does here, spontaneous ideas that are associated merely in the sense that they now appear in the subject's conscious mind contiguously in time; or it can mean spontaneous ideas that were already associated together in this or any of the possible other ways *before* they thus appear contiguously. This is all the more confusing when, as is the case here, what is being asserted is that free associations in the first sense are also free associations in the second.

mount these difficulties that he acquired most of his understanding of the unconscious forces of the mind and most of
his knowledge of how to deal with them therapeutically.

To begin with, for instance, there nearly always came a
moment, sooner or later, when the patient disobeyed Freud's
injunction to tell his thoughts aloud. He would fall silent.
Upon being asked the reason for this he would sometimes
admit that he had stopped talking because he did not want
to say what was in his mind. Either it was too painful or too
embarrassing or too intimate or too absurd to tell; and it
needed a good deal of encouragement and persuasion on
Freud's part to get him to speak about it. This was perhaps
natural enough. But on other occasions the patient would
become silent not because it was disagreeable for him to say
what he was thinking, but because it seemed to him that what
he was thinking about was quite unimportant in itself and
could have no possible connection with the matter in hand.
In this case there appeared to be no sufficient reason why
the patient should have broken the rule, since there was no
great unpleasure involved in telling an idea whose only
demerit was that it was trivial or irrelevant. Further enquiry,
however, and further encouragement to speak what was in
his mind, soon revealed that there were very good reasons
for the patient's silence. It invariably turned out that the idea
in question was connected, in one way or another, with an
idea which had a very great emotional importance for the
patient and of which he did not want to be conscious, and
that he was unwilling to tell the conscious idea because he
did not wish to be led on, through it, to that unconscious idea.

Supposing, for instance, that a young man is describing a
detective story which he has been reading. He is in the middle
of relating a scene in which the hero discovers a dead body in
a trunk. The face of the corpse is so disfigured that the hero
does not recognize it at first. But he then identifies it from its
red hair as being that of an elderly acquaintance of his. At
this moment the patient stops speaking. On being asked why
he is silent, he says, 'Oh, quite a pointless idea has come into

my head; it has nothing to do with what I was telling you.'
Asked to tell the idea all the same, he continues, 'Well, I
suddenly wondered whether, when I became old, my hair
would fall out or become white. It is a little too carroty'. He
is urged to pursue his associations, and it then turns out that
he thinks of himself as the red-haired corpse—that is, that he
is afraid of being murdered. This fear goes back to certain
childhood scenes in which he used to tease and annoy his
younger sister, of whom he was very jealous; and he recalls
violent impulses to attack and hurt her which he consciously
had as a child and which represented an unconscious wish to
kill her—a wish which still exists in his mind. In consequence
of this wish he feels that he ought himself to be killed as a
just retribution for his murderous impulses. Thus he was
afraid to tell these apparently trivial thoughts about his hair,
for fear of giving away the guilty desires that lay behind them.

Finally, the patient might stop talking because there was in
fact no conscious idea in his mind whatsoever. This was nearly
always because the unconscious idea which was occupying it
was on the one hand so obnoxious that none of its derivatives
were acceptable to the preconscious, and on the other, so
powerful that no idea that was not a derivative of it could be
cathected. Here, once again, it took a lot of persuasion and
patience on Freud's part before the patient could be got to
admit the next idea into consciousness.

It sometimes happened, however, that no amount of urging
or encouragement or silent waiting could induce his patients
to tell him what was in their minds or to have any conscious
thoughts at all. Nevertheless, Freud was often able to infer
from what they had been saying just before they stopped
talking, as well as from the general context of their free
associations, what the idea was which they could not be
conscious of or could not tell. So, instead of merely urging
them to say or think something, or waiting patiently for them
to resume their associations, Freud began to tell them what
he believed they were thinking at the moment and why they
were resisting that thought. He found that, provided his

inference was correct, it often had the desired effect. If his patients had been conscious of the thought or feeling in question but had kept it back they usually assented to Freud's statement of it, and if they had not been conscious of it, they sometimes became so; and they were nearly always able to go on with their free associations. Similarly, when their resistance to an unconscious thought made them produce trivial or absurd or irrelevant ideas, an explanation of the probable nature of that thought led to the same satisfactory results.

Freud called his new technique of free association on the part of the patients and interpretation from his side the *Psycho-Analytic Method*. It was on this method alone that he henceforward relied in all his treatments.

Quite early on in his psycho-analytic work, Freud made a discovery which was of great significance both in its practical and theoretical bearings. It very often turned out that when his patients had a specially strong resistance to an idea, it was because they were afraid of his criticism of it, or, more important still, because the idea was about himself. When, for instance, after having stopped talking, they had once more been induced to say what was going on in their mind, they would often declare that what had made them stop was a feeling that Freud was not listening to them, or that he was not sympathetic enough to their troubles, or that he could not cure them; or they were afraid of displeasing or boring him by saying what they were thinking just then. Or if they said that they had had no ideas at all and that their mind had been a blank, it was often clear from what they had been saying before they stopped speaking or what they said after, that they had been repressing ideas about himself.

A patient, let us say, falls silent in the middle of talking about how he once had some money stolen from him. Upon being asked why he has stopped talking, he says, 'I suddenly noticed that the picture on the wall opposite was hanging crookedly. But it seemed such an irrelevant idea that I didn't

mention it.' However, on being reminded that no free association is irrelevant, he proceeds to talk about the crooked
picture. He wonders whether it is allowed to hang crooked
because Freud has not noticed it, or because he likes it that
way. He then mentions the figurative use of the words
'crooked' as meaning 'dishonest', and 'straight' as meaning
'honest'. After that he stops talking once more. But by now
it has begun to seem likely to Freud that the crooked picture
refers to himself. He is the person who lets it hang crooked
and, on the unconscious levels of the mind, a person's belongings are often the same as himself. In addition, Freud recalls
that the patient has, earlier on in his associations, spoken of
having once been robbed by a confidence-trickster. Taking
all these facts together he infers that the patient's repressed
idea was that he (Freud) is stealing money from him; and he
makes an interpretation in this sense. The patient admits that
he may have been having ideas of that sort; for he cannot
help feeling that Freud is taking money from him on false
pretences, since he is not curing him fast enough. After this
his free associations resume their flow.

Freud found that when his patients' ideas about him were
kept back or repressed it was not always because they were
unfriendly. On the contrary, they were often suppressed
because they were too friendly, or involved feelings of a too
intimate or even an erotic kind. A male patient, for instance,
might have an idea of Freud's throwing his arm round his
shoulder in a protective way, and this somewhat remote
derivative of his passive homosexual instincts might be more
than his masculine ego could tolerate. Or a female patient
might entertain the thought of his giving her a kiss, and that
might be a very embarrassing thing for her to have to tell
him if she was inclined to be a prude. Quite crudely sexual
feelings and ideas, too, were often aroused in his patients
towards him, and this created one of the strongest resistances
of all to the production of free associations.

Though somewhat taken aback by this unexpected development, Freud decided to accept his patients' ideas about himself

just as he did the rest of their free associations and interpreted them in the same way. The results which he obtained from this procedure threw much new light upon the analytic situation as also upon kindred ones (notably the hypnotic situation).

It turned out that the patients regularly developed a special attitude to their analyst, owing to the peculiar circumstances of the treatment. In it, as we know, they are in an inferior position to him, being ill while he is well, and they are in a dependent one, too, since they are seeking help from him. They are also in a passive position towards him, since it is he who conducts the treatment and they do what he asks (and, incidentally, they are lying down while he is sitting up). Furthermore, they are alone with him and close to him. In addition, they have to say to him whatever is in their mind, however private or intimate it may be and however much they feel it may shock or anger or excite him. These circumstances combine to create in them what might be termed an 'analytic' *rapport* (on an analogy with hypnotic *rapport*) in which love, trust, dependence, admiration, envy, fear, guilt and defiance all take a hand and in which passive-libidinal instincts, masochistic trends and exhibitionistic impulses play their part.

The patients' attitude to their analyst, moreover, was found to have a further significance. It soon became evident that their feelings and ideas about him were not solely concerned with him as himself. He was also the object upon whom they had for the time being displaced certain impulses, feelings and ideas which they had entertained and were still to a great extent unconsciously entertaining about another object. The male patient's belief that Freud was a crook would, say, turn out to be a displacement or a partial displacement of a belief that a friend of his had cheated him; and the female patient's wish that Freud should give her a kiss might be discovered to have been carried over from a wish that a young man of her acquaintance should make love to her. Such a displacement would, of course, only occur in so far as the patient could not, for some reason or other, adequately implement or be conscious of those desires and ideas in regard to their original objects. If the cheater had not been a friend of the male patient, the latter might have allowed himself to be aware that he was a cheater and would have had no need to regard Freud in that light; and if the man had returned the female patient's love she would not have wanted to be kissed by her analyst. Freud used often to refer to a displacement of the person's ideas and feelings about one object to another, as a 'transference' of them. When this displacement took place from an object to the psycho-analyst, he accordingly named it an *analytic transference* (often curtailed to '*transference*'). If the transference is of a hostile kind, involving fear, suspicion and hatred on the part of the patient towards his analyst, it is called a *negative* transference; if it is of a friendly kind, involving love, admiration and trust, it is called a *positive* one.

As was to be expected from the nature of the analytic relationship and the contents of the unconscious, it most often turned out that the object which the analyst represented to his patients was a parental figure; and if this seemed not to be the case at first it was usually because the immediate object he stood for was itself only a substitute for a parental one. In the rarer cases where the original object was not a parent or an elder, it was sure to be some other person out of the patient's early childhood. Thus Freud would find himself feared by one patient as a forbidding father or hated by another as an evil brother, or even loved by yet another as a tender mother; or he would find himself cast for all these roles in turn towards the same patient, according as the latter's various infantile attitudes and object-relationships came into play in the course of his free associations. Where very early situations were re-activated, he might even become a part-object.

The operation of the transference thus re-created a wealth of situations which had had importance for the patient during his early life and which still had importance for him in his unconscious. If, for instance, the woman patient who vainly loved a married man and had transferred some of that love to her analyst was kept waiting a little longer than usual in the waiting-room, she might not only be imagining that the female patient who came before her was being given a longer session than was her due because the analyst favouritized her, just as the man she loved preferred his wife to her; she might be reviving a scene in which, as a small child, she was being shut out of her parents' bedroom because her father was making love to her mother (or so she thought) in there—a scene which had aroused in her violent passions of jealousy that had had to be repressed on account of its own unpleasure as much as of her love and fear of her parents. And her jealousy and fear *now* will be correspondingly great.

It still remains to understand why interpreting an unconscious idea or feeling to their owner should enable him to become conscious of them. Certainly he becomes conscious of them in the sense that he is aware of them as being put before him by his analyst, and put before him as his own; and he may accept them in the sense that he quite consciously agrees that he must be harbouring such an idea or feeling in his mind. But neither of these things is a making conscious of an unconscious idea in the sense that is meant here. What is meant by it here is that a mental presentation belonging to the subject which has hitherto been unconscious to him should pass through the barrier of repression, so that he should be directly aware of it *as his own*, and should have, and be aware of having, the feelings belonging to it. As a matter of fact an interpretation often fails to achieve this. Very often the patient says, 'I quite understand the impulses and ideas which you are telling me about and I can see from what you point out that I must be having them, but I cannot, for the life of me, *feel* that I am having them!'

It is indeed only in particular circumstances that an interpretation can succeed in making an unconscious psychic presentation conscious in this immediate sense. In the first place it must be made about unconscious psychic material which is being activated at the moment in the patient's unconscious mind; for then the analyst need only reinforce it by putting it before his conscious mind from outside in order for it to gain admission there from within. If the material is not sufficiently highly cathected at the moment of his putting it before the patient then his doing so will not lend it enough added force to carry it through into consciousness. But even if the psychic elements in question are highly cathected, the reinforcement given to them by interpretation may not suffice to make them conscious. For if they are very obnoxious to the preconscious, the ego may increase its resistance to them, so that in spite of their added force they still remain unconscious. All that happens is that the conflict between them and it becomes more violent. Either no visible change occurs in the mind, or the symptoms are intensified or fresh ones accrue. In order, therefore, to be successful the interpretation must in the second place be applied to mental elements which are not only being activated to a significant degree but which are verging upon acceptance by the preconscious, either because they have become sufficiently modified or because it has become more tolerant of them. The interpretation must thus be given not only at the point of most activation but at the point of least resistance. These two points, of course, hardly ever coincide, so that the optimum point of interpretation is nearly always some compromise between them, which inclines now towards material which is comparatively lightly cathected but near the preconscious level, now towards material which, though more deeply unconscious, has a very intense cathexis.

Analytic interpretations, however, do not succeed entirely on their own merits. They also succeed because of the source from which they come. The libidinal attachments of the patients to their analyst make them want to believe what he says, and their reasonable trust in his *expertise* makes them ready to do so. (Though how much this latter purely rational and preconscious confidence in him lowers their resistance so that, apart from *agreeing* to the truth of what he says, they *accept* it in our sense of the word, is another matter.) Furthermore, the patient adopts, to some extent at least, a mentally submissive and infantile attitude to his analyst, who is his authoritative object and stands *in loco parentis* to him; nor is he quite as prompt to assert the critical and rejective functions of his mind as he is in ordinary life. For these reasons the interpretations which his analyst gives not only receive added weight but meet with a lowered resistance.

As in the case of the hypnotist and his subject, moreover, the analyst also partly stands in lieu of some of that portion of his ego and super-ego, small though it may be, which the patient has temporarily abrogated in the analytic *rapport*, so that whatever his analyst puts before him as true and acceptable he is rather more than ordinarily ready to receive as such. Thus his analyst's permissive attitude towards his repudiated ideas becomes in part his (the patient's) own attitude to them. What his analyst tolerates in him this new auxiliary piece of super-ego tolerates too, and gives leave to be conscious.

* * *

The rate at which psycho-analytic treatment proceeds is apt to be very variable. It has many temporary setbacks, owing to the arousal of specially obnoxious ideas and specially strong resistances to them at certain points; it makes sudden spurts forward after the resistance has been overcome; or it marks time while the resistance is being gradually worn down or while new dystonic material is being mobilized. But, as an over-all process the treatment is bound to be slow, and the fact that while the subject is undergoing the treatment he is in full (or almost full) possession of all his mental faculties, including most severely critical, realistic and moral ones, makes it a very laborious task compared to the rapid and brilliant cures which are often effected under hypnosis, where the subject has, for the time being, resigned so much more of those faculties into his operator's hands. Besides, interpretation can only be profitably given when the occasion offers, which is not always. The analyst has often to listen to a long string of associations, or to long silences, from his

I

patients before he can make out what they are occupied with in their unconscious and before he can find the right point at which to give his interpretation. The interpretation must also generally be given repeatedly (though each time in a slightly different form, of course, to suit the different situation in which it arises in the analysis) because the patient often needs to have it presented to his mind from outside more than once before he can accept the unconscious material to which it refers in consciousness. Finally, apart from accepting it consciously and from the abreactive effect of this, he needs time in which to accustom himself to it, to assimilate it to the rest of his mind and to modify it and adapt it to reality —to 'work through' it, as we say. Then again the interpretation can usually only be given piece-meal, in small doses as it were, because the patients cannot bear to become conscious of more than a small portion of their obnoxious ideas at a time. There is a limit to what their ego and super-ego can tolerate in the way of interpretation at any given moment even with the analyst's support, and it is his business to see that he does not overstep that limit, and that his interpretation is not only true and aimed at an effective spot but is appropriate to their capacities to master or discharge, both as to the intensity and the quality of the mental presentation which it arouses and seeks to make conscious. Otherwise, the patients will, at best, reject the interpretation or, at worst, be traumatically affected by it.[1]

Another important factor in the slowness of this process seems to be the reluctance of the mind to give up any position which it has attained and to which it is used—to some kind of conservatism or inertia or whatever it may be. Freud thought

---

[1] Indeed, there may well be more danger in giving a well-aimed but inappropriate interpretation than in giving a false one. For the latter, whether rejected by the patient or mistakenly agreed to, as it sometimes is, does not set up strong reverberations in his unconscious, since it does not correspond to anything in particular there. All it does is to hold up the analysis or falsify it for the moment; and such a falsification is only temporary, since the patient's subsequent free associations will soon put the matter right. (Of course I am not speaking here of *consistently* false interpretations which lead the analysis quite astray and also shake the patient's confidence in his analyst.)

that this conservatism was a particular feature of the ucs. Moreover, he was inclined to attribute a special constitutional quality of adhesiveness to the libido of psychoneurotics and other abnormal persons as compared to normal ones, so that it advanced less easily in their case from its old positions. Finally, the amount of psychic material which has gone in to the structure of the patient's illness is pretty formidable, going back as it does right through his life to his early childhood, and it is wrapped up in a still greater quantity of comparatively unobnoxious material which he produces in his free associations. Much of this must be gone through and elucidated before the core of the illness is reached and brought to light.

Nevertheless, psycho-analysis, though long, is not unending. It is often possible to interpret successfully large amounts of very obnoxious and highly cathected material at a time. Such interpretations, which sometimes tap very deep levels of the mind, can relieve the patient through abreaction of a great deal of mental excitation and clear the way for a big advance.

Moreover the analysis tends, as a whole, to quicken its pace as it proceeds. For in the course of it the preconscious is continually adding more psychic elements to itself from the unconscious. In this way the former gradually becomes enlarged and strengthened at the expense of the latter, which grows correspondingly weak, and the patient is able to tolerate in consciousness and to modify ever larger amounts of obnoxious material at a time. For this reason, too, it is not necessary for the whole of that material (or such derivatives of it as will secure a tolerable and sufficient discharge of its cathexes) to be made conscious *in the analysis* in order for him to be restored to health. For the preconscious is increasingly able to deal on its own with the products of the unconscious. They remain outside the analysis, yet they vanish away during it, quite of themselves, as it seems.

In the last twenty or thirty years, too, the increasing application of psycho-analysis to children has done much to shorten the average length of the treatment, since the pathological material that has collected round the original infantile core of the illness is so much less. Observable neuroses and even psychoses are not seldom met with in the very young, and they can be treated at a quite early age. The first of such cases—known as the case of Little Hans—was successfully conducted under Freud's supervision. It was that of a boy of five who had severe phobia of horses, so that he could not go out of the house for fear of meeting one. Still younger patients can now be treated, and in a more methodical way, by the technique of *Play Analysis*, as it is called, in which the small child's difficulty in lying still and clothing its thoughts in words has been got over by getting it to utter them in games of pretence or in play with toys, chosen by itself—a technique in which free association of ideas expressed in words is replaced by free association of ideas expressed in gestures, and in which all the other essential components of a classical adult analysis, such as interpretation and transference, are present. This technique which has been developed by Mrs. Melanie Klein, a psycho-analyst and a pupil of Karl Abraham, has not only proved eminently successful, but has been responsible for eliciting much of the psychical material present in the infantile mind which is now accepted as part of the analytic theory and of which we have got to know something in earlier chapters of this book.

There is no doubt, too, that many persons who have had to undergo a difficult and tedious analysis in adult life could have been spared this had they had an analysis in childhood. For not only was the illness, or at least the predisposition to it, almost certainly already present at that time so that an adult illness would have been avoided by child analysis; the illness, or its predisposition, was still in a formative stage and the amount of work needed to clear up the trouble then would not have been nearly so great. Thus it is to be expected that the number of child-analyses will progressively gain over the number of adult analyses, to the great advantage of the treatment in respect of its time-factor.[1]

[1] Not to mention other considerations, such as saving the subject many years of unhappiness or wasted effort that cannot be recovered, or preventing him from making important mistakes that cannot be unmade.

Psycho-analysis, moreover, aims at doing very much more than hypnotic suggestion or any of the other kinds of mental treatment which we have discussed. To begin with, it aims at bringing about a permanent removal of the patient's symptoms. Since, unlike hypnotic treatment, it is carried on while the patient is in full possession of his wits, the changes which it effects in his mind are not due to a temporary abeyance of his realistic and critical faculties. Thus when once his symptoms have been removed by it, they do not return when it is over.

Then, too, by having had their transference—or, to be exact, their analytic *rapport*—as well as their original fixations continually interpreted and made conscious as they go along, the patients have never been allowed to accumulate an undue amount of it. Thus the mental health which they recapture during the treatment is not dependent on their operator's continued efforts or presence or well-being or favourable attitude to them, etc., as is so often the case with hypnotic treatment. Indeed, as they get better and lose much of their unrealistic and infantile attitudes and fixations, their relationship to him should gradually change its character accordingly, becoming less unrealistic and infantile, too; until, with complete recovery, *rapport*—including *all* the transference—should have disappeared altogether, leaving nothing more than an atittude of friendliness, respect and, perhaps, gratitude for a job well done.

In addition to this, the range of patients which analysis can treat is much greater than is the case with hypnotism. Whereas hypnotism is best suited to symptoms which arise from repression, i.e. to hysterical symptoms, psycho-analysis can be successfully applied to the pathological products of many other abnormal states of mind—to any, in fact, where the subject has some degree of libidinal object-relationship and is ready to be treated.

Finally, and most important of all, psycho-analysis takes back the patient's mind to the original, infantile situations to which he responded on that occasion in a pathological way and which set the pattern of his later pathological responses; by correcting that first response, it enables him not only to get rid of the symptoms which he has formed, but to get rid of his tendency to *form* symptoms of that sort if he is confronted by similar experiences in the future. In other words it cures him not only of his illness but of his predisposition to it. And more than this. So wide-ranging are his free associations that there is no part of his unconscious which they do not in time touch upon; so that, given a faithful interpretation of them, a great deal of pathogenic, or potentially pathogenic, material not concerned with his particular illness is in due course searched out and corrected. Thus he is cured not only of his predisposition to the kind of mental illness which has overtaken him but of any other pathological predispositions which he may have and which, though they have not so far led to actual symptoms, are liable to do so. He is henceforward immune not only to his kind of illness and able to tolerate the sort of experiences which are likely to bring it on; he is immune to many—if not all—other kinds as well and can tolerate the sort of experiences which conduce to *them*.

Chapter XVIII

CONCLUSIONS

THERE is no doubt whatever that the psycho-analytic method provides us with an instrument which is able not only to cure mental illnesses and the predisposition to them but largely to correct those dispositions of mind of the averagely normal person which render him such a bad risk on the international scene.

This being so, it follows that our most important recommendation is that this method should be universally applied as a prophylactic measure.

But clearly such a programme is, at present at least, outside the bounds of practical possibility, if only for want of enough analysts. The next best thing to do, therefore, is to pick out those people whom it would be most profitable to analyse. These fall, I should say, into five categories. The first consists of persons who are more than ordinarily hostile, aggressive and destructive—persons who are in any case dangerous to others. The second consists of persons who have a marked instinct of domination—the natural leaders whose talents, if wrongly directed, can do so much harm. The third consists of all who occupy positions of authority over others or positions in which they have especial influence over the minds of others. The fourth consists of those whose life places them in situations which are highly charged with State-mentality. The fifth consists of persons who are exceptionally group-prone. Scientists, artists, engineers and business men, whose work does not put them in a position in which they govern human thought and action to any great extent, can be more safely left to their own devices than can, say, school-teachers, who come into contact with the powerful instinctual desires of the child and who must help it to master them, or those concerned with the prevention or punishment of crime, or politicians who guide the destiny of their nationals or who come up against this particular kind of group-mentality in some of its crudest forms and may be tempted to exploit it, or are themselves carried away by it.

Unfortunately, the most important class of persons indicated under the third heading—to whom, perhaps, even teachers come second—are parents of children. And since this class covers virtually the entire population there is no chance whatever of meeting the demand.

In addition to this excess of demand over supply, psycho-analysis is beset by another practical disability. This is that it can only be applied to people who have attained a requisite degree of civilization and whose reason and knowledge are sufficiently advanced for them to grasp all the implications of a modern war, and where it is mainly a matter of bringing a rebellious unconscious under the management of an informed but weak preconscious. This—until education has raised their understanding to the proper level—rules out many backward countries as beneficiaries of the method. Fortunately, so far, the sole possessors of world-destroying weapons are progressive countries, who have attained the necessary standards of enlightenment. But how long this will remain so, who can say?

Thus we see that the usefulness of psycho-analysis as a therapeutic *method* is bound to be extremely limited for many years to come. As far as more immediate measures are concerned, we must rather look to those recommendations which flow from it as a *theory*, as they have been put forward with qualified approval a few chapters ago. Nor should we under-rate the more conventional measures many of which are beginning in any case to find general acceptance and even tentative implementation. Improvements in the social, economic and political conditions of people everywhere, and in especial their educational advancement, should be pressed forward as fast as possible, and international relationships and organizations should be energetically fostered. For even if, as psycho-analysts and acquainted with the deeps of the mind, we are less optimistic than many about the success of such measures, we do not deny that they will do *some* good.

Then, too, we must not minimize man's will, or instinct, to go on living and to ensure the continuance of his race. Perhaps he will employ still more ingenuity in protecting himself and his country against the lethal arms he invents than he has in inventing them, and that he will find some defensive weapon against the hydrogen bomb. But, alas, the scientist holds out no such hopes.

Again, it is undeniable that a great change has taken place over the centuries in the moral attitude of man towards war. This change, though it may not apply to his unconscious attitude, is absolutely genuine and does affect his attitude as a whole. The civilized person of today is much more intolerant of war than were his ruder forefathers not so long ago, not only because of its increasing destructiveness but because of the increasing value of the things it destroys—the ever richer field of his cultural achievements and material prosperity—and also because he puts a higher value upon human life and can less and less bear to commit acts of violence and blood-shed. This, as Freud has suggested,[1] may represent a genuine process of cultural evolution which may eventually lead mankind quite away from its warlike impulses. At present, however, the process seems to be uncertain and liable to constant relapses. Moreover, it is, once more, a slow business and will not have time to advance far enough or consolidate itself sufficiently to meet the present danger. Nothing short of a universal transformation overnight would do. And miracles do not happen. In this connection, too, it should be borne in mind that much of modern man's hatred of war is due to a reactive formation against, or overcompensation for, his own destructive instincts rather than a genuine absence

---

[1] At the end of an exchange of letters with Einstein on the subject, entitled *Why War?*

of them, and this is not the most secure foundation for a peaceable state of affairs.[1]

Then, too, it must be remembered that the destructive instincts which, when all is said and done, are the greatest single cause of war, *are* instincts and that they are impossible to eradicate altogether, greatly though they may be modified. Nor would it be desirable for them to be so eradicated. For fatal though they now are to mankind in war, they are still indispensable for fighting many other ills and dangers.

Here, perhaps—who knows?—the growing independence of the female sex and their increasing entrance into public affairs, which are such a new and striking feature of the present day, may yet bear unexpected fruit. For they may do much to dilute the total amount of operative destructiveness in the world, seeing that, besides being relatively immune to State-mentality, women as a whole possess much less destructive energy and more libido than men. But these are, perhaps, fanciful ideas.

Lastly, I do not wish to underrate the power of the human intellect. It may be hoped that, faced with the horrors of the new weapons and with the prospect of extermination, mankind will in fact make the necessary effort to abolish war. One of the essential things for this is that a true and full knowledge of just how complete that extermination will be should be brought home to everybody by every possible means, and as soon as possible. This is the first task of statesmen and scientists.

For the same reason I think that it would be very useful if people were to know more about the background of the psychological obstacles that stand in the way of peace—about the unconscious motives which do so much to promote war and hinder its abolition. For, seeing how unrealistic and unacceptable most of them are to the conscious self, it cannot but be that when a person—all except the most barbarous and backward sort—comes face to face with them he will be sufficiently critical of them to resist their influence with all his might, even if he cannot conjure them away. At least he

[1] As Edward Glover points out in his *War, Sadism and Pacifism*.

will know where to direct his efforts. It therefore seems to me highly desirable that a knowledge of the findings of psychoanalysis, especially in its bearings on this topic, should be as widely diffused as possible; and this has been one of the main purposes of the present book.

BIBLIOGRAPHY

ABRAHAM, K. (1911) 'Notes on the Psycho-Analytical Investigation and Treatment of Manic-Depressive Insanity and Allied Conditions', *Selected Papers*, London, 1927.

(1924) 'A Short Study of the Development of the Libido', Chap. iv, 'Mania', *Selected Papers*, London, 1927.

ADLER, A. (1907) *Studie ueber Minderwertigkeit von Organen*, Vienna.

FERENCZI, S. (1900) 'Introjection and Transference', *First Contributions to Psycho-Analysis*, London, 1952.

(1913) 'Stages in the Development of the Sense of Reality', *First Contributions to Psycho-Analysis*, London, 1952.

FLUGEL, J. C. (1945) *Man, Morals and Society, a Psycho-Analytic Study*, London.

FREUD, ANNA (1936) *The Ego and the Mechanisms of Defence*, London.

FREUD, S. (1900) *The Interpretation of Dreams*, London and New York, 1955.

(1905) *Three Essays on the Theory of Sexuality*, London, 1953.

(1909) 'Notes upon a Case of Obsessional Neurosis', (The 'Rat Man'), *Standard Ed.*, Vol. X, London, 1955.

(1909) 'Analysis of a Phobia in a Five-Year-Old Boy' ('Little Hans'), *Standard Ed.*, Vol. X, London, 1955.

(1911) 'Formulations on the Two Principles of Mental Functioning', *Collected Papers*, Vol. I, London, 1924.

(1911) 'Psycho-Analytic Notes upon an Autobiographical Account of a Case of Paranoia (Dementia Paranoides)', *Collected Papers*, Vol. III, London, 1925.

(1912–13) *Totem and Taboo*, London, 1950.

(1915) 'Instincts and their Vicissitudes', *Collected Papers*, Vol. IV, London, 1925.

(1915) 'The Unconscious', *Collected Papers*, Vol. IV, London, 1925.

(1916–17) *Introductory Lectures on Psycho-Analysis*, London and New York, 1929.

(1917) 'Metapsychological Supplement to the Theory of Dreams', *Collected Papers*, Vol. IV, London, 1925.

(1917) 'Mourning and Melancholia', *Collected Papers*, Vol. IV, London, 1925.

(1918) 'From the History of an Infantile Neurosis' (The 'Wolf-Man'), *Collected Papers*, Vol. IV, London, 1925.

(1922) *Group Psychology and the Analysis of the Ego*, London, 1949.

(1923) *The Ego and the Id*, London, 1949.

(1925) *An Autobiographical Study*, London and New York (under title *Autobiography*), 1935.

(1930) *Civilization and its Discontents*, London, 1949.

(1932) *New Introductory Lectures on Psycho-Analysis*, London and New York, 1933.

(1932) 'Why War?' (with Einstein), *Collected Papers*, Vol. V, London, 1947.

(1938) *An Outline of Psycho-Analysis*, London, 1949.

GLOVER, E. (1947) *War, Sadism and Pacifism: Further Essays on Group-Psychology and War*, London and New York.

ISAACS, SUSAN (1933) *Social Development in Young Children*, London.

JONES, E. (1923) 'Rationalization in Everyday Life', *Papers on Psycho-Analysis*, London and New York.

(1923) 'The Theory of Symbolism', *Papers on Psycho-Analysis*, London and New York.

(1933) 'The Phallic Phase', *International Journal of Psycho-Analysis*, Vol. XIV.

(1941) 'Evolution and Revolution', *International Journal of Psycho-Analysis*, Vol. XXII.

INDEX

GEORGE ALLEN & UNWIN LTD
London: 40 Museum Street, W.C.1

Auckland: 24 Wyndham Street
Bombay: 15 Graham Road, Ballard Estate, Bombay 1
Calcutta: 17 Chittaranjan Avenue, Calcutta 13
Cape Town: 109 Long Street
Karachi: 254 Ingle Road
New Delhi: 13–14 Ajmeri Gate Extension, New Delhi 1
São Paulo: Avenida 9 de Julho 1138–Ap. 51
Sydney, N.S.W.: Bradbury House, 55 York Street
Toronto: 91 Wellington Street West

The Interpretation of Dreams

By Sigmund Freud

Translated by James Strachey

This entirely new translation of Freud's most important work contains a number of features not to be found in any previous edition, whether in English or German. Freud made a great many changes and additions to the book over a period of some thirty years, and the present edition indicates for the first time the exact nature of these changes and additions and the dates at which they were made, thus enabling the reader to trace the gradual development and modification of Freud's view. This edition also includes numerous explanatory notes and a historical introduction, as well as enlarged and revised bibliographies and very full indexes. In preparing the translation Mr. Strachey has enjoyed the advantage of regular consultation with the author's daughter, Miss Anna Freud.

'. . . Mr. Strachey, quite rightly, has decided to keep scrupulously to Freud's own narrative, quoting and annotating the German where occasion demands. The index, bibliographies and supplementary notes are invaluable. As a result, both the psychological specialist and the general reader now have available a richly documented edition of what is after all one of the most original contributions to science published during the present century.'   *Sir Cyril Burt, in 'Nature'*

'. . . a true variorum edition, for Mr. Strachey has edited as well as translated the original. For the first time we can perceive easily and clearly the various changes Freud introduced in the eight German editions. . . . We have here a classic model of how an important scientific work should be presented, one of which the editor, his assistants, and publisher may all be proud.'

British Medical Journal

'A definitive and superb new translation of this masterpiece. The work is a 'variorum' edition, indicating all the additions and modifications which Freud introduced into the eight editions published in his lifetime—so elegant is the style, so precise the translation, that it can now be read with more pleasure and profit than has ever been possible for people without a complete command of German. It is a desirable, as well as an essential, possession for all who wish to understand one of the most influential trends of our time.'   *The Listener*

'. . . The results of his brilliant editing will be of great value not only to students of Freud, but to all who care about the scholarly presentation of classical works of science.'   *The Times*

Demy 8vo.   21s. net

Freud or Jung

by Edward Glover

The rapid post-war expansion of psychiatry in this country has given new life to the vogue of "eclectic psychology." Modern mental specialists are interested more in the application of various forms of treatment than in the principles on which they are based. Similarly, writers on applied psychology are more and more given to indiscriminate quotation, citing in support of their aesthetic or political views little bits of Freud, Jung and anyone else they fancy, without apparently being aware of the fundamental incompatibility of the systems in question.

Dr. Glover, now the foremost Freudian in this country, has written a book vigorously opposing this tendency to eclecticism. Believing that the psychology of Jung has many attractions for the unthinking, he has subjected Jungian theories to a searching analysis and comes to the conclusion they are little more than disguised forms of the old "conscious" psychologies. Some interesting chapters are devoted to Jung's views on politics, religion and art. This is a challenging book which no student of psychology can afford to neglect.

'This book is an extremely important work. It is carefully put together, scholarly, and erudite. To those interested in psychopathology Dr. Glover is always worth reading, and perhaps never more so than in this his latest book.'

Manchester Guardian

'The tone of this book is throughout polemical: unashamedly so in fact. . . . Yet this polemical tone is not altogether out of place. The liveliness of Dr. Glover's writing, as well as its obvious sincerity, cannot but appeal. He is partisan; but why not? . . . Many may feel that on final estimate Dr. Glover has done scant justice to Jung; but they will not regret having read his book.'

Times Educational Supplement

'In his sustained polemic Dr. Glover exposes the nebulosity, vagueness, and self-contradictoriness of the Jungian system, in which psychological, philosophical, and metaphysical elements are all combined.' *British Medical Journal*

'It presents in a condensed and yet accurate form the Freudian analytical presentation of mental development. For this alone the book is well worth while reading and it certainly does what it sets out to do, i.e. presents to the world a clear, concise and logical critique of Jung's psychology.'

The Medical Press

Demy 8vo. 15s. net

War, Sadism, and Pacifism:

FURTHER ESSAYS ON GROUP PSYCHOLOGY AND WAR

by *Edward Glover*

This is a new and greatly enlarged edition of Dr. Glover's well-known book of the same title which was first published in 1935.

It was reprinted several times in its original form and the author has now expanded the book to more than double its original length with the addition of several new chapters which deal with unconscious causes of war, unconscious factors in peace, problems of war prevention and group psychology.

Apart from his work as a consultant in medical psychology, Dr. Glover is widely known for his writings on sociology and for his broadcast talks.

Crown 8vo.   9s. 6d. net

Ego, Hunger and Aggression

A REVISION OF FREUD'S THEORY AND METHOD

by *F. S. Perls*

The author, a practising psychoanalyst, aims in this book to examine some psychological and psycho-pathological reactions of the human organism within its environment. His central conception is the theory that the organism is striving for the maintenance of a balance which is continuously disturbed by its needs, and regained through their gratification.

The author is critical of orthodox psychoanalysis, and claims that the use of the new intellectual tools *holism* (field conception) and *semantics* (the meaning of meaning) can greatly improve our theoretical outlook. Instead of looking at aggression from a purely psychologistic point of view, the holistic-semantic approach is made and reveals a number of shortcomings even in the best-developed of the psychological methods: namely, psychoanalysis. After showing the inadequacies of psychoanalysis in the first part, the author proceeds in the second to outline the larger scope of the new concept. In the third and final part of the volume detailed instructions are given for a therapeutic technique resulting from the changed theoretical outlook.

The book should be of great interest and value to the psychiatrist, psychologist and medical practitioner, also to dental surgeons, sociologists and politicians. Though it challenges orthodox conclusions, it does constructively offer a new theoretical outlook, and is original and stimulating.

Demy 8vo.   12s. 6d. net

A Primer of Freudian Psychology

by Calvin S. Hall

Freud's system of abnormal psychology and psychoanalysis, and his techniques for treating the mentally sick have become a part of popular language. But few people realize that Freud developed a complete system of *normal* psychology over a period of forty years. *A Primer of Freudian Psychology* represents the first attempt to bring together, in a concise form, Freud's ideas on the organization, dynamics, and development of normal personality. The reader will find here his answers to such major questions as: What is personality? What forces motivate our behaviour? What factors are responsible for shaping personality?

Stripped of extraneous material and technical jargon, it presents material from many of Freud's books and articles in one clear and logical pattern. Carefully chosen examples illustrate the various concepts. The primer is short but nothing essential to the complete picture of Freud's system has been omitted.

'It brings out Freud's contributions to modern dynamic theories of the normal personality, and while not ignoring neurotic mechanisms does succeed in putting them in perspective. Primarily it is a text book for psychology students who want a balanced impersonal survey, rather than for the layman. But it is clearly written.'   *Times Educational Supplement*

Demy 8vo.   13s. 6d. net

Instinct in Man

by Ronald Fletcher

The nature of instinct and the extent of its importance in human experience and behaviour is one of the most important, as it is certainly one of the most controversial subjects in the whole of psychology.

In this book, Dr. Fletcher systematically examines the whole doctrine of human instincts and argues for the reinstatement of the theory of instincts in psychology. Three bodies of work are critically assessed: the work of the earlier psychologists, from Darwin onwards (James, Lloyd Morgan, MacDougall, Drever, and others); the recent findings of the Comparative Ethologists (Lorenz, Tinbergen, Thorpe, etc.) on instincts in animals; and the account of instinct given in Psychoanalysis. He demonstrates that these three bodies of work are not in conflict, but support and supplement each other, and then formulates a reliable and comprehensive theory of instincts. The more important implications which this theory has for other areas of study—such as education, social psychology, moral and social philosophy, and sociology—are pointed out and discussed.

Most writers have approached the subject from one position only. Dr. Fletcher gives a valuable assessment of every aspect. His thorough and up-to-date knowledge of the subject makes his excellent book a most useful contribution to literature on psychology.

Sm. Royal 8vo.   About 42s. net

GEORGE ALLEN AND UNWIN LTD

DATE DUE